P9-DVO-320

NOTLEY
NATION

NOTLEY
NATION

How Alberta's Political
Upheaval Swept the Country

SYDNEY SHARPE | DON BRAID

DUNDURN
TORONTO

Copyright © Sydney Sharpe and Don Braid, 2016

All rights reserved. No part of this publication may be reproduced, stored in a retrieval system, or transmitted in any form or by any means, electronic, mechanical, photocopying, recording, or otherwise (except for brief passages for purpose of review) without the prior permission of Dundurn Press. Permission to photocopy should be requested from Access Copyright.

Printer: Webcom
Cover image: © shutterstock.com/ illpos

Library and Archives Canada Cataloguing in Publication

Sharpe, Sydney, author
    Notley nation : how Alberta's political upheaval swept the country / Sydney Sharpe and Don Braid.

Includes bibliographical references and index.
Issued in print and electronic formats.

ISBN 978-1-4597-3603-0 (paperback).--ISBN 978-1-4597-3604-7 (pdf).--ISBN 978-1-4597-3605-4 (epub)

1. Alberta--Politics and government--2015-. 2. Elections--Alberta. 3. Alberta. Legislative Assembly--Elections. 4. Alberta New Democrats. 5. Alberta--History--21st century. 6. Canada--Politics and government--2015-. 7. Canada--History--21st century. I. Braid, Don, 1942-, author II. Title.

FC3676.2.S58 2016   971.23'04   C2016-904843-8
                                              C2016-904844-6

1   2   3   4   5   20   19   18   17   16

We acknowledge the support of the **Canada Council for the Arts** and the **Ontario Arts Council** for our publishing program. We also acknowledge the financial support of the **Government of Ontario**, through the **Ontario Book Publishing Tax Credit** and the **Ontario Media Development Corporation**, and the **Government of Canada**.

Care has been taken to trace the ownership of copyright material used in this book. The author and the publisher welcome any information enabling them to rectify any references or credits in subsequent editions.

— *J. Kirk Howard, President*

The publisher is not responsible for websites or their content unless they are owned by the publisher.

Printed and bound in Canada.

VISIT US AT

dundurn.com | @dundurnpress | dundurnpress | dundurnpress

Dundurn
3 Church Street, Suite 500
Toronto, Ontario, Canada
M5E 1M2

For Norma Sharpe
Rielle and Jamie
Gabriel, James, and Rasa
And
The inspirational Patricia Leeson

CONTENTS

CHAPTER 1

"A LITTLE BIT OF HISTORY"

It's voting day — May 5, 2015 — and a political earthquake is about to rumble through Alberta. It catches pundits and seasoned politicians off guard. Premier Jim Prentice expects his Progressive Conservative government to shake, perhaps, but not tumble from power.

The leader of Alberta's New Democratic Party, Rachel Notley, knows what's about to happen. She may be the only party leader prepared for such a dramatic upheaval. But she is still shocked by the results on that tumultuous Tuesday night.

Soon after the polls close the extent of the PC collapse becomes evident. The NDP captures fifty-three of eighty-seven seats, securing the first left-of-centre Alberta government in eighty years. Notley has managed to unseat a forty-three-year-old Progressive Conservative regime, the most famous in Canada for longevity, if not recent accomplishment. She becomes the province's seventeenth premier, instantly shattering every myth about Alberta being eternally conservative.

WHEN PRENTICE CALLED the election the Progressive Conservatives commanded seventy seats; on election night only nine PCs managed to win their ridings. The Wildrose Party, initially formed as a right-wing alternative to the PCs, earned twenty-one seats, four more than it had in 2012 when the party seriously challenged the Tories until the final week of the campaign. Wildrose would remain the Official Opposition. Conservatism lost the province that night, but it was far from dead.

This political upheaval in the unlikeliest province also signalled a vast political shift across Canada. Within five months Prime Minister Stephen Harper's Conservative government would be defeated by Justin Trudeau's Liberals, who would benefit from the same storming of the polls by urban, progressive, young voters.

The reasons for the Alberta upheaval, although fascinating in detail, are not wildly complicated. Notley was an appealing new leader who ran a brilliant campaign, while the PCs were out of touch with the modern province they believed they owned. Their seeming sense of entitlement, combined with their record of infighting and constant leadership crises (there had been four PC premiers in four years) had eroded public respect. The once-great party was creaky, top-heavy, and slow to adopt modern campaign methods. And yet, until the very last moment, the PCs failed to grasp that they might not be invincible.

It took a Prentice-led PC platform full of controversies and blunders, combined with a faultless NDP campaign that connected with a new generation of voters. Notley and her Orange Crush rushed the province with their talk of helping the struggling underclass, reviewing oil and gas royalties, and raising taxes on the well-to-do. Millennials and other alienated Albertans voted in droves for the first time. Many later said they had never cast a ballot in their adult lives because they thought nothing would change. This time they suddenly realized that something could actually happen, and they shook themselves out of their long political torpor.

The roots of the Alberta PC disaster were visible and growing years earlier, with the election of Calgary Mayor Naheed Nenshi in 2010. Notley saw them for what they were. The Alberta Tories did not; nor did Harper's Conservatives.

While the Alberta Progressive Conservatives were mired in leadership schemes and scandals, they failed to notice their province had changed. It started with clear signs that even in Canada's most right-wing province younger voters were feeling ignored and dispossessed, that social concerns like LGBTQ rights were treated with contempt, and that the Tory government no longer connected with big-city voters. The election of Mayor Nenshi was a sharp sign that the youth of urban Canada were finally stirring. A bold thirty-eight-year-old Calgary academic, Nenshi organized his Purple Revolution, trounced two candidates who were heavily favoured over him, and became the first Muslim mayor of a major North American city, a fact that fascinated American networks like CNN. In Alberta, the more important political point was that he represented a victory for well-educated, urban progressives who were culturally and ethnically ecumenical. Rather than learning from his rise, however, both provincial and federal conservatives largely ignored it. They thought Nenshi was a political fluke — a "big mistake," as one PC MLA said on Twitter. But the mayor was the future.

A generation that felt powerless now believed change could come through the ballot box. One PC premier, Alison Redford, had grasped the trend and tried to put a progressive face on the PCs. "Not your father's party," she called it, to the annoyance of traditionalists. Redford resigned in March 2014, brought down by her own foibles and a party rebellion. When the PCs elected Jim Prentice as leader he felt forced by economic conditions into a tax-and-cut stance that seemed to belie his own more moderate brand of conservatism. To the end, the PCs never imagined that progressives would unite with fed-up moderates and take hold of a provincial election.

But Notley's NDP swept the province, riding heavy support from the eighteen-to-thirty-four-year-old generation, as well as the resentments of older voters who felt the more-than-four-decade-old regime was completely out of touch. By election day, Notley topped the polls in every age category.

NOBODY SHOULD HAVE grasped the meaning of this more quickly than Stephen Harper. From his Calgary riding he had a perfect vantage point to sense and assess the profound changes that threatened his Alberta fortress, and his government in the country beyond.

But Harper chose to fight rather than adapt. The Conservatives' summer-and-fall campaign of 2015 became a reactionary spasm against change. It sought to stifle, dismiss, and discredit the looming generational shift. The backlash against Harper was exactly like the one that ended the career of Prentice only five months earlier.

Liberal Leader Justin Trudeau, derided as "not ready" by Harper, proved to be the exact opposite on the campaign trail.

Trudeau was saying what many millennials, seniors, and those who felt politically abandoned wanted to hear. He had expanded the conversation far beyond Harper's predictable and confined fiscal Conservative message. Stalwarts like Conservative MP Tony Clement explained to the *Globe and Mail* how those constraints played into their election defeat. They were wrapped into a "straightjacket of only talking economy, generally, and security," noting that they didn't even go into crucial social issues such as "poverty reduction, environment, indigenous rights," because they were considered "off message." In the end, continued Clement, "We didn't have anything to say to city dwellers, we didn't have anything to say to millennials."[1]

The federal Conservatives failed to acknowledge the Alberta signs pointing to a massive voting shift, much to the benefit of Trudeau and the Liberals.

OVER TIME, SUCCESS can make politicians stubborn. Harper refused even to try extending his party's reach beyond his own comfort zone. The Prentice PCs became positively sclerotic, convinced that whatever they offered, the voters would endorse. The apparent stability of Alberta politics certainly encouraged that belief — twelve straight victories can breed a great deal of confidence in a party. Other Canadians too had some reason for seeing Alberta as stable to the point of paralysis.

But, in fact, Alberta has always been a cauldron of discontent; it has bred a long list of upstart rebels, including, amongst others, Social Credit, the Reform Party, the Wildrose movement, the modern Conservative Party of Canada, Harper himself, and even the CCF, precursor to the NDP.

But the peculiar quirk of Albertans, who have often felt threatened by federal enemies, real and imagined, has been to pour their discontent into a single party for long stretches. In essence, voters have preferred to make the governing party change rather than to change the government themselves. The Progressive Conservatives had three major makeovers during their forty-three years in power, each of which led to more majority victories. The first PC premier, Peter Lougheed, managed an elegant exit. Following his departure the party made its stately way through six more premiers and eight more victories before the final flurry of changes that made Alberta politics seem like a French farce of entries and exits through slamming doors. The departure of each leader after Lougheed seemed messier than the last, and in the end public confidence in the party simply eroded.

The script for the May 2015 election was a new one, however. A week before the election Notley knew the NDP was gaining momentum, although she still had no idea that she would be premier. Then she found herself staring at new party polling numbers. Everything pointed to an NDP victory.

She realized that her final campaign blitz was now biting into critical time she would need to plan the transition to power. She knew that she should be bracing herself not just for victory but for government changeover, a complex job that hadn't been necessary in Alberta since 1971.

Very few politicians or officials in Alberta had any experience with a task that's fairly routine in other provinces. Before the PC run, Social Credit had ruled Alberta for thirty-six years. The kind of multi-generational one-party rule that has characterized Alberta politics was last seen in Canada thirty years earlier, when Ontario's PCs fell from grace on June 25, 1985, only four months after long-standing Premier Bill Davis retired. The Ontario PCs had presided over Queen's Park since August 17, 1943. The 2015 Alberta Tory rout left Manitoba's NDP as the longest serving twenty-first-century government, at seventeen years. That lasted until April 19, 2016, when the province booted Greg Selinger and his party out of office and ushered in Progressive Conservative Premier Brian Pallister.

Alberta's new reality was hard to absorb, even for seasoned observers and politicians. The PC way of politics had been woven into the fabric of daily life for so long, so ground into the Alberta spirit, that some people viewed the election result as radical and even illegitimate. They expected a calamitous collapse of government.

So extreme was the reaction of some to the NDP victory that there arose a "kudatah" (*coup d'état*) movement. (The inventive spelling started on Twitter and took off with the hashtag #kudutah.) Its aim was to eject Notley by plebiscite, a procedure for which there is no legal mechanism in Alberta. "I'll be making the announcement at 12:15 p.m., by 12:30 we will be back in charge of Alberta," founder George Clark said. This was a polite Canadian insurrection, however, so he added: "Pass it on and thanks."

Notley was still in office at 12:30. Clark won a great deal of publicity but no change of government.

Despite the pushback from the margins, a large portion of the electorate, if not necessarily the majority, was clearly content with the election results. Indeed, Notley had said for years that Alberta was becoming far more progressive than many traditional PCs recognized, especially in the big cities. Still, the transition from a significant group of voters who felt this way to a government that always acts this way was so profound it almost required provincial therapy.

Various shades of conservatism had ruled Alberta since 1935, when Social Credit and its evangelical leader, William Aberhart, swept fifty-six of sixty-three seats. Social Credit secured its reign over three and a half decades once Ernest Manning — father of Preston — succeeded Aberhart after he died in 1943. But Harry Strom, who followed Manning as premier in 1968, proved no match for the young and charismatic Peter Lougheed.

As leader of the Progressive Conservatives, the moribund party he took over and rebuilt, Lougheed joined arms and intellect with his first six-person caucus, and cruised into a 1971 win with forty-nine of seventy-five seats. Lougheed was in some ways the Rachel Notley of his era — a liberal-minded premier who represented large cities that were coming of age and no longer had much use for rural-based Social Credit. Lougheed was also interventionist, quick to use government power as an economic lever. He even bought an airline, Pacific Western, because Air Canada refused to serve small northern communities. Sometimes the NDP of that day had to work hard to dislike him.

One riding Lougheed's PCs had trouble capturing was Spirit River-Fairview, the northwest rural seat held by the highly respected Grant Notley, leader of the provincial NDP and father of Rachel. The elder Notley died tragically in a plane crash on October 19, 1984, when Rachel was still a university student. Grant Notley was one of the very few Albertans who actually believed his party would someday govern Alberta. Thirty-one years later, his daughter proved him correct.

Two forms of conservatism have long been at war in Alberta. The Progressive Conservatives battled Social Credit and its various splinters and survivors, including Preston Manning's Reform Party. Conflicting loyalties between Reformers and traditional PCs often threatened to split former premier Ralph Klein's caucus down the middle, even though Reform was never a provincial party. The latest battle is between right-wing Wildrose, another heir of Social Credit, and the surprisingly resilient rump of the defeated PCs.

Former federal Conservative minister Jason Kenney plans to end all that. In July 2016 he announced his intention to win the leadership of the PC party, and then unite the right with Wildrosers, all dutifully merging into a new party that he would lead to government. Former prime minister Stephen Harper quickly endorsed him, as did interim Conservative leader Rona Ambrose. Kenney hoped to accomplish provincially what Harper had engineered federally in 2003. Harper had helped unite heirs of Reform, who took the name Canadian Alliance, and the federal PCs under then-leader Peter MacKay. Only when this final deal was reached in late 2003, with the formation of the Conservative Party of Canada, was it once again possible for federal conservatism to defeat the Liberals.

Kenney's plan for Alberta provincial conservatives exactly mirrored that federal strategy. It immediately opened the old fissures between the progressives and the social conservatives in the provincial PC party. One veteran progressive said Kenney's move "recalls the last time the Reform Party hijacked the Progressive Conservatives."

Kenney's appeal to right-of-centre Albertans is aimed at bringing the Wildrosers back into the conservative fold, likely to the exclusion of many centrist and progressive members. He hopes to recreate a new party more in the image of Ralph Klein than Peter Lougheed. For Kenney, "Conservative Party of Alberta" would be a perfect name for this hypothetical party. As Kenney began campaigning, Wildrose chief Brian Jean said he'll talk to any new Tory leader who is keen on unity. While still intent on enlarging the Wildrose Party, Jean was open to a change of name.

"I believe the future for the Wildrose is to consolidate conservatives over one banner," Jean said in an interview in mid-May, 2016. "The PCs have turned their back on us. As a result of that, we have to try and win the hearts and minds of Albertans. The members will decide our future. I think Wildrose is a great name but if our members decide on Conservative or Conservative Wildrose or Alberta Conservative Party or Wildrose Alliance or Reform Alliance, that's fine.

"We're going to work really hard and have some small and big ideas: smaller government and less taxes," Jean continued. When asked what he sees after the next election, Jean replied: "In three years, I see a province with a lot of hope because they've just elected a majority Wildrose government."

That may be tough for Jean who hopes to unite the right. In his home city of Fort McMurray, as Jean talked about "beating the drum" for seniors' issues, he actually said: "But it's against the law to beat Rachel Notley." Although he quickly apologized, many Albertans, especially women, were appalled that the thought would even enter Jean's mind. It's no joke that abuse statistics are climbing and shows a worrisome lack of judgment for the man who wants to be premier.

LARGELY FORGOTTEN IN all the day-to-day battles is the fact that before the eighty years of dominance by the two squabbling twins of Alberta conservatism, the province lived under generally liberal rule for thirty years. In 1905 the brand-new province elected Alexander Rutherford and his Liberal Party. Although he would resign amidst a railway loan scandal, the party prevailed until 1921. The United Farmers of Alberta fought for change in a time of economic erosion. The province's farmers, pummelled by drought and low commodity prices, brought the UFA into power.

There they remained for fourteen years, until scandal and Aberhart swept them away in 1935. United Farmers Premier John Brownlee was sued for an alleged affair with a former family friend, who was a clerk in the attorney general's office. Brownlee denied everything, countering that Liberal Party opponents and an angry suitor put Vivian MacMillan up to a lie. The case went to the Supreme Court of Canada, which found in MacMillan's favour. Brownlee resigned as premier.

In 1932, UFA party members and federal MPs met with other progressives in Calgary to form the Co-operative Commonwealth Federation (CCF), which would become the NDP in 1961. Notley loves to point out that the movement began in Alberta. "I was born into the NDP," she told a stone-silent business crowd in Calgary five months after the election, referring to her family, but also alluding to the NDP's birth in that very city.

The reality for more than forty years had been that the PCs owned Alberta. But the man who first made that happen, and watched his PCs log twelve straight victories, never expected them to outlast the Roman Empire.

Ten years before the NDP victory, Lougheed himself had predicted this massive electoral shift. "The largest political change in decades ahead could be an adjustment from dominance of one party; that will change as the province becomes more diversified and more newcomers get involved," he said.[2]

The PCs paid little heed to such warnings, though. They had come to expect they would never lose because the voters would forgive them anything: policy reversals, leadership rumbles and tumbles, corruption scandals, sudden reversals of spending commitments, and Cabinet ministers who sabotaged each other as often as they did the opposition. The fall of Canada's greatest political dynasty happened just the way many experts always said it would — with a sudden toppling of the pedestal, a crash, and a fading cloud of dust.

FOR ALBERTANS, THE defeat of the federal Conservatives and the re-election of the Liberals, with a Trudeau as leader no less, proved especially shocking. Not only was a party that many regarded as the "enemy" of Alberta in power in Ottawa once again, but their own province was now headed by a left-wing government whose leader seemed willing to make friends with the Liberals. To conservative traditionalists who had so mistrusted Justin Trudeau's father, Pierre Elliott Trudeau, that sounded like the script for a horror movie. And yet, Albertans themselves effected the first change, and played a significant role in the second.

Of all the consequences, the most important was the new NDP-Liberal alignment on issues of major national importance. Notley cast off Alberta's often cranky and contrarian approach to national relations, painting the province as a full partner and even leader in Canada and abroad, especially in environment and climate change.

Even United States president Barack Obama took note. When he addressed the House of Commons in Ottawa on June 30, 2016, Obama said: "Alberta, the oil country of Canada, is working hard to reduce emissions while still promoting growth. So if Canada can do it, and the United States can do it, the whole world can unleash economic growth and protect our planet. We can do this."[3]

Prime Minister Justin Trudeau's 2015 victory created the oddest sight of all — an NDP provincial government more closely aligned with Liberal Ottawa than Alberta's previous PC governments had ever been with their federal Conservative counterparts. In her quest for pipelines, Notley also applied a new tactic with Ontario and Quebec: the pressure of open friendship. Alberta would simply be too collaborative and agreeable, just too darned nice, to turn down. Some called it *Care Bear* diplomacy. Part of Notley's rationale was that since nothing else had succeeded in getting pipelines built, it only made sense to try a different approach.

"Canada is a collection of provinces. Historically some people play that feature off against one another. I don't think that's typically resulted in progress. It is not in any way, shape or form the appropriate frame for this conversation. And we're not going to do that with it," she said to Alexander Panetta of the Canadian Press.[4]

ONCE THE EXTENT of her victory became clear on election night, Notley told her exuberant supporters, "Well, my friends, I think we might have made a little bit of history tonight.… I believe change has finally come to Alberta. New people, new ideas, and a fresh start for our great province."

A striking example of that "fresh start" was the equal number of women and men in Notley's first Cabinet: six each, including the premier. Gender equality was no longer a political dream, but a working reality. The premier's new caucus was 47 percent female. She used this as a springboard to equality action everywhere, from the legislature itself to the heart of government and the private workplace. Then Prime Minister Trudeau created his own gender-equal Cabinet. Asked why, he said: "Because it's 2015." He didn't need to add: "Because of Alberta, too."

Rachel Notley has dreams, so many that she alarms a good percentage of the population with the sheer scope of NDP change. She also has a relentless practical drive to make the dreams come true. Those that do have national consequences, with gender parity only a beginning.

Notley wants to completely rebuild the province's fraught relationship with indigenous people. She takes every chance to show respect. Her swearing-in ceremony began with a declaration that everyone present stood on Treaty 6 land. Behind this push for reconciliation, which is by no means forced or false, lies the certain knowledge that without mutual respect in dealings with First Nations, pipelines aren't even a remote possibility.

Notley harbours intertwined dreams for the economy and the environment and, more prosaically, those pipelines. World-leading climate policy will lead to approval of pipelines. Energy revenues, supplemented by a general carbon tax, will kick-start new green industries, thus realizing the age-old Alberta dream of a truly diversified economy. The oil and gas industry will inevitably fade, but with dignity and respect. (Early and ugly battles over the phase-out of coal-fired electricity, however, do not suggest that every industry will happily lead its own funeral march.)

The premier also dreams of dignity and resources for the poor and disadvantaged. She and her caucus despise the province's booming payday loan industry, which they wanted to effectively disable with legislation. She believes a higher minimum wage creates jobs, rather than destroys them, by pushing more spending power into the economy. She knows the province has to collect much more revenue — especially with resource royalties down sharply — but she's flexible about the methods. In the spring 2016 budget, the government actually lowered the small business tax, from 3 percent to 2 percent.

Notley also knows, along with nearly everybody else in Alberta, that this former fountain of wealth is no longer cruising toward a future guaranteed to be even modestly prosperous. Albertans see their main industry being pinched into oblivion by inexplicable hostility. They watch provinces that resist Canadian pipelines casually accepting Saudi oil by both tanker and pipeline. They find it peculiar, when they are being polite, that Quebec refiners are lukewarm about the Energy East pipeline because they get plenty of crude from the United States — by tanker. They detect no sympathy, during a savage local recession, for the fact that Alberta doesn't benefit from equalization, and hasn't in any year since 1963. And these Albertans ask — in an equally polite way — what kind of country is this anyway?

Part of Notley's mission is to reframe the future for Albertans, both in reality and in their minds. She's trying to foster hope that this whole system can be rebuilt into something larger and more generous that works for everybody. This is a noble goal, but fraught with risk, because if it doesn't succeed the premier and her province will have nowhere else to go.

Aging pipelines often develop a technical problem called stress corrosion cracking that can lead to ruptures. Now, the whole nation exhibits symptoms of the same syndrome. For Notley, the local and regional hostilities around pipelines are her biggest long-term challenge. Such tensions always lurk just below the thin crust of national civility, waiting for some irritant to draw them out.

One of the best things to be said about Notley, and Justin Trudeau, is that they refuse to play the regional cards that have been so destructive in the past. The prime minister appears to be with her on the pipeline issue, at least in principle. And he certainly owes her for the rushed Alberta climate-change plan that he was able to wave at the Paris summit in December 2015. It impressed French President François Hollande, who later praised Trudeau at the G7 meeting in Japan in May 2016: "Had it not been for Canada, with the enthusiasm Justin Trudeau was able to bring, but also the quality of the proposals, I'm not sure that we would have had such a complete record," the *National Post*'s Matthew Fisher reported.[5]

"I have been crystal clear for years now on pipelines," Trudeau said. "One of the fundamental responsibilities of any Canadian prime minister … is to get Canadian resources to international markets. In order to get our resources to market in the twenty-first century, we have to be responsible around the environment and we have to respect the concerns of communities, and we have to build partnerships with indigenous peoples. That's the only way to get our resources built responsibly and sustainably now."[6]

Alberta, of course, has created many of its own problems with lax environmental performance and policy, and responses to criticism that were often arrogant. At first these assaults on the oil sands and the province seemed trivial, but they gradually grew into a massive practical and environmental problem.

Notley's goal is to create a whole new image by completely rejecting the past and vaulting to a level of environmental stringency unmatched in Canada. This will take years to sink in, but already she has succeeded to some degree. In her travels she presents Alberta as an environmental patron and a province that is serious about combating greenhouse gas emissions and taking climate action. Ontario Premier Kathleen Wynne certainly suggested that Alberta's pipeline quest would have a more receptive audience because of the province's climate-leadership plan. When she met Notley in the Alberta legislature in May 2016, Wynne said: "It convinces me that this conversation, which is a national conversation, is a much easier one because of the work Alberta is doing, absolutely."[7]

RACHEL NOTLEY AND her NDP dealt with many problems in their first year of government, from crashing oil prices to massive deficits and controversy over the new carbon tax. But nothing prepared them — or anyone in Alberta — for the raging Fort McMurray wildfire that swept into the northern city on May 3, 2016. Called the "beast" by Fire Chief Darby Allen, this dreadful natural disaster destroyed more than two thousand homes and sent riveting images of the "ocean of fire" (Notley's striking term) around the world.

Almost immediately it also became a test of national empathy and understanding toward Alberta and the oil sands region. The displays of courage were inspiring. Wildrose leader Brian Jean lost his house to the fire. Photos showed an ash pit where the family dwelling had stood before. Despite his own pain, Jean spent three days driving around the fire sites, shooting video for people who wanted to know what happened to their homes but weren't yet allowed back in. Jean praised the premier for including him, as Official Opposition leader, in daily briefings, and also for admitting him to the city when it was under blanket evacuation order. "We get along on a personal basis very well. We have a very cordial relationship; she's reached out to me," Jean said in an interview.

The vast outpouring of sympathy and practical support that swept across Canada thrilled Albertans, many to the point of tears. Those few Canadians who crowed about climate karma were aptly called "miserable bastards" by Rex Murphy in a *National Post* column.[8] It's one thing to talk honestly about the impacts of climate change, including drought and the lengthening Canadian wildfire season, but quite another to gloat in revenge at a catastrophe that uprooted ninety thousand people, many of them children.

Albertans were powerfully moved by a far more generous group: the new Syrian refugees in the province who, with very little to their names, donated as much as they could manage to the relief effort. "Canadians gave us everything, and now it's time to return the favour," wrote Rita Khanchet in an Arabic Facebook post that started this movement.[9]

In a sense the national response was a validation of what Notley is trying to do. It showed a store of goodwill beneath the political and environmental animosity. It revealed, as disasters often do, the fundamental bond that holds Canadians together. Notley has counted on that spirit all along. She deeply believes in its power.

The premier herself was so effective during the fire, so restrained, sensible, and reassuring, that she may have taken the first steps from being merely the premier to being seen as the provincial leader. Albertans everywhere, including many who will never agree with her policies, such as Brian Jean, had to agree that she was admirable through the whole excruciating ordeal, including the dreadful day when it seemed possible the whole city might burn to the ground.

Jim Stanton, president of national crisis communications firm Stanton and Associates, said he's rarely seen a better performance from a leader under the intense stress of an escalating disaster. "The premier has become the benchmark for how a political leader should show up," he says. "She was consistent in her messaging and looked like she really cared. There were times when you thought she'd burst into tears. There was no political grandstanding at all."

RACHEL NOTLEY WILL face many more trials before she achieves her ambitious goals. But then she's stared down quite a few already just to get where she is. Whether Alberta will be reborn into its familiar wealth and influence, or simply slump into post-oil irrelevance, is the great question for Notley's regime and for the nation that for many years has benefited from Alberta's energy industry. Whatever the result, Notley's victory is proof of a Canadian political reality. Much of Canada's raw political energy in the past thirty years has been spawned in Alberta, from hard fiscal conservatism to a new, purely Albertan, form of progressivism.

CHAPTER 2

THE HOPE-MONGERS

"My name is Rachel Notley and I'm running to be your premier."

It was the Alberta NDP leader's opening line at every forum, rally, and truck stop during the 2015 Alberta election campaign. Much more than a mantra, this was a declaration. Clear, concise, and accessible, Notley seemed to speak directly to each person in the audience. Five months later Justin Trudeau assumed a similar style, with his "sunny ways" shining over the dour aura of Stephen Harper during the federal election. Notley's optimism placed her directly apart from the pessimism of her main opponent, Progressive Conservative leader and premier Jim Prentice. The campaign pitted a dynamic Notley riding a horse called hope against a gloom-laden Prentice, astride a nag named doom.

The election was supposed to be an easy sprint to the finish for Jim Prentice. Yet it was Notley's flawless run that energized the province and propelled the NDP to victory. A generation of youth born under an unending PC government, first elected in 1971, suddenly felt empowered. No longer a detour to the past, the voting booth became a door to the future.

"[The PCs] were no good at politics," Calgary mayor Naheed Nenshi told the authors. "They talked about their great ground game, but they didn't have a great ground game. They didn't have an air game. They'd gotten a bit sclerotic around this." At their peak the Tories excelled at both. Identifying their supporters during their door-knocking and canvassing constituted their good ground game. Their mass media advertising, including ads targeting specific groups, plus the leader's tour and its attendant media coverage, formed the solid air game. As David McLaughlin, a former federal Conservative chief of staff, states in the *Globe and Mail*: "The air war is to persuade voters. The ground game is to identify voters. The two [get] together in what is known as GOTV — get out the vote."[1]

Nenshi noticed that the PCs had failed to keep their volunteers "excited and engaged on the constituency level. They'd gotten very complacent, even though they still have got a great base. Add to that a leader who couldn't connect an air game with the majority of Albertans, there was no way they could win that election. It was all a façade by the end."

A TORY ROUT HAD seemed unfathomable only a few months earlier. Going into the election, Prentice was the most popular leader in the province and absolutely, unalterably sure of what he was doing. After easily winning the Progressive Conservative leadership on September 6, 2014, Prentice quickly distanced himself from former premier Alison Redford and her government. Sworn in as the sixteenth premier of Alberta on September 15, 2014, Prentice declared: "As of this moment, Alberta is under new management. This is a new government with new leadership, new voices and a new way of doing things."

On October 27 the Prentice team appeared invincible, as "new leadership" brought a PC sweep of four by-elections, three in Calgary and one in Edmonton. Looking back at that triumph more than a year later, some senior PCs felt the victories "went to Jim's head." He appeared to believe a thirteenth straight PC majority was preordained.

The new premier's confidence soared again when he engineered the most remarkable mass floor crossing in the history of Canadian politics.

On November 24, 2014, Wildrose MLAs Kerry Towle and Ian Donovan joined Prentice and the PCs. Wildrose leader Danielle Smith seemed shocked by the apparent betrayal. "I suspect they're going to be in for a bit of a rude awakening on the other side," she said.

Then Smith herself stunned the province — and enraged many conservatives — when on December 17 she crossed to the PCs, taking eight other Wildrose MLAs with her. Only five MLAs were left behind to guard the flame of this right-wing Official Opposition.

"It is my sincere hope that you will join us and encourage your fellow members to come together under Premier Prentice's leadership," Smith wrote to the Wildrose executive committee.[2] She was not only leaving, but counselling the party to vote itself out of existence. Wildrose was supposed to vanish with gratitude after Smith abandoned all her former colleagues. She genuinely admired Prentice, and to her, the floor crossings seemed simply a coalition of like minds — not the traitorous betrayal many Albertans would perceive.

Prentice's "new way of doing things" was immediately blasted by people at every point on the political spectrum. Never had an Official Opposition been so decimated by a premier and his party without benefit of an election. The MLAs who stayed with the Wildrose caucus bitterly painted the crossings as a personal back-stab and a betrayal of democracy. Their leftover caucus was now equal in number to the Liberals, each with one more seat than the four-member NDP caucus.

The floor crossings suddenly gave the legislature two parties vying to be the Official Opposition. A day after Wildrose appointed Calgary MLA Heather Forsyth as temporary leader, Speaker Gene Zwozdesky ruled that the party would keep its Official Opposition status. Zwozdesky, himself a Progressive Conservative, was unwilling to hand Wildrose its legislative death sentence.

Few were surprised when Liberal leader Raj Sherman stepped down as leader on January 26, 2015. One week later, veteran MLA and former leader David Swann assumed the interim role while Sherman remained an MLA until the election call.

Prentice thought he had folded the right-wing opposition under his wing and decimated Wildrose as a viable opposition party. The Liberals, also-rans in Alberta since the first Liberal government was defeated in 1921, appeared as weak as they'd been since the heady days of Laurence Decore's leadership in the 1990s. Prentice had every reason to gaze happily at a legislature where his government was utterly dominant.

At that point, however, dangerous perceptions were already taking shape among the voters. Wildrose was momentarily on the ropes, but the gravest political damage would be to the PCs. The floor crossings blurred their identity and infuriated many party loyalists who wanted nothing to do with the more right-wing opposition party. Many other voters simply felt it was undemocratic, as well as ethically wrong, for so many MLAs elected under the banner of one party to join another, especially after negotiations that were kept completely private.

WHILE THE PCS and Wildrose were already conducting merger talks in deep secrecy in mid-2014, Rachel Notley was running for the leadership of the NDP. She impressed many people from the start with her warmth, humour, and conviction. On October 18 a triumphant Notley was handed the mantle by retiring leader Brian Mason.

"I'd just become leader, and I thought as soon as the leadership is over, I'm going to get a rest. Then, literally three days after I was elected leader, Prentice made this comment," Notley recalls. He had urged voters to compare his record to that of other premiers — language that sounded suspiciously electoral. "I went back to my office and said, 'Did you hear that comment? It's suddenly different. The guy is going to call the election in four months, not sixteen months. So we're not getting our break.'"

Notley notified her election committee and broke the unwelcome news. "We accelerated our candidate search and all our preparation and all that work, which allowed us to be better prepared than the other opposition parties. But how could the Wildrose possibly have been well prepared? How could the Liberals be well prepared? Losing their leaders, it was craziness." When Prentice dropped the writ, the NDP was as equipped as it could be for a snap election. "We were the only opposition, the only one who announced we were running for government. That was us."

THE PCS HAD always seen one use only for the provincial NDP: it was a handy tool to split the left-wing vote and keep the Liberals away from power. If the NDP seemed especially weak, the PCs were always happy to pass on some extra legislature funding to keep it viable. The one thing they never imagined was that the New Democrats would threaten their government.

But now the NDP was suddenly the only party that seemed predictable and stable. People began to take a serious look at Notley. Her personal story resonated with many Albertans; her father, Grant Notley, had been leader of the NDP and one of the most respected politicians in Alberta history. He had been killed in a plane crash in 1984, exactly thirty years and one day before his daughter succeeded him as leader of the party he helped create.

Largely oblivious to these factors, Prentice was laying the groundwork for a PC budget and a spring election by preparing the province for hard economic times. He employed the old PC strategy that had worked for every premier since Ralph Klein — essentially, running against the record of his own party and painting his regime as something entirely new, even though the only real shift was in the premier's office. But this line was wearing thinner with each election. Alison Redford, preaching the same doctrine of internal transformation, had pulled off a victory in 2012 only because mid-campaign "bozo eruptions" tainted Wildrose. It was inevitable that one day the voters would hear all the PCs' self-criticism as a reason to defeat the government rather than reform it once again. Prentice himself was cultivating the ground for his own defeat.

The danger escalated when Prentice suddenly seemed to blame regular Albertans, not just the government, for the sorry state of provincial finances that had been brought on by escalating deficits even in boom times for the oil and gas industry. "We all want to blame somebody for the circumstance we're in," Prentice explained to CBC Radio's Donna McElligot on March 4, 2015. "In terms of who is responsible, we all need only look in the mirror. Basically, all of us have had the best of everything and have not had to pay for what it costs."[3]

Considering that the Tories had been at the helm for forty-three years, the suggestion that the voters were somehow responsible for the government's fiscal plight ignited a storm of criticism. Within moments Twitter erupted and a new hashtag went viral: #PrenticeBlamesAlbertans.

Opposition leaders blasted Prentice. "That is a profoundly insulting comment to all Albertans," Notley declared in the legislature. She immediately showed her gift for catching and reflecting exactly what the public was thinking. "I think there is no question that what this has revealed is an incredible level of arrogance. If this is what the premier will say to Albertans now, before an election, heaven forbid what he'll say after an election."[4]

Prentice was forced to retreat from that comment, but he continued to preach that economic decay required public sacrifice. Every move he made on this front, however, was an admission that the PCs had failed to deal with the province's main structural problem, overreliance on oil and gas. When he tabled his document of doom on March 26, 2015, many Albertans reacted as if a skunk had been dumped at the door.

The PC budget contained fifty-nine new taxes and fee hikes. The 10 percent flat tax was gone, replaced with progressive increases for those making more than $50,000 per year. A health levy, linked to income over $50,000, would top out at $1,000 per family. Taxes were to jump for alcohol and gasoline, while fees rose for mortgages, land transfers, and land registry searches. Public-sector jobs would drop by two thousand in addition to cuts in agencies, boards, and commissions. In health care and education, services would be rolled back and positions eliminated. Even with all that, a $5 billion deficit loomed because of the oil price crash. But Prentice promised to balance the budget by 2017.

As often happens when a government makes complex changes, the public focus turned to a detail that was relatively small but symbolically powerful.

Prentice pruned back the tax credit for charitable donations over $200, to 12.75 percent from 21 percent. But he left the credit for donations to political parties untouched at 75 percent, arguing that this was healthy for democracy. The contrast was devastating; the premier appeared to care more about his party than charity. Prentice took more than three weeks to consider his folly. "Today I need to admit that we've gotten one very important thing wrong in our budget proposal," he admitted on April 21, 2015, after meeting leaders from the charity sector at the University of Calgary campus. He restored the 21 percent credit, but it was far too late. The damage to his image and party was palpable. He appeared to be the corporate man through and through.

This impression deepened dangerously with his obdurate refusal to raise corporate taxes by the slightest fraction, even though he was imposing many new levies on individuals. He held his ground despite the fact that 61 percent of Albertans supported an increase in corporate tax, while only 26 percent were opposed, according to a May 1, 2015, Leger poll conducted for the *Calgary Herald* and *Edmonton Journal*.

No less a figure than revered former premier Peter Lougheed, who died in 2012, had believed the corporate sector wasn't paying its fair due. He certainly didn't want punishing taxes that destroyed jobs; generally speaking, Alberta is a very pro-business province. But Prentice's hard-line stand created resentment. Voters saw in him a premier who not only thought they were responsible for government errors, but expected them to pay the entire bill while his corporate pals got off free. Yet Prentice still believed his budget would bring him decisive victory.

The Harper Conservatives ran into the same mood only months later, with no more apparent concern for its dangers. Their platform for the October 2015 election, 159 pages long, read more like a cold-blooded financial statement than a political manifesto. It was Harper's familiar mantra of balanced budgets and job creation through tax policy rather than direct action. Unlike Prentice, Harper promised to lower personal taxes, not raise them, but national voters had heard all that before.

Thomas Mulcair's NDP followed the Conservatives into the balanced-budget thicket — a strategy that seemed barely credible from a party that also promised more spending on health care, universal plans for both drugs and child care, renewed home delivery from Canada Post, and much more besides. Then Liberal Leader Justin Trudeau did something unique in recent elections; he "promised" larger deficits, in order to get the economy moving and put people back to work. The hunger for change was so powerful that voters flocked to the Liberals, whose New Age platform was at least consistent, and as different from all the works of Stephen Harper as it could possibly be.

But classic western conservatism still had a major role to play in Alberta. Even as Notley's victory was taking shape, Wildrose was quietly reviving. The party had been stripped of most of its MLAs, but it still commanded a substantial war chest. Interim leader Forsyth, a Calgary MLA, had insisted from the day of the floor crossings that supporters had not abandoned the party. She proved to be right. Many members, furious at the floor-crossers, had indeed decided that only the voters, not the pundits or the PCs, could declare their party dead. Wildrose still faced the dismal prospect of fighting an election with a temporary leader who had already said she intended to leave politics. The party executive, with Forsyth's full approval, rushed a process to elect a leader before the expected spring vote.

On March 28, 2015, a former Harper Conservative MP, Brian Jean, launched his provincial political career as leader of the Wildrose. By coincidence, that was the same day former Wildrose leader Smith, now a backbench PC MLA, lost her bid for her new party's nomination in Highwood riding. At the Wildrose leadership event in Calgary, news of her stunning defeat at the hands of PCs was greeted with more cheers and applause than the announcement that Jean had won the leadership vote. It was a troubling omen for Prentice — proof that Progressive Conservatives despised the floor crossings as much as Wildrosers did.

Jean positioned his party as hard right on economic issues, but decreed that Wildrose wouldn't pronounce or agitate on social issues like gay rights. "I will not legislate on a social agenda. I don't think that's what governments are for," he later told columnist Gary Mason of the *Globe and Mail*, on April 22, 2015. "Governments are for making a better quality of life for people, and I think I should stay out of their personal business and that's exactly what I intend to do. That sort of thing only splits Albertans, splits Canadians, and there's no benefit in it."[5]

Jean made his point by responding to the comments of two aspiring Wildrose candidates, one on a blog post, another on an open microphone, that were considered insensitive.

Just before his leadership win was announced, all Wildrose provincial candidates flocked to the stage at the Calgary hotel. "We need lots of brown people in the front," candidate Bill Jarvis blurted out.[6]

The remark, caught on a microphone, brought rebuke from the new leader in a party statement the next day: "The comment was disrespectful, and while I accept that Mr. Jarvis did not intend to insult, I will not accept inappropriate statements that fail to show respect for all Albertans."

In that same statement, a contrite Jarvis resigned as a candidate and apologized: "I recognize that my comments might have caused offence. That was certainly not my intent."

On April 15 another candidate, Russ Kuykendall, was denied a Wildrose nomination after a 2007 anti-gay blog surfaced in the *Western Standard*. In it, Kuykendall complained about a gay pride brunch hosted by then-Edmonton mayor Stephen Mandel in a Catholic church. "The message that appears to be sent to Catholic Christians who don't accept this 'lifestyle' as acceptable is that 'equality' means that gay activists can take their agenda not just to your front door, but inside the door to places that are consecrated to the Catholic faith."[7]

Jean wouldn't comment on the reasons for denying Kuykendall a candidacy run, remarking only: "As a result of going over that paperwork, I felt he would not make a good candidate for the Wildrose."

Jean was doing his best to avoid any appearance of homophobia in the party that lost the 2012 election primarily because of that. The "lake of fire" controversy erupted over a 2011 blog posted by Wildrose candidate Allan Hunsperger. In that post, Hunsperger said that gays "will suffer the rest of eternity in the lake of fire, hell." Then-leader Danielle Smith refused to censure his remarks or ask him to step down. After holding an early lead in the election campaign, Wildrose support plunged in the final campaign days after the post became public.

Even as Wildrose tried to stay away from "social issues," a campaigning MLA managed to steer a little too close for party comfort. Running in the rural riding of Drumheller-Stettler, Rick Strankman asked supporters: "Take a break from calving, farming, spring work and NHL playoffs to join your neighbors from near and far" for an "old-fashioned pie auction." The April 16 Wildrose post urged them to "BYWP (Bring Your Wife's Pie!!)."[8]

This was no lake of fire, but many women were offended. One launched a witty hashtag: #bakeoffire. Asked about Strankman, Notley laughed: "It's clear he has a sweet tooth, but he needs a wisdom tooth."

Jean quickly contacted Strankman, who said he was sorry but blamed a volunteer for his tweet: "I apologize for our poster. It was posted by our volunteers through my account. As soon as I saw it, I asked them to take it down."

Strankman remained the candidate and went on to win the riding for Wildrose, but the episode showed the extreme Wildrose sensitivity to even a hint of such issues running loose. The episode did intensify the party's image as rural based, especially during the 2015 election. Wildrose wouldn't win a seat in Alberta's two largest cities until a later by-election in Prentice's former Calgary-Foothills riding. Retiring interim leader Forsyth's Calgary-Fish Creek seat narrowly went PC over the NDP, followed closely by third-place finisher Wildrose.

FOR THE PREMIER, the timing of this election appeared to be as good as he would get. He considered his austere budget ideal for tough times. Surely Albertans would understand and climb aboard the PC election express. The budget was tabled on March 26, and the premier gave Albertans twelve days to absorb the pain. With the PCs' proposed deficit, borrowing, and massive tax hikes, Prentice dropped the writ on April 7 for an election on May 5, 2015. "Albertans have the opportunity to make a choice — a realistic, honest plan or frankly betting the future on some extreme ideas and ideologies," he declared.[9]

It wouldn't take long for hindsight to reveal the folly. "The warning signs were there that this election was possibly not the smartest call," Mainstreet Technologies pollster Quito Maggi told the *Calgary Herald*'s Darcy Henton.[10]

It was already clear that voters in all age groups were more irritated by Prentice every day. Now he exasperated them by calling the election a year earlier than his own government had mandated. Prentice argued that he needed public approval for his budget, but many saw only that he was breaking a provincial law, passed by the PCs themselves, in order to take advantage of Wildrose disarray and nail down another majority. The election also seemed unnecessary and wasteful for a government preaching austerity. But the province's deepening economic slide promised to be prolonged, and senior PC strategists calculated that waiting another year would bring a far more serious risk of defeat.

Calgary Mayor Naheed Nenshi jumped in to voice the thoughts of many voters. "I don't think I would have called an election now," he told reporters. "I think that there is a pretty good mandate. And I think that if we're in a world where it's difficult to find $200,000 to investigate the deaths of children in care, to then find $30 million to run an election, it's a tough argument for me to make if I were in that shoe."[11]

TWO DAYS AFTER the election call, Wildrose released its own economic strategy. It started and ended with a battle against new taxes. This would be Brian Jean's mantra throughout the campaign as he directly targeted the provincial public sector, in particular its managers.

Wildrose would chop 3,200 jobs, slashing one-third of the managerial staff in government and fully one-half of those in Alberta Health Services. The harsh cuts would clearly affect programs and services, but Wildrose never wavered in its belief that less government would eliminate the need for tax hikes while balancing the books by 2017. The PCs immediately criticized the plan, saying it would leave the province with a $29 billion funding hole.

Notley, like the federal Liberals in the later national campaign, had no objection to deficit spending in difficult times. She correctly judged that many Albertans were fed up with the PC habit of cutting education and health spending whenever oil prices dipped.

From the beginning, Notley promised to halt PC funding cuts to both and to safeguard civil service jobs in the name of stability. On April 19 she presented the NDP's economic platform, calling for a balanced budget by 2017 (later revised to 2018 because of an embarrassing accounting lapse). The party would stop the PCs' planned health levy and add two thousand new long-term-care beds over four years. Notley vowed to fund classrooms for twelve thousand new students and provide lunch for children who arrive at school hungry and empty-handed.

Targeting a long-dormant political underclass in Alberta — the highly educated, underemployed young people struggling to get enough hours in the coffee bars and restaurants — the NDP promised to boost the minimum wage from $10.20 per hour to $15 by 2018. Notley would also stimulate twenty-seven thousand new jobs through employer tax credits of 10 percent up to $50,000 for each new hire. She promised to restore a student summer employment system that had been axed by the PCs. Notley insisted that her fiscal plan would be less onerous than that of Prentice for 90 percent of Albertans. But personal taxes would rise for upper-income earners; those earning over $125,000 per year would see an incremental income tax hike according to their tax bracket.

In sharp contrast to the PCs, the NDP would also make profitable companies pay more. A corporate tax hike of two points, from 10 to 12 percent, would kick in after profits reached $500,000. Notley noted that the tax hike would target "profitable corporations — not small business." The increase would still give Alberta the lowest corporate tax in the country, she said. This left Prentice hanging out on a shaky limb as the only major leader who wanted to raise taxes for individuals, but not business.

Notley also promised a full review of the province's oil and gas royalty regime, a crucial revenue source Prentice had declared untouchable. Combined with his refusal to raise corporate taxes by even a fraction of a point, this deepened his image as "Diamond Jim," a pal of business. Even Lougheed, after he came to power in 1971, realized that royalties needed to increase when prices and profits rose, and hiked them twice within a decade. Prentice was also acting against the results of a recent survey by his own finance department; it showed that most Albertans wanted both a higher corporate tax and a review of the royalty system.

Another key Notley promise was to abolish Canada's most lax and corporate-friendly system of political financing. She vowed to ban union and corporate donations to political parties. The NDP would no longer see its treasury grow from union contributions. Nor would the PCs reap the corporate donations that had long been their major source of funds. All parties would need to cultivate more individual donors, which the Wildrose was doing much more efficiently than its rivals.

Popularity, however, was already erasing the NDP's funding problem. Individual donations to the party began to rise dramatically as the campaign progressed. "There were different points in the campaign where we realized that there was massive support that we'd never seen before. We felt really good about it," Notley said in an interview. "It just told us that we were going to do well. That was very exciting."

As the campaign progressed, volunteers and money poured in, to the delight of Notley's election crew. "The increase in fundraising was extraordinary," says Brian Topp, Notley's director of tour and communications, and now her chief of staff. "It felt like we were in a Harry Potter movie: the mail courier just came by and a million dollars blew through the mail slot, all by itself. It felt like the office of money." The other shock was the wave of volunteers rushing to participate. "There was a whole bunch of people who showed up. We were rushing to catch up with them. We were constantly running out of stuff and had to keep reprinting signs and pamphlets at a scale we were not used to in this market."

THE MAJOR NDP breakthrough of the campaign occurred the evening of April 23, 2015, as four provincial leaders stood behind their podiums staring into the cameras, for the only televised debate. An NHL playoff game between the Calgary Flames and Vancouver Canucks, scheduled to start right afterward, drew an unusually large audience to the TV.

Brian Topp coached Notley through the two opposing tactics that Prentice would likely wield — attack or shun. Whom would he face and whom would he ignore: Wildrose leader Jean, or NDP leader Notley? (Liberal leader David Swann was respectfully disregarded.) In the end, Prentice made the decision for her; he chose Notley as his main foe. This crucial move backfired explosively and further launched Notley's rise in the polls. Albertans saw a massive political shift happening in real time, right before their eyes: a reigning PC premier was directly attacking an NDP leader, and being shredded, while effectively ignoring the Official Opposition. Prentice both legitimized Notley and lost the debating contest. This proved to be the moment of his undoing.

Disaster struck as leaders debated corporate tax rates. Prentice accused the NDP of planning a "20 percent corporate income tax." Notley immediately countered with her party's proposal for 12 percent. At that point Prentice, a head taller than Notley, turned and looked down at her: "I know that math is difficult," he said, "but 12 percent is a 20 percent increase."

Whatever his intention, Prentice must have sensed at that very moment that he'd lost it. He was accused of "mansplaining" to Notley, and the twitticisms rolled in. Jenna Greig (@jlgreig) spliced a picture of Barbie in a pink-striped halter dress and carrying a large pink purse. At the top, she shouted in caps: "MATH IS HARD"; at the bottom: "LET'S GO SHOPPING."[12] Then @jlgreig posted: "It's a good thing Jim Prentice is here to save us from ourselves."

Twitter erupted with a new hashtag — #mathishard — while the debate was still on the air. Steve Ladurantaye (@sladurantaye) of Twitter Canada asked: "Pop quiz: When did Prentice tell Notley that math is hard? That got Twitter all riled up."

For Albertans, this would prove to be as decisive a political moment as Brian Mulroney's evisceration of John Turner in 1984 ("You had a choice, sir"), or Justin Trudeau's later 2015 performance that showed he wasn't the bumbling fool of Conservative myth. But at the moment it happened, everything depended on how Notley handled the opening Prentice handed her.

She responded perfectly, first letting the comment pass without showing any outrage or raising allegations of sexism. And then, when the discussion shifted to oil and gas royalties, she pounced. In response to Prentice, she said, "Albertans are always told, 'Don't worry your pretty little heads.'" Another woman tweeted: "Right there, that was the moment that I decided how to vote."

The PC premier and his advisers had clearly misjudged the NDP's gifted female leader. Prentice also appeared rude when he literally turned his back on Wildrose leader Jean in mid-sentence. During one of the few exchanges when Prentice faced Jean, to slam the Wildrose economic plans, Notley adeptly stole the scene. "That's no way to talk to a donor," she said. Her zinger shrewdly reminded voters that Jean had donated $10,000 to the premier's PC leadership campaign only the previous autumn.

Overall, Prentice seemed jolted by Notley's quickness. She played him adroitly without appearing angry, just indignant. Sometimes Prentice seemed exasperated. Danielle Smith, the former Wildrose leader now on the sidelines, watched the debate and tweeted via @ABDanielleSmith: "I'm in a room full of business conservatives. Feedback so far is the men look grim and Rachel looks great."

Post-debate polls showed Notley was the clear winner. The premier and his advisers had grossly underestimated her. They should have known that a woman who had managed to rise to the top of the field as a labour lawyer and a politician might be tough under pressure.

"She just comes right back at you. She is spring-loaded to be an effective debater," a top Notley adviser told Maclean's magazine columnist Paul Wells.[13]

The debate was just another sign of the PC Party's stunning loss of contact with the public throughout the campaign. For a politician once considered an heir to former Conservative prime minister Stephen Harper, Prentice seemed surprisingly insensitive to modern Alberta. And his clangers didn't end with the debate.

The day after, Prentice declared: "Alberta is not an NDP province." Once again, Notley showed her sharp political instinct. She agreed with him. "Alberta is not an NDP province," she said. "It's not a PC province. It's not a Liberal province. It's not a Wildrose province. Alberta belongs to Albertans." Like most of her comments in the campaign, this was pitch-perfect. The PCs simply couldn't get past their belief that only they defined and represented the province. They didn't see that many thousands of young people were ready to shape Alberta in a new way.

When Notley met with the *Edmonton Journal* editorial board she expressed her deep belief that the province was as progressive as "many other parts of Canada. I had one senior Tory tell me, on the eve of the 2012 election: 'We've done all this polling, and Albertans don't know it, but they actually are New Democrats.' We are a different province than we were 20 years ago."[14]

Notley had a similar message for the *Globe and Mail's* Mason: "There is a national urban myth about the values of Albertans. We are a young province, a very diverse province. We are very progressive and forward-looking on a lot of issues, more so than a lot of other parts of the country."[15]

As the campaign pressed on, the polls began to reflect Notley's rise. In every age group — including those over sixty-five — she was the leader Albertans trusted most. Change, trust, and accountability trumped the nuts-and-bolts issues — health and education — that make up nearly half the government budget and affect everyone. After nearly forty-four years of PC rule, many people were fed up with late-regime leadership instability, internal conflicts, and constant vacillation between funding cuts and increases. They were looking for something more.

The signs had been visible for nearly five years, for those who cared to see. Nenshi's 2010 mayoral victory, and his second win in 2013, signalled that change was waiting to happen far beyond the municipal arena. Don Iveson's 2013 mayoral victory in Edmonton carried the same message: younger, progressive voters were on the march, and they wanted change. Well-educated millennials were looking for leaders who not only understood them but promised something more than pothole politics. Notley fit that bill. Prentice did not. He generally ignored those outside the carefully tended Tory tent of entitlement. As the oil-price crash destroyed jobs across the province, his platform contained no plan for direct job-creation, or anything whatever for young people, beyond the standard conservative pleas to trust tax and fiscal policy to provide employment eventually.

Prentice made no effort to modify his campaign as the headwinds began to rise. If anything, he intensified it, and business leaders piled on to dismiss the NDP's policies on taxes and royalties. To one of his attacks Notley responded: "I don't exactly know how a [royalty] review would be devastating one way or another. I don't know how talking to Albertans, with Albertans, in an independent, transparent, accountable forum about a resource that belongs to Albertans is going to kill the industry."[16] For more than five years, despite the fierce opposition of the industry, polls had shown the majority of Albertans wanted a review of the royalty regime.

Major business leaders struck a sour note when they tried to get involved. The CEO of Cenovus Energy, Brian Ferguson, told *Bloomberg News*: "I don't think there's any room for any increase in royalties. If there are changes that make the structure uncompetitive, that will be negative for investment in Alberta."[17] But Notley had never said that royalities would be raised, only that the system would be reviewed.

Prentice presented Notley and the NDP as enemies of energy, especially the bitumen produced from the oil sands and the new pipelines needed to get the crude to market. Notley called him out for "fear-mongering." She insisted she was not against bitumen or new pipelines but preferred to champion those with the best chance for success: TransCanada's Energy East pipeline that would pump Alberta crude to New Brunswick refineries; and the Kinder Morgan Trans Mountain pipeline to the southwest British Columbia coast.

Notley felt the other two pipeline projects were too tangled in land-owner and regulatory opposition that could take years to unravel. Enbridge's Northern Gateway project was intended to carry crude from near Edmonton, Alberta, to Kitimat, B.C., for tanker shipment to Pacific markets. TransCanada's Keystone XL would pipe bitumen to the U.S. Gulf Coast. Notley's political judgment proved prescient. In a landmark decision, U.S. president Barack Obama vetoed the Keystone project on November 6, 2015. A week later, Prime Minister Justin Trudeau's new Liberal government declared its intention to rule the northern B.C. coastline off limits to tankers, thus paralyzing Northern Gateway's moves. Later, that position seemed to soften as the government hesitated on actually imposing the ban pending discussions on a different site for the port. Trudeau was adamant, however, that "the Great Bear rainforest is no place for a pipeline." But the whole issue seemed to become moot in July 2016, when the Federal Court of Appeal ruled that the original approval was invalid because the federal government had failed to properly consult indigenous people.

As for Keystone, Gary Doer, the former Canadian ambassador to the United States, wonders: "You ask people, do you want your oil from Canada or petro-dictators? I do believe it will be part of an energy and environmental security policy with Canada, the U.S., and Mexico."

Prentice continued his campaign push against the NDP, calling its corporate tax increase "symbolic ... of a fundamental distrust of business and the creation of jobs in this province." Speaking to 1,600 supporters at the $500-per-plate Edmonton leader's dinner, Prentice criticized Notley for being too cozy with federal NDP leader Thomas Mulcair: "We don't need a pipeline policy in this province that feels like it was scripted by Thomas Mulcair. Fundamentally, the NDP could undermine the heart of Alberta's economy. And we must not let that happen."[18]

When asked about the remarks as she voted at the advance poll on May 1, Notley laughed and replied that she hadn't spoken to Mulcair in months. She added that the campaign "has deteriorated into groundless name-calling, and it's certainly not the strategy that I would take."[19] (In fact, the 2016 NDP national convention held in Edmonton would show the rift between not only Notley and Mulcair, but between her and the hard-left, anti–fossil fuel wing represented by the Leap Manifesto proponents.)

The PCs assumed their late TV and radio ad campaign to demonize the NDP would pay off with victory. During the campaign period they managed to raise a massive $3.4 million, far outflanking the NDP and Wildrose.[20] But the PCs also spent more — so much more, $4.3 million, that the party plunged into a huge red hole of $930,000. The largest expense, $1.7 million, went to advertising and communications, more than double the $726,000 the PCs put into research and direct voter contact. The competition, however, managed to steer the balance sheet into the black. The Wildrose spent far less, $1.2 million, and banked an impressive surplus of over $500,000. The NDP spent a little more, $1.64 million, and ended with a campaign surplus of just over $7,000.

"We were conducting a very focused ground game aimed at what looked like targets when the plan was put together two to three months before the campaign," says Topp. "The party focused resources tightly on a tier of seats expected to win on the ground. The big air campaign didn't mean we were conceding anywhere. In the balance of seats that didn't have this kind of organizational focus, we were going to campaign anyway. There was a second wave of ground operations that were driven by volunteers. We were running to keep up with this incredible demand for the ability to participate in the campaign."

About a third of the way through the campaign, as NDP strategists assessed their increasing support, they watched the momentum continue into seats they hadn't targeted. "We had to take advantage of this growing enthusiasm by people seeing us," adds Topp. The second-wave volunteers set up billboards and signs throughout the province and in places where the NDP hadn't pushed before. "We weren't used to seeing this happening. The campaign was catching up with volunteers on the ground. "

The original NDP media buy didn't fit the campaign any more, explained Topp. "Suddenly we were competitive all over the place, fueled by a whack of donations from ordinary folks who wanted Rachel Notley to do well. We redesigned our media buy at least twice. The first extension was in Calgary, where the leader always said the key to victory lies." As with her leadership launch, Notley continued her first focus on Alberta's two big cities and then broadened the election tour across the province. The candidates with their pamphlets, signs, and billboard messages actively campaigned throughout their constituencies in a push that hadn't really happened before in an Alberta NDP campaign. "We went quite wide so people could see our candidates and see us as a real option that they could make," continued Topp. "So people weren't wasting their vote."

Topp believed that Notley was the New Democrats' "key asset and key communication vehicle. Her events were often quite extraordinary, and so we kept rethinking and recalibrating. The tour grew like an onion as we added layers. Where she was going is where we thought we were going to win." Which, in the end, was every urban centre and rural corner of the province, as Notley's first to last waking hours were spent with Albertans listening, questioning, and then considering an alternative to what simply was, and had been, for nearly forty-four years.

The PC ad campaign was supposed to thwart all that and convince the province that only one party could govern effectively. Instead, it created a backlash. For the first time ever in Alberta, all that money, collected mainly from business, backfired on the PC Party and its leader. The ads just made people angrier, exactly as federal Conservative ads would ultimately hurt Stephen Harper's government in the federal campaign in October 2015.

Both cases showed that contrary to popular stereotype, and to the behaviour of every governing party, money is not always everything in politics.

By the end of the provincial struggle the PCs were in full panic mode. It led them to a spectacular final blunder. Business friends and associates of the premier held an Edmonton news conference to warn Albertans they "weren't thinking straight" in supporting the NDP. "These are about clear choices, let's make no mistake," said lawyer Doug Goss, who was the PC-appointed chair of the University of Alberta board of governors, and also a central figure in the Prentice campaign. "At a time when we have every opportunity to go to another level, we just cannot afford to go backwards and take a misstep."[21]

The news conference was held in the offices of Melcor Developments, a major land developer in Alberta and British Columbia. Its executive chairman, Tim Melton, said NDP governments "don't understand how economies work," and praised the PCs as a "very solid government.... I don't understand the unhappiness and disenchantment that appears to be out there."

John Cameron, CEO of Keller Construction, added: "I can't imagine what this province will look like if we don't make the right choice next week.... I risk everything I have because I am a small business, and then I have somebody tell me that I should be paying more tax. Why? Why is it me? Why is it the corporation?"

Ashif Mawji, CEO of NPO Zero, a company that provides services to non-profits, implied that charitable funding would dry up under the NDP: "If there is no bottom line ... there's no money that goes to charities. We all make donations to charities, there is no more excellence at the Stollery [the children's hospital in Edmonton], as an example, or great programs at the university. There's all those things that businesses contribute to. So it's an important ingredient and we can't forget that."

The angry reaction was immediate on social and mainstream media commentary. Within minutes, a new hashtag, #PCAAHostageCrisis, trended across the country. There was more to come after the *Edmonton Journal* reported that the five businessmen and their companies had donated $95,000 in total to the Progressive Conservatives in the previous five years, and some had received millions in government contracts.[22]

The late-campaign news conference, which had been approved by Prentice's campaign, solidified the impression that the PCs had become a compliant government in the pocket of business interests. After the election, Canadian Press reporter Dean Bennett wrote: "Notley said she remembered watching the group and thinking 'this is it?' She said she then realized how profoundly the Tories had misread the electorate."[23]

In their desperation, the PCs had tried a version of the fright-wig ploy they had pulled off brilliantly against Wildrose in 2012. But Notley was a target both more impressive and more elusive. To many voters she didn't appear scary at all, but reasonable and appealing. The business assault backfired. Erupting on May 2, the Friday before the 2015 election, it probably contributed to a late burst of NDP support over the final weekend.

Even as the polls showed the popularity of Notley's platform, Prentice believed he could still convince Albertans they were wrong. He had spent months arguing that finances were a wreck and the province was on the verge of ruin. But rather than marshalling Albertans to action, he was sending a dismal message that seemed devoid of hope; and in the end, it was all about his own party's long record in government. His manner was that of a gruff general waging war against the past. His message earned him a new nickname: "Grim Jim."

Despite the emerging hard times, most Albertans weren't so pessimistic. What they wanted was a government that understood their obvious fears but offered a touch of inspiration, along with a plan that protected essential services. Many younger people saw that Notley promised both a direct job creation program and a higher minimum wage.

For every dark cloud that Prentice forecast, Notley countered with a ray of hope and confidence in the spirit and innovation of Albertans. She allayed the fears of the voters by presenting an image of poise and tenacity. The hope-monger bested the fear-monger. It was exactly what many Albertans, especially the younger ones, wanted to hear. Toward the end, NDP supporters rose from unexpected Tory places. The late Ralph Klein's eldest daughter, Angie, posted a YouTube call for NDP victory.[24]

On the final weekend, a member of the PC Party executive called the party's Ottawa-based pollster and asked for a précis of the findings. There was a pause, and then the pollster said: "You're screwed."

When Canadian political campaigns run off the rails, they often go so wildly wrong that some malign force seems to be working against the party that's about to be obliterated. So it was, right to the end of the PC campaign.

An uproar involving the recently deposed justice minister, Jonathan Denis, exploded into the media. He was embroiled in a bitter divorce with his estranged wife, Breanna Palmer, who was granted a restraining order against him. A publication ban on court proceedings was lifted the day before the election. That led, on the very day of the vote, to a front-page *Calgary Herald* story containing allegations that were never proven. The judge ruled that there was no basis to Palmer's claim she was in physical danger.[25] Aside from the allegations, what made the story such a hot topic was how Prentice treated Denis. The leader supported him, although rather weakly, by accepting his resignation as justice minister while allowing him to remain as a PC candidate. "We move on," the premier said without noticeable enthusiasm.

But the PCs were finding it ever harder to move on. Denis stayed in the PC fold even though another committed Tory, Jamie Lall, had been stripped of his nomination by the party, ostensibly because his ex-girlfriend once had a restraining order against him. The order was made in 2007, when the former girlfriend said she felt threatened after they broke up. By 2015, however, she told the CBC, "We are diplomatically civil now."[26]

That didn't help Lall, who was dumped from the Chestermere-Rocky View riding, while Bruce McAllister, a Wildrose floor-crosser, was appointed as the PC candidate. The appearance of a double-standard — a former justice minister got to remain a candidate while a PC volunteer did not — suggested the background reason. The PC brass were alarmed that Wildrose floor-crossers, especially Danielle Smith, kept losing PC nominations. They needed those floor-crosser candidates.

Lall then decided to run against McAllister as an independent, and soon proved to be a lethal weapon aimed at his old party. He released a series of texts between himself and former PC Party executive director Kelley Charlebois, which seemed to support the political rather than the personal motive behind Lall's ouster. "Don't want you in Chestermere [the riding]," wrote Charlebois on January 31, 2015. "I think it has more to do with who you're running against than you," Charlebois later wrote.

When the PCs put a private investigator on Lall's trail, he sought support from his friend Jonathan Denis. "Buddy, you are being set up," texted Denis. Lall replied that the party said all candidates were vetted this way.

Denis said: "BS. BS. BS," and added that Lall should "hire a lawyer."[27] All that emerged even before Denis ended up in court with his estranged wife.

Then, on April 29, Jim Prentice found himself defending Mike Allen as a suitable PC candidate, while he said Lall was not.[28] Fort McMurray MLA Mike Allen was convicted of soliciting two prostitutes — at the same time — in July 2013.[29] His problems began when they turned out to be undercover cops and arrested him. Allen was attending a conference in St. Paul, Minnesota, as an Alberta government representative. After the news broke, Allen quit the PC caucus and paid back his conference expenses of $2,061.44, but remained an independent MLA. In December he pleaded guilty to soliciting and received a fine of $500 plus costs. A year after his eventful Minnesota trip, Allen was accepted back into the PC fold. Prentice said that Allen had taken responsibility for what he did, while Lall had not disclosed that his former girlfriend once held a restraining order against him eight years before.

The bitter root of all these party skirmishes was the Wildrose floor crossings. "The anger that was directed toward me when I got defeated in my riding, I think it ricocheted," Danielle Smith told a Spur Festival forum on April 26, 2015. "That anger had to go somewhere, so I think it just sort of ricocheted back onto Prentice and the PCs."[30] Not one of the eleven floor-crossers would be in the new legislature after the May 5 election. They either decided not to run, tried for PC nominations but lost, or captured nominations one way or another and then lost in the general election. McAllister, after being appointed, lost to Wildrose candidate Leela Aheer. As for Allen, Prentice's defence didn't help him. Wildroser Tany Yao won his riding.

The PCs no longer had the luxury of fighting their internecine squabbles in public while strolling to another easy victory. They were upended by voter disgust that had spread deep into their own support base. Their policies were out of step with the public, and Prentice had made one blunder after another. They'd walked straight into a force they never expected to face — a sharp, focused NDP led by a new leader who shocked them with her skill, even though they should have seen her coming. Notley had been in the legislature since 2008, right across from the PCs, showing growing skill as a debater as well as a great force of personality. She had all the ingredients for success: a warm manner, quick intelligence, humour, and a gift for saying exactly the right thing in the heat of political exchange

("Alberta isn't an NDP province …"). Yet the PCs never took her seriously because, in their darkest nightmares, they simply couldn't imagine being defeated by the NDP.

"You could tell from afar that things had turned in Alberta during the election campaign," said Gary Doer, who was in Washington at the time. "Rachel Notley has charisma and the ability to articulate her vision. Her platform was pretty solid as well. Some very definite proposals fit with the vision of the NDP." When he saw the old regime tumble, Doer, once the NDP premier of Manitoba, also blamed the PCs' very longevity for the fall. He recalled the old political adage: "You have to get out before the grim reaper or the grim voter gets you."

As Notley approached the finish line, she was met with large, enthusiastic crowds. She declared to avid listeners: "It's time for renewal. It is time for change. It's time for new people with new ideas, better ideas, ideas about making things better instead of worse. And I say this to every Albertan in every community of this province: You don't have to repeat history. This Tuesday you can make history."[31]

That they did, to the shock not only of the PCs but of the entire country. The climate for change had created a swell that Calgary's Naheed Nenshi rode to the 2010 mayor's chair. In 2013, it swept Edmonton's Don Iveson into his mayoralty spot. Notley caught the same rising waves that would go on to crest with Prime Minister Justin Trudeau's victory.

NOTLEY GOT WORD of the decisive poll just over a week before the election. "There were other polls that were already suggesting that we were positioned to win. But this particular poll, just being a bit of a geek that I am, was done in a way and asked questions in a way and asked the right people in a way that made me go, 'Oh, my God. This is real. This is actually real.' I still remember the day because I got briefed on the poll on the road, between events."

But Notley carried on with her packed schedule into the night just as the reality of what was about to happen began to dawn on her.

"I was already a bit tired and a bit grumpy, so when I got back to my hotel room around nine o'clock, I called my husband and told him about the last poll." While she downloaded her concerns, her fatigue spread through the line as Lou Arab, her husband and closest confidant, quickly absorbed that this election would change history. Notley continued, "We don't appear to be doing any transition planning yet," but Arab quickly stopped her and said, "Call your campaign manager."

She immediately phoned Gerry Scott with her pressing plea. "This is actually going to happen. And every free moment over the next six to eight days has to be focused on transition. We've done nothing and we're not ready," she told him forcefully.

As Notley looks back she doesn't recall ever being frightened. "I was just urgent. If urgency can be a sentiment, it was just urgency." She knew, as she settled into the notion of an NDP government, that she wasn't stranded in a political wilderness. "Part of it was sitting down and talking to key people to sort of map out the architecture of this." After all, they had the brain trust of past NDP governments from across the country.

Topp recalled how the team was "quite sobered with the implications. We were tackling a big job taking on the government of Alberta basically from a standing start." Just as Notley had "urged" her inner core to prepare for transition, Topp got "down to brass tacks quite quickly and what the transition team looked like, turning to that a week before the campaign ended."

On the night of her election victory, a euphoric Notley reflected on the historic win. "I believe that change has finally come to Alberta," she told the boisterous crowd in the Edmonton Weston Hotel's bulging ballroom. "New people, new ideas, and a fresh start for our great province."

She was right — but only to a point. People finally wanted a change from the PCs. But for that change to happen, the PCs had to run the worst campaign imaginable, and the NDP had to run the best. As new governments always will, Notley chose to see her mandate as a full endorsement of every line in her policy book. The reality was much more complex; her support was a combination of yearning for the new, a desire to move to younger leadership, a visceral rejection of a stale-dated party, and an embrace of a fresh direction that ranged, depending upon the voter, from enthusiastic to tentative.

But Conservatism itself was far from dead in Alberta. The NDP won 40.6 percent of the popular vote; the PCs and Wildrose together took 52 percent. Talk of a conservative merger began almost at once. The provincial economy quickly sank to a level even Prentice hadn't forecast in his scariest scenarios. Notley had taken office in the toughest circumstances faced by any new premier since William Aberhart became the first Social Credit premier in 1935, during the dark heart of the Great Depression.

The remarkable Rachel Notley was premier. She'd earned that job. But nothing would be easy for her, especially after it became clear that she was intent on driving through the most aggressive social and economic changes ever seen in Alberta.

CHAPTER 3

THE MIRROR CRACKS

Albertans awoke with a political hangover after decades of imbibing the PC brand.

The triumphant Rachel Notley and her New Democrats seemed as stunned as the nation. The reigning PCs were defeated and with them Jim Prentice, who was winning his riding when he abruptly quit.

All those years of PC power had prepared Prentice for one thing only: another striking win. It took the highest Alberta voter turnout in a generation, 58.3 percent, to push the PCs from their perch. A new generation had taken to the polls and helped trigger a colossal upset.

"Well, Prentice did promise us 'generational change.' But he obviously didn't have this in mind," wrote *Edmonton Journal* columnist Graham Thomson. "Prentice thought he had it figured out — undermine the Wildrose with a mass floor-crossing, appoint his favourites as candidates, call an early election — but it all backfired."[1]

Just as Notley and her NDP were embracing the extent of their victory, Prentice was recognizing his historic humiliation. He resigned his party leadership, and his Calgary-Foothills seat, even before his personal victory by more than 1,500 votes was fully recorded. "My contribution to public life is now at an end," Prentice told his supporters. "While I am personally saddened by the decision, the voters are always right in our democracy. Rachel obviously ran an excellent campaign and clearly has the confidence of Albertans, and I have spoken to her this evening and wished her the very best." Prentice was gracious at the end, living up to one of his several nicknames — "Gentleman Jim." He took full responsibility for the defeat, and then went underground. For nine long days Prentice remained silent. His absence from his government underscored both his personal and his party's profound blow. Even though he was still premier, he appeared to be mostly uninvolved in the complex transition of government.

"He wasn't necessarily thinking about how to help us," Notley said in an interview. "But no one was thinking, 'Let's go to this guy, who has his own disappointment to manage, and bring him in and ask him to work.' I think that would have been a bit disrespectful. I did speak to him very soon after and we met very soon after as well. He was very gracious. He'd say, 'Here's a file we're working on and I hope you continue working on, and here are some opportunities for you.' We just debriefed, honestly, about the campaign in large part too, because you've both been on the road. It's a very exhausting thing being on the election campaign.

"It was a good conversation and we were able to talk about things we had in common. There're plenty of things about being a politician that are the same for people. It's not hard for me to sit down in a room with a politician from another party and find lots of common issues to talk about; trials and tribulations and joking matters that politicians would know about regardless of which side of the floor they're on. And so we had that kind of conversation."

Notley was understanding of Prentice's profound pain and why it would be hard for him to advise on any transitioning. "I wouldn't say there was help per se. To be perfectly honest, I would say that Premier Prentice was under his own form of stress." It was indeed a hard thing for Prentice to be known as the final PC premier of a forty-three-year-old regime, the one who brought it all crashing down.

When he finally emerged in public on May 14, to speak at the party's pre-scheduled leader's dinner, the sombre crowd heard "an emotional Prentice," reported the *Calgary Herald's* James Wood. "The obligation of leadership rests squarely on my shoulders," Prentice said. "I will carry those decisions and the electoral consequences of it for the rest of my life." Then he added: "I am sorry I let you down as leader."[2]

Prentice wouldn't talk to waiting media and retreated into silence. He was still premier until Notley could be sworn in. Yet the legislature that had bustled with Tory pride fell listless. The only discernible bursts of government activity were shredding machines coughing up the scraps of documents past.

"What an ignoble exit," wrote *Calgary Herald* columnist (and co-author) Don Braid. "Such a shabby segue into obscurity. Silent and pouty, the Progressive Conservatives leave one final image behind after nearly forty-four years of government. Shredding. Clear plastic bags bloated with paper strips in legislature hallways, the unreadable debris of a frantic cleanout in the first three days after the May 5 election defeat."[3]

The shredding prompted a news release from the province's information and privacy commissioner, Jill Clayton. "There are rules for government ministries and their employees relating to the retention, destruction and preservation of records, and these rules apply and must be followed during the government's transition period."[4]

The question of what was being destroyed after four decades of Tory rule fired up fears that critical records would be irretrievably lost. The *Calgary Herald's* Matt McClure searched the government's record guide, noting that "the legislation says those containing information that will have future legal, financial, research or archival value should be retained."[5]

The Service Alberta manual is explicit: "If you're in doubt, keep the record."

Prentice, still premier, needn't have allowed such an embarrassing display of defeat to become the symbol of a fallen dynasty.

Only eight months before, he had won a decisive leadership contest, with abilities that had long seemed lacking in previous premiers. Finally, the party had the Jim they needed, noted a number of party regulars, with a sad nod to the previous Jim — Dinning, about whom many still say, "Jim Dinning is the best leader we never had." On September 6, 2014, Prentice, with 76 percent, easily defeated former Cabinet ministers Thomas Lukaszuk and Ric McIver to become the head of the PC Party and the new premier of Alberta.

But there were signs that the PC brand was in trouble, with the most obvious being the vast drop in votes cast in the leadership contest — only twenty-three thousand compared to fifty-nine thousand in the victory of Alison Redford in 2011. The PC troubles stretched far beyond the new electronic voting system that created havoc over the two-day voting period. The controversies of previous premiers made for a distrustful public and disillusioned party. But Prentice was determined to bury the past. "This is a viable party with a future," he insisted. "Albertans will see that immediately and we will re-earn trust and respect one vote at a time."[6]

PRENTICE SEEMED PERFECT for his new job. He had polished his political career by running successfully for the federal riding of Calgary Centre-North in 2004. When Stephen Harper's Conservative government won a minority in 2006, Prentice became minister of Indian affairs and northern development. In 2007 he was appointed minister of industry, and then minister of the environment after Harper's 2008 majority victory.

"I have a lot of respect for Jim Prentice," says former Canadian ambassador to the United States Gary Doer. "He brought in vehicle emission standards, on which we worked together. It led to a profound drop in greenhouse gas emissions."

Prentice had left federal politics on November 4, 2010, to join the Canadian Imperial Bank of Commerce as a senior executive, starting January 1, 2011. In March 2014 he took a break from his CIBC duties to jump aboard pipeline giant Enbridge and its multi-billion-dollar quest to build the Northern Gateway pipeline from near Edmonton, Alberta, to Kitimat on the British Columbia coast. With his experience and understanding, Prentice hoped to thaw the frozen negotiations between Enbridge and the First Nations along the project route. "It is never too late to sit down and hear what people have to say, to hear what their concerns are and find ways to address them," he told CBC News. "I will sit at the table as long as I need to sit at the table to see that through."[7]

Only two months later, on May 16, 2014, Prentice left the corporate table to run for the leadership of the Alberta PCs. His victory brought a quick jump in the polls for the party. He soon moved to put his personal stamp on the government, appointing two Cabinet ministers who weren't yet elected for critical portfolios. The health ministry went to Stephen Mandel, the popular Edmonton ex-mayor; while the education portfolio was assumed by Gordon Dirks, a former Saskatchewan social services minister and Calgary Board of Education chair.

There were four ridings at play when Prentice called the by-elections for October 27, 2014, with Wildrose expected to win at least one. But the hard-fought, innuendo-ridden battle saw Wildrose come up empty. In Calgary, Prentice handily won his seat, as did Dirks, while Mandel also won by a wide margin in Edmonton. The only squeaker was the tight Calgary race between the high-profile Wildrose candidate, Sheila Taylor, and the little-known Tory, Calgary Police Sergeant Mike Ellis, who finally won by just over three hundred votes.

That night, the opposition Wildrose couldn't put a dent in Prentice's popularity. Leader Danielle Smith conceded: "Albertans have told the PCs they are willing to give them one last chance, but certainly not a blank cheque. Albertans have put Premier Jim Prentice on probation."[8]

Her remarks would later seem hollow. Was the probation really a time for Smith herself to weigh a floor crossing? By the end of the year, Smith and ten of her Wildrose colleagues would themselves lift the probation period to sit with Prentice and his PCs.

It was a triumphant, confident premier whose by-election victories now set the stage for his self-described "new beginning for Alberta." The floor crossings would only add to the PCs' sense of invincibility.

But problems continued to erode the PC base, especially in the cities. In late 2014 Prentice and his caucus managed to paint themselves into a social-conservative corner much as Stephen Harper's Conservatives would do in the 2015 federal election. For the latter, it would be the niqab ban coupled with the "barbaric cultural practices" snitch line. For the Alberta PCs, it featured a discriminatory mess called Bill 10, which seemed to deny basic human rights for gay youths. The PC bill was a reaction to the Liberals' Bill 202, which had been astutely presented by Liberal MLA Laurie Blakeman to give students the right to form gay-straight alliances (GSAs) in schools.

The root of this legislative turmoil was an earlier attempt by then-Liberal MLA Kent Hehr to support GSAs in schools. His private member's Motion 503, introduced in April 2014, was defeated, although the NDP, the Liberals, and a smattering of PCs and Wildrosers, such as Smith, supported it. Six months later, Blakeman, taking guidance from Hehr, introduced Bill 202.

"Motion 503 failed but it was a start. It built momentum for this issue," says Hehr, the Calgary Centre Liberal MP, who became federal minister of veterans affairs after the 2015 Trudeau victory. Hehr explained that Blakeman had won one of the MLA draws to present a motion in the legislature. "I worked with her on framing it, and sure enough it was on the Order Paper. The PCs knew it was coming up."

But they rejected Blakeman's Bill 202 and replaced it with the clumsily written and widely condemned Bill 10, which was supposed to prevent bullying by supporting GSAs in schools. Except that it didn't, because a school or school board could refuse a student's GSA request. The students could still form their alliance after rejection — by winning an appeal in the Court of Queen's Bench. Critics conjured the absurd image of fifteen-year-olds trooping into court to plead their case, like a pack of government lawyers.

The PCs then amended the bill to allow students who were refused an alliance to appeal directly to the minister of education. The minister would be required by law to mandate the club — but it couldn't be on school property unless the school board agreed. This raised more howls of protest. What kind of school club wouldn't be allowed at the school? The answer was clear: only a club designed to foster friendships between gay and straight kids. No other club would face such a stricture.

While trying to reconcile the decision-making power of school boards with the rights of students, the PCs lost sight of how much damage this public, highly emotional debate was inflicting on LGBTQ students. The NDP and Liberals had both provided convincing cases that these alliances not only make youth feel more secure, but can actually save them from suicide. Prentice and the PCs, by presenting the alliances as such a special category, actually found themselves promoting the sense of difference and alienation among gay youths.

During the emotional debate, the NDP's Brian Mason compared the bill to the racist "separate but equal" Jim Crow laws that segregated African-Americans in the United States. "It's institutionalized apartheid of gay students," he said.[9]

Some of the more enlightened PC caucus members refused to be part of their government's misguided effort. An appalled Doug Griffiths, once a PC Cabinet minister, argued passionately for GSAs. Standing defiantly in the legislature, he spoke of his sons who attend a Catholic school. "I taught them the values of defending people and to stand up for people and to have everyone treated with respect. There is no way I would accept a school board of any religious background or non-religious background to dictate to my sons whether they're allowed to partner with gay students to set up gay-straight alliances."[10]

Thomas Lukaszuk, a former deputy premier who also had children in Catholic schools, was equally angered.

"We didn't give women half a vote," he tweeted.[11]

Both he and Griffiths voted against their government's bill, along with PC floor-crosser and former Wildroser Ian Donovan, who had the very opposite reason for his vote. Donovan said his constituents were opposed to any gay-straight alliances, regardless. The three Tories joined the NDP, Liberals, and Wildrose in voting against the bill. Every other member of the PC caucus, armed with a backpack of reasons, appeared to crawl up the cliff of intolerance.

The bill created a firestorm within the province and beyond. When Prentice made the comment "Rights are never absolute" during a conference call on December 3, 2014, the popular CBC host and comic Rick Mercer (@rickmercer) tweeted: "Nice ring to it Jim maybe that should be on the license plate."[12]

Hehr was shocked by Prentice's remark and then saw the @rickmercer tweet. "Suddenly the whole country was looking at Prentice, who's sort of a reasonable, level-headed guy who was largely on the left side of the Harper regime. They wonder, 'Who is this guy and what kind of party is he running? Who are these people voting against these kids who just want to be accepted and included?' They couldn't understand why his government was still discriminating. The damage was done. It was the first real nick in the armour of the Prentice regime."

The great Calgary Stampeders' running back and Grey Cup champion, Jon Cornish, who was raised by a lesbian couple, didn't mince words when he talked to reporters.

"I want my kids growing up in a world where it doesn't matter who you love, it doesn't matter the colour of your skin. I want my kids to understand that none of that matters."[13]

The president of the Calgary-Bow PC riding association, Josh Traptow, was so upset that he immediately resigned. Party stalwarts Brenda Meneghetti and Chris Harper also left the PC Party over Bill 10. The highly regarded former PC MLA and senator, Ron Ghitter, who has spent his life fighting for human rights, labelled the bill "backwards." Speaking with the *Calgary Herald*'s James Wood, Ghitter commented on the bill: "It takes a particular identifiable group and we're setting a different standard or procedure for them. Why are we doing that?" Ghitter supported the Liberal legislation, explaining that "the Tory government should have simply allowed Blakeman's bill to come to a vote."[14]

But Prentice hadn't trusted Blakeman's straightforward bill, which many PCs felt had been introduced just to embarrass them. It was a strange dilemma for the premier because he appeared to be going against his own admirable record on LGBTQ issues. Prentice was an opposition Conservative MP when, in 2005, he voted with his principles and the ruling Liberals to support same-sex marriage. It was a bold move that brought a swift reaction from constituents. As Dean Bennett of Canadian Press reports, riding staff quit and the veranda of Prentice's house in Calgary was set on fire.

"The pressure [to vote no] was incredible," Prentice said, in recalling the incident after he became premier. "[But] I believe in the rights of individuals, including the rights of communities of faith. There's a duty to balance and protect the rights of everyone."[15]

For a politician who had courageously voted with his conscience rather than with his conservative colleagues, the whole Bill 10 debacle was oddly out of sync, a sign that he wasn't fully in control of his caucus. Prentice finally put Bill 10 on hold, calling a halt to the drama playing out on the legislature floor. He cited the pain the debate was inflicting on gay students. Then he and his education minister, Gordon Dirks, turned to the province to consult students and groups directly affected.

Dirks in particular had been baked in the media roaster as homophobic because of his evangelical beliefs as a pastor. Yet it was Dirks who later gave an impassioned speech for the revised Bill 10 after weeks of meeting young people and hearing how GSAs improved their lives. "Some of those moments were very moving moments as you heard students telling their stories of being bullied, discriminated against, feeling suicidal. When you have those kinds of intimate, frank conversations with students, it goes from your head to your heart."[16]

On March 10, 2015, Prentice did the right thing. He backpedalled completely and adopted Blakeman's approach in a freshly revised Bill 10. Gay-straight alliances would be allowed in all government-funded schools.

"It's hard to contain my joy," Blakeman said of the historic bill born out of her courage and tenacity.[17] The vote would have been unanimous except for the opposition of two former Wildrose floor-crossers, PC MLAs Ian Donovan and Bruce Rowe. It was an especially emotional vote for Blakeman, who had realized one of the most amazing feats possible for an opposition MLA. (Blakeman's heroics, however, didn't help her during the May 2015 election. She lost to David Shepherd in the NDP sweep of Edmonton.)

NDP Leader Notley acknowledged in the legislature that "the PCs had to be dragged across the finish line on this one, but, that being said, they are here now. It's a testament to the strength of the youth that kept pushing it, to the strength of the activists and frankly, to some extent, to the strength of the opposition in forcing the government to come to terms with this issue."[18]

Kristopher Wells, a University of Alberta professor with the Institute for Sexual Minority Studies and Services, watched the bill's passage on the legislature floor. "It's hard to believe but we are no longer the redneck, roughneck province," he told CBC News. "Today we took a stand for human rights. Today, we're in the lead."[19]

As students and young adults lobbied across the province, Prentice listened and acted as he had ten years before. He was widely applauded for embracing a changing Alberta where intolerance and homophobia would become a distant echo of politics past.

IT WAS A REMARKABLE moment in legislature history, and one that should have ensured Prentice remained premier of Alberta for many years. But then his time for listening seemed to stall out. He didn't appear to see Bill 10 as an omen that signalled both a generational shift and far more diversity in Alberta.

In the decade where he was often away, the province had changed. Yet Prentice proved unable or unwilling to alter the course of his unwieldy forty-three-year-old PC vessel.

He had won all four by-elections and compromised successfully with Bill 10. For him, the next steps were clear: table the budget of deficit and sacrifice; drop the writ; call the election; and fixed dates be damned. It would be his undoing.

"Jim Prentice believed he needed a mandate from the people," said a source close to the campaign. "He especially felt he needed a mandate on this tough budget. He knew the economy would be in substantial turmoil, which he predicted accurately. He also knew that calling the election in 2016 was virtual suicide."

But the reaction to the snap election call was swift and hostile. The anger toward the premier and the PCs had festered since the dramatic December floor-crossings. The temporary goodwill that his revised Bill 10 got was now gone.

"The PCs didn't get focused on the issues. At the beginning of a campaign after two weeks, there's usually a compare and contrast moment. But that didn't happen this time. The story got out of hand and the PCs couldn't form the narrative," said the source. At the same time, the Liberal vote collapsed and Wildrose proved resilient. "The Wildrose continued nipping at our heels, and we couldn't consolidate the vote with them. Instead, they split the vote." And the messages between the two parties became blurred.

By the end, there were three decisive factors that brought the PCs down: they lost message; their nearly forty-four-year history finally caught up with them; and the NDP ran a smart campaign. "Rachel Notley was fresh, new, exciting, and charismatic. She was a very good candidate, very smart and with a great pedigree. She was not the usual candidate," concluded the PC insider.

The warning was there that the old ways of doing things were crumbling. Even the PC election slogan, "Choose Alberta's Future," seemed wildly inappropriate, given that the past four decades once represented the PC future. The slogan was dangerous for a party that had held power longer than any other governing regime in Canada. It appeared to be an argument not for another term with the PCs, but for the election of a whole new government.

Then came an episode that showed how out of touch the PCs were with the political opportunities, and perils, of social media and the Internet. They stood by while the smallest opposition group, the Alberta Party, literally took over their slogan by registering the domain names "ChooseAlbertasFuture.com" and "ChooseAlbertasFuture.ca." Anyone searching the PC slogan was routed directly to the Alberta Party website.

"It's a classic case of the PCs not seeing the trees for the forest. Details are important," Alberta Party leader Greg Clark told the *Calgary Herald*'s Trevor Howell. "All of us were tuned into the [Prentice election call] webcast ... and one staffer just happened to go after the [domain names] — '.ca,' and the other, '.com.' It wasn't a planned thing. The opportunity was there and our team took it."[20]

Not to be outdone, the NDP and its Web crawlers grabbed another domain name, "prenticeteam.ca," sending searchers to the Alberta NDP website. The PCs appeared to have no response to this. Their failure to grasp the nimble wit of Web-youth was clear even before the election campaign began.

"We loved the battle between staffs on social media," Notley strategist Brian Topp said in an interview. "The other side was not used to having us there and pretty much had the space all to their own. We were able to acquire a voice in social media. Some in the war room focused on this. We had quite a good crew of happy warriors. We cleaned their clocks on social media and they didn't know how to respond."

Topp said many battles on social media are generated by paid staff, sitting in little cubicles, "drinking too much coffee and pretending they're different people so they can try and persuade the public to think like they do." But this time he saw regular people getting engaged. "Posts from real voters indicate a wave of goodwill. Another positive indicator is retweeting and reposting."

When Topp saw voters picking up New Democrat messages and tweeting them, it was a validation of the Notley campaign. "Social media can be a real wildfire. Look at populist campaigns ... it can be the source of a prairie fire."

Perhaps the silliest attempt by the Prentice team to connect with the younger generation occurred two days before the PC budget, during the premier's paid televised address to the province. In his speech, the premier said: "And just as I asked for the help of Alberta's public servants, essentially I am talking about a spirit of openness across every segment of Alberta — from oil executives to dentists and welders — from loggers to bloggers."[21]

Seconds later, Twitter took off with all kinds of "loggers to bloggers" posts. The funniest came from the droll Alberta blogger Dave Cournoyer. "Logger AND blogger," he tweeted, posting a picture of himself holding an axe while dressed as a lumberjack.[22] Wearing a red and green plaid flannel shirt, he earnestly looks forward as a plant inches menacingly towards his back. This witty riposte to the premier's clueless reference to the Web generation generated kudos for Cournoyer rather than plaudits for Prentice.

At least Prentice appeared to stop blaming Albertans. This time he explained the expected deficit much more sensibly: "Fundamentally, we've not always had realistic expectations, and our leaders must bear a considerable part of the responsibility for that."[23]

THEN POLITICAL INSIGHT evaporated once more as Prentice fell into the trap of the past and the conviction that only the Tories had the divine right to govern. He and his team would orchestrate the inevitable win. The group included his friend Jason Hatcher, who had been his "anonymous spokesperson" even before Prentice announced his run for the PC leadership. Another close friend, Randy Dawson, came onboard, soon to be campaign manager. A confident Prentice dropped the writ, knowing that Dawson, the legendary kingmaker, would be running things.

Dawson is an astute and charming political insider whose clever strategic insight propelled Ed Stelmach to the premier's chair in the 2008 PC leadership election. Four years later, Dawson nimbly navigated Alison Redford through a stormy party leadership election into the office of Alberta premier. The conventional wisdom was that if there was a hole in an opponent's platform, Dawson would not only find it, he would drive a dump truck through it.

When not volunteering for political ventures, Dawson and Hatcher were managing principals in Navigator, the self-described "high-stakes" national consulting firm. Its trademarked motto: "When you can't afford to lose." But lose they did, even after Dawson took a leave of absence from Navigator to run the campaign.

"The party forgot who the people were who were voting," said former PC president Ron Nicholls. The eighty-five-year-old party stalwart first started volunteering with the PCs when Peter Lougheed ran. Nicholls and his wife, Jeanette Nicholls, have worked every campaign since. "The people are what matters most — or the rest of it doesn't matter, as we've seen.

You must keep the constituency alive and vibrant. If you don't focus your attention on every one of the constituencies and know who the people are, you've missed the point. The constituency meeting is the most important business of the party. Politics always is a grass-roots organization." That was exactly what the PCs' two rivals, the NDP and the Wildrose, understood all the way to the ballot box.

By 2015, the PCs had lost touch with the unfolding transformation of their province, including the growing political impact of the millennials. Their corporate image and style no longer fit modern Alberta. On May 5 at 10:05 p.m., when the results of the provincial election were finally clear, Prentice quickly resigned, to the surprise and annoyance of supporters and detractors alike. He was regarded as petulant, but in fact he was behaving like the corporate executive he had become, leaving the building without looking back, his box of personal effects under his arm. In this view, his time was over, and a leader who loses yet stays around presents a problem. Leaving is the only solution.

But politics is not a business, although it has been confused with one over decades of ideological identity crises. Businesses rely on shareholders, with a few possessing many more shares — and hence, power — than the majority of smaller investors. Politics relies on its voters, with everyone having an equal vote — and power — in an election. At least that's the theory. One thing is certainly true, though. Voters are not shareholders, they are equal partners in a democracy. Over the years, the PC leaders forgot that they were running one of the most fought-for and also one of the most fragile of institutions known to history — a democratic government.

Once the party of integrity, the PCs had slowly slipped into dusky entitlement. Transparency gave way to obfuscation. Leadership toppled into "an aura of power."[24] That's how Alberta's auditor general, Merwan Saher, described former premier Alison Redford's office. For a party that one time governed from the bottom up, the top-down tone was striking. When Redford quit in March 2014, she was blasted by both the public and her own party for offences such as her misuse of government planes and construction of a personal "sky palace" near the legislature. Many people agreed that the party would have one more chance to find a solid, competent leader. And the vast majority thought Prentice was the deliverer.

But the problems ran much deeper than that. Government culture had grown increasingly corporate-minded. It had lost sight of individual Albertans, as PCs focused on their corporate donors — by the end, the vast majority of their funding was corporate. Ordinary Albertans began to think they were only afterthoughts. Many felt disenfranchised and stopped voting. No Albertan younger than forty-three had lived in the province when the PCs weren't in power. They were a dynasty that expected to govern forever.

MONTHS LATER, THE failings of the federal Conservative campaign would have eerily similar elements — the overarching business and economic focus, the exclusion of environmental and social policies, the sudden move away from core principles. Prentice appeared not to value charities, a PC priority for decades. Harper seemed to turn away from immigrants after a decade of courting them. Suddenly the identities of both regimes were blurred, to the confusion even of the public and previously loyal supporters.

And so, the Alberta PCs' fabled big tent, which had lured in elements of both left and right through twelve elections, simply collapsed. What followed was a PC campaign that party candidates didn't always buy into. The Tory team seemed to possess a collective tin ear to the public mood: respected party stalwarts didn't feel their voices mattered. Even some of their own candidates felt alienated from policy and budget decisions as well as campaign platforms. On May 5, 2015, the PCs realized the extent of their alienation. But conservatives across the province were far from silent.

The *Edmonton Sun*'s Matt Dykstra spoke to a number of defeated Tory candidates who described the former premier's decision making as "catastrophic." "Things changed on the ground like a wave," an MLA told Dykstra. "After that, there were a lot of people who just wanted to see what change looked like after forty-four years and I have to give credit to the NDP and the Wildrose who really hit that message home."[25]

The storied Tory machine of past finally seized up. Its leaders failed to focus on the changing landscape and completely lost their messaging map. Rather than destroying the opposition with their takeover tactics, they watered the seeds of public anger with their own hubris. Their complete disregard for the growing resentment positioned the charismatic Notley as an amiable alternative. She considered the Wildrose crossovers one of the tipping points that led to her victory.

"There were a few points even before the campaign. I won't say this is what propelled us into winning, but [it] certainly propelled us into a position where we believed we were going to do very well. One of the keys was when Wildrose crossed the floor. We'd known three or four days beforehand that it was going to happen, and that's again with the ability to talk to people from the other side. We didn't want it to happen. So there was no particular benefit to us prompting it.

"But we were prepared for it, and I felt at the time, we were able," Notley continues. "There were a lot of rumours twenty-four hours before it was actually announced. And we sort of leapt into the abyss and, I thought, did not a bad job of framing it as a betrayal of Albertans and betrayal of democracy. It was a backroom deal. People were angry, and people did feel betrayed; we were able to help frame what they were thinking about it. Because when it first happened, everyone was sort of saying, 'Oh look at this great Machiavellian leadership move.' But people didn't really quite like it and they didn't quite know why, and we were able to get out there and help them with their narrative. That was not necessarily what propelled us into governance. But it was the start of a number of well-timed and well-positioned responses to things throughout the next few months.

"I used to joke around on the campaign trail and say, 'Should they, hypothetically … Can you imagine if they didn't win? Let me tell you, it's going to be called *Look in the Mirror;* the book is going to be *Look in the Mirror.*' That had nothing to do with us. That had everything to do with Prentice. That was probably his tipping point, in many respects."

CHAPTER 4

BRIMSTONE AND FIRE

In 2015 and 2016, Canadian governments in Alberta, Manitoba, Newfoundland and Labrador, as well as Ottawa, were ripe for defeat. They faced roughly parallel problems: voter mistrust, perceived lack of integrity, and broken promises. With the exception of Prince Edward Island in 2015 and Saskatchewan in 2016, where the parties in power won their third straight majorities, voter fatigue was threatening aging governments. Nearly ten years of Stephen Harper was plenty for many voters, while almost seventeen years ran out the string for Premier Greg Selinger's Manitoba NDP. Alberta's peculiar substitute for real change — picking yet another leader for the government party — was also wearing extremely thin with voters.

After forty-three years in office, the Alberta PCs were truly a unique case — a government and party with deep internal problems that were never properly addressed while the victories came easily. Other Canadians wondered how the party that was called the Miracle on the Prairie by the populist premier Ralph Klein could lose its way so dramatically.

A clue: only one PC leader ever left of his — or her — own accord. That was Peter Lougheed, the visionary who, in 1971, nurtured his band of Progressive Conservatives into a stunning defeat of a tired, decades-old dynasty, Social Credit. The next four PC premiers — Don Getty, Ralph Klein, Ed Stelmach, and Alison Redford — were all forced out by their party, triggering leadership votes that became increasingly divisive. Each contest embittered losing factions and further weakened party cohesion.

After Redford was bumped from office, the next premier, Dave Hancock, a long-time Cabinet minister, was appointed by the PC caucus. As agreed, he resigned when Prentice became the leader. Prentice then fell heir to all the party fractures and schisms, problems that helped convince voters it was finally time to force an eviction on their own.

TO MANY ALBERTANS, it still seems remarkable that a party forged in greatness had collapsed into such confusion. Peter Lougheed was considered one of the most brilliant politicians Canada has ever seen. He took over a moribund party in 1965, fostered its growth by sheer force of work and character, and by 1971 made it a credible alternative to aging Social Credit. That party's thirty-three-year-old regime had begun with an evangelical preacher, the fiery William Aberhart, who was followed by a milder and wiser acolyte, Ernest Manning, father of future Reform Party founder and leader Preston Manning. The final Social Credit premier was Harry Strom, an earnest, hard-working farmer who never really wanted the job after Manning retired. In the 1971 campaign he told a rally in Lethbridge: "A victory for the Conservatives would be the first step in the takeover of Alberta by Socialists." That tactic was no more successful in 1971 than it would be in 2015. Albertans gave the PCs forty-nine out of seventy-five seats.

Lougheed brought a youthful vigour to the staid legislature, with his insight, intuition, and optimistic plans for a province that was poised to play an important role in Confederation. He kick-started a natural resources policy that included funds for research into the nascent oil sands. That would earn him the moniker "the blue-eyed sheik." He instituted a heritage savings plan that would maintain Alberta through lean times but also provide low-interest loans to other provinces.

He fought with Prime Minister Pierre Trudeau over the National Energy Program (NEP), spending nearly two years going head-to-head on resource ownership and revenue sharing. Lougheed faced Trudeau again over the Constitution, insisting on the inclusion of a "notwithstanding clause" that would ensure all provinces had a voice in the country's direction. (In what is sometimes called the Alberta formula, the clause called for seven provinces with 50 percent of the population to effect any amendment.)

Lougheed won four consecutive and decisive elections and would likely have won more, but after fourteen years as premier he decided to leave politics in June 1985, stepping down officially in February 1986.

Lougheed had been deeply affected when his great political foe, Grant Notley, died in a plane crash on October 19, 1984. He so respected Notley's intellect and dexterity in debate that he was always attentive as Notley rose to speak. It was an even match when Notley and Lougheed sparred. Both were sharp, skilled, and devoted to their respective paths. Notley won his riding in 1971 as the lone Alberta NDP to sit across the aisle from the new premier. It wasn't until 1982, when he was joined by Ray Martin, that Notley had ideological company. Martin's election also led to Notley, amazingly, becoming leader of the Official Opposition. That's because Lougheed's PCs won seventy-five of the seventy-nine seats. The only others to break the PC sweep were two independents.

When Lougheed left politics his PCs were in solid shape. Lougheed believed that there must be a strong connection between the party and the government. One thing he did almost daily was phone a few riding association presidents and ask what was going on in their area. He insisted that his MLAs be in constant touch with local party apparatus. When he asked an MLA to discuss the riding issues, Lougheed expected a detailed account, and woe to the member who tried to wing it.

The premier was a tough boss, but he had great respect for his caucus. That respect was reciprocated. Caucus was included in all major decisions; the most striking example occurred at the constitutional talks. As Lougheed considered a slight change to Alberta's position, he called from Ottawa to speak with all his PC MLAs on the phone. They conferred, voted, and effectively armed Lougheed with the confidence of his caucus, and his province.

Lougheed understood that consultation and collaboration are precisely what keep a leader strong in a democracy. They help to build respect and confidence within the caucus and the party, while creating a synergy that boosts loyalty and enhances the authority of the leader. This basic political truth has eluded too many leaders since Lougheed. In May 2012 he was named the best Canadian premier in forty years by *Policy Options,* the magazine of the non-profit, independent Institute for Research on Public Policy.

LOUGHEED WAS AN almost impossible act to follow, and his successor, Don Getty, who died in February 2016, hasn't always been given his due. While Getty lacked his predecessor's drive, ability, and luck, he did try to govern well during challenging economic times. He took over on November 1, 1985, just as the province was pulling out of the effects of an economic recession and the NEP. Then oil prices crashed. A barrel of oil sold for less than US$10 in August 1986.

Getty didn't deal with the province's revenue crisis early enough. One year he expected his treasurer, Dick Johnston, to deliver not simply a balanced budget, but a surplus. The treasurer did as he was told, on paper; in reality the budget produced not a surplus but a deficit of over $2 billion. Despite this, Getty believed his government was on the right track with the province's economy. He always preferred to focus on the net assets of the province that far outweighed the deficit. In his view, Alberta was debt-free.

As poor prices continued to batter the province, however, Getty responded by slashing spending in health and education. While cutting social services, the government also provided hundreds of millions of dollars in loans and guarantees to agriculture and business, especially the energy industry.

What would ultimately prove Getty's undoing was the collapse of two provincial banks in 1985, the Canadian Commercial Bank and the Northlands Bank, along with a trust company, the Principal Group in 1987. To make matters worse, Gainers, a meat-packing plant owned by Peter Pocklington, defaulted on loans from government and landed in the hands of its largest creditor. Ultimately, the company closed.

To help boost the government's balance sheet, in 1990 Getty began to privatize its Crown corporation Alberta Government Telephones for a subsequent public share offering. To that end, the government formed a holding company, Telus Communications, which it sold to AGT for $870 million. But it removed from the offering AGT's trouble-plagued cellular subsidiary, NovaTel, which ultimately cost the government between $544 million and $614 million to cover the company's liabilities.[1]

As the provincial debt soared — it would reach a numbing $23 billion by the time Getty left office in 1992 — the premier's public persona suffered. When the Principal Group collapsed in the summer of 1987, media were told that Getty "was working out of the office." A photographer caught him on the golf course, working on his swing.

Getty had considerable skill, especially in federal-provincial relations. He played a strong role during the Free Trade Agreement, the Charlottetown Accord, and the ambitious failure known as the Meech Lake Accord. Getty didn't have the kind of enthusiasm that his predecessor — or his successor, Ralph Klein — had for the job. But he was an able conciliator and performed skillfully on the national level.

When the next election was called for March 20, 1989, Getty's Conservatives handily won the contest, taking fifty-nine of eighty-three seats. Unfortunately, that night the premier was not among the victors, losing his Edmonton-Whitemud riding to Liberal Percy Wickman. Getty would have to wait until a May by-election, held after the loyal PC MLA Brian Downey relinquished his Stettler riding, to safely sit back in his legislature chair.

But he would not retain that position for long. The party was particularly unhappy with its unlucky leader and the way he was handling the economy. The provincial PC victory did little to quell the anger looming over Getty's leadership, quickly compounded by his initial riding defeat. As the decade turned, so did much of the PC Party, especially the Calgary wing. Fundraising was at a standstill, always a death-knell for a party leader. To compound PC fears, the Liberals, under popular former Edmonton mayor Laurence Decore, started to surge in the polls. In 1992, when it became evident the party wanted him gone, Getty announced his resignation, with a leadership vote to be held in December.

Neither the party nor the premier could imagine they were sowing the first seeds of the eventual PC implosion. It would take more than two decades before the PCs and their leader descended into an inglorious collapse. But the years of caucus solidarity created by Premier Lougheed were already fading. And in the end, the resulting plot line was deceptively simple and perhaps somewhat inevitable: the party banished one premier after another and the voters be damned — until May 5, 2015, when the voters, like the party members before them, finally rebelled.

THE DECEMBER 1992 PC leadership convention presented two very different paths for the party and the province. The progressive wing of the PCs wanted Lougheed protegé Nancy Betkowski (later Nancy MacBeth.)

The strict conservatives preferred former Calgary mayor Ralph Klein, a bold upstart who was now provincial environment minister.

When he won his legislative seat in a 1989 by-election, Klein had been offered higher-profile portfolios by Getty. But he chose environment — then a sleepy corner of the government — because it provided opportunities to travel around the province, building up rural support. Klein and his trusted aid, Rod Love, were already looking far beyond the environment ministry into the premier's office.

Bctkowski had been minister of education and then health in the Getty government. Considered a Red Tory, she was clearly the front-runner and appeared to have a visceral dislike for her main opponent, Klein. He was definitely the dark horse, but his populist persona captured the hearts of rural voters. Many were won over by the Klein campaign's second-ballot drive to convince them that Betkowski was dangerously left-wing.

The PC Party brass had failed to fully understand Klein's populist appeal. But it wasn't lost on his own inner circle, led by Love and a crew of Calgary businessmen and women. (They were known from Klein's mayoralty days as FORK — friends of Ralph Klein.) After Klein won the leadership on December 5, 1992, he offered Betkowski a premium Cabinet post. Instead, she disappeared for a time and ultimately left the party. She returned briefly to politics in 1998 with a new name and new party. Now Nancy MacBeth (after marrying Hilliard MacBeth), she joined the Liberals and became their leader, only to lose her seat and more than half of her fifteen-member caucus in the 2001 election.

With Klein as PC leader, the province went to the polls in 1993 at the height of Liberal leader Laurence Decore's popularity. Both campaigns were largely interchangeable: balance the budget and eliminate the debt. Decore, with his Liberals, would become the most formidable foe to face the ruling PCs until Danielle Smith and her Wildrose Party were poised to wipe clean the PC slate of Alison Redford. In each case, social issues stopped the challengers cold.

Decore wandered into the political minefield of a woman's right to choose, which he was against. After an offhand response to a reporter's question, Decore faced an angry wave of betrayed women who expected a far different response from a Liberal leader. Klein then said it was a matter between a woman, her doctor, and God. At that point Klein picked up the vote of many progressive women. Some even took out ads in the province's newspapers. What had been Decore's election to lose became Klein's first provincial victory.

Klein won both the leadership and the election by promising to get the province's finances in order. It was a political position that he came by honestly. He had an innate frugality, born on a hardscrabble childhood. He learned very early that life could be wildly unfair and that abuse could lurk in places that deceptively promised peace. He escaped from the alcohol-fuelled rage of a stepfather in the middle of a blizzard blasting the night in a tiny town, taking his younger brother with him. It was only one of many harsh realities that taught Klein the power of self-reliance and resisting the status quo. He didn't trust authority because it never intervened when the dark side took over. For a long time, alcohol would make it all a bit easier.

A military career was a tough route for an anti-establishment teenager, and basic training left Klein aching for his past life. The more he thought about his pals, his education, and a life gone awry, the more depressed he became. Klein broke down and landed in hospital. Ultimately, he received an honourable discharge and returned to Calgary, where he enrolled in Calgary Business College. Klein graduated with honours and was hired to teach. He took the necessary courses and was later appointed the college's principal. He loved standing before students whom he considered his peers, listening, talking, teaching, and giving them what he had earned: another chance.

The pain of his past never dulled his ambition, and Klein vowed to make his life a success. A school counsellor told him he'd make it to city hall — as a janitor. Klein remembered the remark, not just as a put-down of him but of every hard-working man and woman whose job was so easily dismissed in the eyes of authority. Klein was anti-establishment, as a journalist and later as candidate for mayor. When he won in 1980, with the help of a mutton-chopped, horn-rimmed Houdini named Rod Love, the two built a political shop that has yet to be replicated. It took Klein to the premier's chair in a province that wasn't quite sure what hit it. Getty had begun a budgetary slash and burn, but it was too slow for Klein — and for opposition leader Decore. Even though Klein was now very much part of the establishment, he took his anti-authoritarian persona to policy and politics. He eventually cut spending by an accumulated 20 percent, starting with a 5 percent pay cut within his own caucus. It was called the Alberta

Advantage, except by the thousands who lost their jobs or saw their salary sliced. Klein's winning political art — making a promise and actually keeping it — made him popular at home and famous across the country.

But his demons were always there. One dreary night in 2001, Klein finished a bout of drinking with a stop at an Edmonton homeless shelter. Annoyed at something one of the residents said, he told the men to get a job and then dropped some bills on the floor. The shocking display became a news story. Klein apologized, but the episode created an image of him that he was never able to escape.

"I'm ashamed I did that. That is not who I am," Klein said in an interview over a decade later. "That could have been me in the shelter, if life had gone a different way. I stopped drinking the next day."[2]

Colleen Klein remembered the rant and her husband's subsequent regret. "He was so humiliated by his actions. It was very out of character for him. It was bizarre. That's when he quit drinking."

She recalled the time he picked up a family roaming the Calgary streets after midnight. "Ralph brought them all home, fed them, and gave them blankets to sleep with. They were homeless and they stayed the night. That's where Ralph's heart was."

Three years later, Klein said the 2004 election would be his last. Yet he wouldn't name an actual date for leaving office. The party's executive director, Peter Elzinga, prodded him for specifics, but Klein lingered. With a leadership review looming at the end of March 2006, Klein announced on March 14 that he'd resign at the end of October 2007. He then changed the date once more, noting that his actual resignation would become effective in early 2008 after a new leader was chosen.

By that time party members felt they needed to move on quickly. The result cut Klein to the core. The landslide 90 percent support of previous reviews plummeted to a paltry 55 percent. "When the party dumped him, it was heartbreaking," says Colleen Klein. "After that, it was just like he gave up."

Klein would sink into dementia and die from complications of chronic obstructive pulmonary disease in late March 2013. His great friend Rod Love, stricken with pancreatic cancer, would also die in late October 2014.

When Klein's popularity pushed past gravity, the party loved him. But he was never a party man, and his connection to the PC Party apparatus was always weak. As his popularity soared, the party's influence waned and the Tory riding structure atrophied. Yet the annual meetings, head-lined by the premier, were hugely successful as delegates bathed in his star touch. The polls continued to show a premier more popular than his party, always a strong position for a leader. The positions were reversed for most of his successors.

THE PC PARTY ushered out a still-popular premier and then selected, through a Byzantine process, a weak successor in Ed Stelmach. He was not the first choice among the eight candidates — that spot belonged to the charming and hugely experienced Jim Dinning, who was, as expected after the first ballot, number one at 30 percent. The formidable Ted Morton was second, with 26 percent, while Stelmach managed third with just 15 percent. But Stelmach won because preferential balloting allowed party voters to rate their first and second choices. Morton and Dinning had attacked each other like wolverines, virtually ignoring Stelmach, who quietly became the favourite of northern Albertans fed up with what they saw as dominance by Calgary politicians.

Known as "a nice guy,"[3] Stelmach was never able to display the authority and gravitas needed to be a strong leader. Instead of cultivating province-wide support, Stelmach surrounded himself with a small group of his northeastern Alberta favourites. Others he cast into outer darkness, leaving his personal political posse riding with an agenda that didn't sit well with his caucus or the public. In major matters, Stelmach tended to impose policy decisions rather than debating them with caucus before delivering a critical bill. But the opposition remained weak. After governing without a mandate from voters for fifteen months, Stelmach won the March 3, 2008, election with 53 percent of the popular vote. Only 41 percent of voters made it to the polling stations, however, making this election's turnout the lowest in provincial history. Stelmach's huge major-ity masked a steep drop in enthusiasm for the governing party.

As politicians almost always will, Stelmach interpreted the Tory win as a resounding victory for his leadership. This led him into making a number of mistakes. Arguably the worst was imposing higher royalties just when energy prices were crashing. Another clunker was driving through, by Cabinet fiat rather than public consultation, a series of electricity transmission lines that were extraordinarily controversial in rural Alberta, largely because decision-making power was taken away from regulatory bodies and handed to Cabinet. Stelmach drove another nail into the coffin of his rural base by enabling legislation that was perceived as threatening property rights.

As a rule, Alberta premiers can get away with all that and much more, as long as the economy is booming and oil prices are soaring. And the economy did roar for months after the election, until, on one glorious July day, the price hit US$147 a barrel for West Texas crude. Then prices began to slide and the world financial crisis hit. By January 2009 the price for a barrel of oil slipped into the $30 range — a disastrous plunge for Alberta. And it happened just as Stelmach was abolishing health care premiums — a source of $700 million in annual revenue for the government — as well as raising oil and gas royalties charged to energy companies.

A projected surplus of $1.6 billion in the April 2008 budget became a $1 billion deficit by the end of the fiscal year. The premier started to lose control of a caucus whose confidence in him had already been weak. Political fundraising plunged, and the PC Party erupted in furor. All the while, the right-wing Wildrose Party began to grow rapidly, with a dynamic new leader, Danielle Smith. "Donations skyrocketed from $230,000 in 2009 to $2.7 million in 2011," wrote the *Edmonton Journal*'s Karen Kleiss.[4]

Former Wildrose Party leader Paul Hinman took a 2009 Calgary by-election from the Tories. Soon, the PCs' Heather Forsyth and Rob Anderson walked across the aisle to join Hinman. Later, Guy Boutilier, who was booted out of the PC caucus after criticizing the Stelmach government, also went over to the Wildrose caucus. With four MLAs, the Wildrose now had access to more government funding.

Even as his public numbers tumbled, Stelmach won a party leadership review in November 2009 with 77 percent support of the delegates, largely because the PCs were unwilling to risk more rage and change with an immediate leadership fight. But the caucus clash continued in 2010 as Morton, now treasurer, went into virtual rebellion over the new deficit-ridden budget. Stelmach faced another caucus crisis when Raj Sherman, a PC MLA and a doctor, sent out an email accusing the premier of breaking faith with doctors over health care. Stelmach suspended

Sherman in November 2010; the emergency room doctor left the PCs and became leader of the Liberals. Facing unending caucus and party turmoil, Stelmach declared on January 25, 2011, that he would be quitting, triggering another leadership contest.

When the next leadership marathon, almost nine months long, neared its end on September 17, 2011, Gary Mar led the six-person pack, with 41 percent after a first ballot, with a second scheduled for two weeks later, if needed.

It was needed, because the party's clear favourite didn't have the magical 50 percent. Far below Mar were Alison Redford, at 19 percent, and Doug Horner, with 15 percent. The other three challengers — Ted Morton, Rick Orman, and Doug Griffiths — dropped off the second ballot and moved their vocal support to Gary Mar. "If the race to replace retiring Progressive Conservative leader Ed Stelmach had any natural justice to it, [the winner's] name would be Gary Mar," wrote *National Post* columnist Kevin Libin.[5]

Somehow, "natural justice" never seemed to find its way into a PC leadership contest.

As Mar, Redford, and Horner worked their resources to the limit, real life swiftly stepped in. On September 28, Redford's ailing mother suffered a setback. The candidate and a sister rushed to Helen Redford's side and were with her as she died. When death intervenes, even the most cynical stop cold. Politics took a break as all the leadership hopefuls sent their sympathies while Redford dealt with her personal loss.

When the second ballot results were announced at the Edmonton EXPO Centre on October 1, the contest was clearly not over. Mar still led, at 43 percent, managing just a two-point bounce from the first ballot. The surprise momentum went to Redford, who now had 37 percent of the delegates' support, an eighteen-point leap. Horner, with 20 percent, dropped off, having asked his supporters to make Redford their second choice on the preferential ballot. Of those two-thirds that selected a second choice, four out of five picked Redford.

And then Alberta went down the rabbit hole. The Horner voters' second choice was added to the two front-runner's first-choice numbers, at which point Redford magically hopped over Mar with 51 percent to his 49 percent.

The party's peculiar preferential balloting had again prevailed, but this time it ushered in a leader who had never been the first choice of more than 37 percent of votes cast in the second ballot.

How did Redford manage to achieve even that in the two intervening weeks between the two ballots? Her caucus support was negligible, save that of longtime Calgary MLA Art Johnston. Redford, astutely, went to the Alberta School Boards and the Alberta Teachers' Association, stating explicitly her plan to restore $107 million in funding if she became leader and premier. On September 22, 2011, Redford wrote to ATA president Carol Henderson: "I will commit to restoring the education cuts ... within ten days of being sworn in as premier. This funding should not have been removed from the budgets of Alberta School Boards. I only regret that the timing of the leadership contest means that unacceptable disruption has already occurred that must be reversed. If elected premier, I will not allow that to happen again."[6]

After Redford's win, the October 11, 2011, ATA newsletter, noting her letter to Henderson, explicitly stated that "many of Redford's supporters, including her campaign manager, Stephen Carter, are citing Redford's funding commitment and her appeal to teachers as key to her victory."[7]

Redford had attracted a coalition of unionists, Liberals, and New Democrats, not the PC Party's natural constituency — a tactic with a mixed record of success. Nancy Betkowski (MacBeth) had tried the same tactic in her run against Ralph Klein and failed. Yet, the October 2010 election of Calgary mayor Naheed Nenshi proved that a charismatic outsider could rise swiftly when the public grew tired of the establishment. That's exactly what had happened in 1980 when Klein beat the status-quo candidate, Ross Alger, to become Calgary mayor.

Both Redford and Nenshi employed the same campaign manager, the brash and shrewd Stephen Carter. After the initial shock, Redford's win turned into an era of hope, especially for women and progressives. She was a successful human rights lawyer and a Queen's Counsel, with international experience at the United Nations. Now she was leading a province that boasted a long tradition of breakthroughs for women.

In 1916, Prairie women were the first in Canada to vote, with Manitoba gaining the right in January, Saskatchewan in March, and Alberta in April. It would take British Columbia and then Ontario another year. The Dominion of Canada finally granted women the vote on May 24, 1918, a full two years after the Prairies. Also in 1916, Edmonton author Emily Murphy (who wrote under the name Janey Canuck) was appointed the first female magistrate in the entire British Empire. Louise McKinney, in 1917, won her Claresholm, Alberta, riding and became the first female legislator in the British Empire. Alberta minister without portfolio Irene Parlby was only the second woman in the British Empire to become a Cabinet minister — British Columbia's Mary Ellen Smith was the first.

In 1927 five Alberta women challenged the Supreme Court to rule that they were "persons" under the British North America Act, and thus eligible to sit in the Senate. In what became "the Persons Case," Murphy rounded up McKinney and Parlby as well as popular author and Alberta MLA Nellie McClung, along with journalist and artist Henrietta Muir Edwards. When Canada's Supreme Court ruled they were not "persons," the five petitioned the British Privy Council, the highest court of appeal in Canada at the time. On October 18, 1929, reason prevailed; the "Famous Five," as they would later be called, won. Nellie McClung, with her usual wit, noted that Canadian women had not known they were not persons until they heard that they were.[8]

Alberta's list of social and political firsts was vast, but "woman premier" had eluded the province. Ever since Parlby there had been exceptional women in Cabinet, but none had served as premier until Redford. Klein believed his deputy premier and minister of finance, Shirley McClellan, was the best person for the job when he retired. She didn't take him up on it.

All of this leaves a reader wondering what *Globe and Mail* headline writers were thinking when they wrote, "Alberta Steps into the Present."[9] Writers and pundits from across the country sneered at the condescension. Unfortunately, there was no such headline to inform *Globe and Mail* readers when, more than a year later, Ontario finally "stepped into the present" with Kathleen Wynne's ascension to the position of premier.

The growing number of women leaders was heartening for the baby boom generation that had struggled for gender equality. Millennials grew up with the expectation that women had earned equal access to all jobs. That played especially well in Alberta, where the PC premier and the Wildrose Official Opposition leader were women. Redford and Smith were ably matched, dynamic speakers who were quick on their feet. The other two opposition parties also boasted exceptional women debaters, Liberal Laurie Blakeman and New Democrat Rachel Notley. Each of these energetic legislators has played an auspicious role in Alberta politics.

Redford won because she went beyond the mundane expectations of a tired party and pursued those who felt left out, the progressive wing of the Tories plus union members. She offended traditionalists by campaigning with the line that her PC Party was "not your father's party." Many, especially in the big cities, joined up to vote for Redford.

A number proved to be "two-minute Tories," departing soon after the job was done and leaving behind a well of discontent in the traditional conservative ranks. Redford had a major job to do: win over her own party and convince the traditionalists that she was on their side — that she needed them as much as they needed her. That campaign slogan still rankled among long-time volunteers.

But Redford didn't win the party over. Not only did she fail to keep the new members, she didn't reach out to party stalwarts, the senior Tories who'd stuck with the party through the Stelmach years and before.

By the time she tabled her first budget and then called the election for April 23, 2012, her government was in trouble. Spending was high, with a predicted deficit of $886 million. This added to public annoyance over revelations about the so-called "no-meet committee," which hadn't convened since 2008 but still awarded each of its twenty-one MLAs a monthly stipend of $1,000. The government also had problems with the influential medical community. A report by the Health Quality Council of Alberta described a culture of intimidation and bullying of doctors in the health system.

The polls favoured Danielle Smith's Wildrose. So did political donors. During the campaign period Wildrose amassed $3.1 million and spent all but $29,000. The PCs, meanwhile, collected just $1.6 million yet spent $4.6 million, running a $3 million deficit. In the two weeks leading up to the election, Wildrose was ahead and it was Smith's to lose. That she did with three quick strikes.

She challenged the validity of climate change. "We have always said the science isn't settled and we need to continue to monitor the debate," Smith stated in an online forum on April 16, 2012. The next day, celebrated University of Alberta scientist David Schindler retorted, "I wonder if she thinks the flat Earth debate is settled."[10]

On April 15, 2015, Wildrose candidate and former pastor Ron Leech offered his peculiar view of ethnic relations: "I think as a Caucasian I have an advantage. When different community leaders such as a Sikh leader or a Muslim leader speaks, they really speak to their own people in many ways. As a Caucasian, I believe that I can speak to all the community."[11] He later offered a convoluted apology that did little to stifle Calgary mayor Naheed Nenshi's ire. On April 18, @Nenshi tweeted: "All I'm saying is don't say 'I shouldn't have said offensive thing.' Say 'I don't actually believe it!'"[12]

Then there was Edmonton Wildrose candidate and pastor Allan Hunsperger, who, as noted earlier, blasted gays in a June 2011 blog, writing: "You can live the way you were born, and if you die the way you were born, then you will suffer the rest of eternity in the lake of fire, hell, a place of eternal suffering."[13]

The blog shocked the province, and it was clear that it would not be enough for Smith to just censure Hunsperger for his comments. She would have to remove her candidate. Smith refused, even as her closest advisers urged her to act decisively against intolerance. Her defence was that she had talked to Hunsperger, noting that the party "won't be legislating on contentious social issues." Smith later added: "We accept that people have a broad diversity of viewpoints, but the way we get along is that we focus on the things on which we can agree."

Hunsperger quickly took down his offensive post, but the damage was done. Smith's dreams of victory died in the lake of fire. Redford won a resounding majority, thanks primarily to her campaign manager, Randy Dawson. His inspired tag line for the PCs' late ad campaign, "Not Worth the Risk," resonated with urban voters as Smith lost both the white-collar and youth sectors.

Redford, like Stelmach, took her victory as a resounding personal endorsement. She appeared to forget the centrists and progressives who had helped her win not only her leadership but the critical 2012 election. Redford's 2013 budget broke the promise to teachers and slashed education spending, a startling rebuke to the ATA and the teachers who had trusted her government. She went after collective bargaining rights, introducing some of the most draconian legislation public-sector unions had ever seen in Alberta.

Redford was also the first premier since Don Getty to borrow significant amounts of money. The peculiar style of her government was to start doing something and then make it seem as if everyone should have known it was already being done. For example, the borrowing initiative was obliquely mentioned at a PC convention, shocking reporters because it had been unheard of for more than a decade. Doug Horner, by then the treasurer, said it should have been obvious because there had been a reference to it in an obscure government document.

Suffering already from her government's own mistakes, Redford had the political misfortune to be premier when one of the largest disasters in Canadian history happened. The great flood of June 2013 swept away businesses and homes in parts of Calgary and rural southern Alberta. The signpost test of her government was how it handled flood relief. What seemed to start from a strong and positive position dissolved into a miasma of struggles for money for the people afflicted.

"I promise you that, on behalf of the government of Alberta, we will do everything that it takes for people to rebuild their homes and rebuild their lives and rebuild their communities," Redford told reporters on June 24, 2013. In a question and answer session with the *Calgary Herald* a few days earlier, she said: "We're going to do what it takes to get people back to their homes so that they can rebuild."[14]

She was asked: "Will the government cover the entire costs?"

Answer: "Yes."

Question: "So, anybody who is in High River, that's obviously a big concern, those people will have their entire costs covered?"

Answer: "Yes."

Question: "So, you'll rebuild all those people's homes?"

Answer: "Yup."

The statement immediately raised concerns, even in southern Alberta, that Redford was making promises neither she nor the taxpayers could possibly keep. And, in fact, they didn't.

The politician who seemed to be everywhere and show the most concern was Calgary Mayor Naheed Nenshi, who got to the point where he looked so haggard from the exhausting hours he was spending trying to help people and effectively oversee the relief efforts that citizens were advising him to take a break. Sleep was the luxury he would take on the fly as he criss-crossed the city and outlying areas.

People loved his genuine dedication and showed their appreciation. Few could manage that degree of adulation, and Redford, up against

Mother Nature and Nenshi, never had a chance. She did her part, but there always seemed to be a certain distance that no hug could overcome.

Throughout her tenure rumours and questions were raised about her leadership style, her use of government airplanes, and her foreign travel. Redford's popularity plummeted to 18 percent, the lowest ever for a PC premier, while the party didn't do much better at 19 percent. Fundraising dwindled.

Len Webber, a respected PC backbencher, left his party to sit as an independent, calling the premier "a bully." (In September 2015 Webber won his federal Conservative riding.) Then Donna Kennedy-Glans, the associate minister for electricity, quit the PCs. Redford's party was almost in open rebellion, with at least another ten caucus members threatening to leave. She seemed to seal her own fate when questions were asked about her air travel excesses and the penthouse her office had stickhandled through the bureaucracy. On March 19, 2014, Redford abruptly announced she would be stepping down as premier on March 23 — four days later. She kept her Calgary-Elbow seat — and salary — but didn't show up for two months, amid much controversy. Cabinet warhorse Dave Hancock stepped in as interim party leader and premier, signalling yet another PC leadership struggle.

On August 6, 2014, Redford also resigned her seat. In a guest column that appeared in the *Calgary Herald* and the *Edmonton Journal*, she stated that "mistakes were made," but did not specifically state who made them.

"I recognize mistakes were made along the way. In hindsight, there were many things I would have done differently," she wrote. "That said, I accept responsibility for all the decisions I have made."[15] Within moments, Twitter had a new hashtag, #MistakesWereMade.

The day after her resignation as an MLA, Auditor General Saher issued his scathing report, which only strengthened a CBC story that had been released on Redford's spending excesses. "Premier Redford and her office used public resources inappropriately," Saher stated. "Premier Redford used public assets (aircraft) for personal and partisan purposes. And Premier Redford was involved in a plan to convert public space in a public building into personal living space."[16]

The auditor general's report confirmed that Redford's office block-booked flights with false names of passengers who would magically disappear before departure. In what Saher termed "a personal benefit," Redford had flown her daughter on fifty occasions when it wasn't warranted. Her office had also booked the government plane for an uncle's funeral in Vancouver, Saher's report stated, "and only later did the former premier book two meetings there." The auditor general also noted that Redford's reported cost of her trip to India, $131,000, was not the actual amount, which was "$450,000, well above the published cost."

"How could this have happened?" Saher asked. "The answer is the aura of power around Premier Redford and her office and the perception that the influence of the office should not be questioned."[17]

Another hashtag was born: #auraofpower; and as soon as each of these hashtags landed on Twitter, they immediately trended. Twitter wits rushed their tweets, making the government a laughing stock, and prompting prospective PC leadership candidates to consider their options.

WHILE HANCOCK SERVED as a calming temporary premier, nobody in the PC Party wanted a leadership bloodbath. Conservative insiders conscripted Jim Prentice, the former federal Cabinet minister under Stephen Harper. Edmonton's Thomas Lukaszuk and Calgary's Ric McIver, both former Cabinet ministers under Redford, made it a three-way contest. But not really; this time the easy winner was Prentice. To many in the bedraggled party, Prentice appeared the saviour because of his federal experience, management skills, and business career as vice-president of the Canadian Imperial Bank of Commerce.

In the end, though, this party was not to be saved. The dynasty dissolved into a farrago of broken dreams. What Peter Lougheed had given, the PCs had themselves taken away. They gradually lost that storied connection between the party and the province, and even between the party and the premier. There was a looming paradigm shift that the party particularly refused to see. The educated urban millennials were underemployed, restless, and angry. This double-disconnect occurred because the Alberta population was changing rapidly as it became more urban and progressive minded.

Redford had actually understood this clearly and, with Stephen Carter's strategic advice, had presented herself as a progressive waiting to listen and govern accordingly. She promised a fresh and innovative approach that initially excited hopeful young Albertans. Many women were particularly optimistic with the first female premier of the province, who seemed to successfully juggle the jobs-overspill of the modern woman. All those roles of lawyer, politician, mother, and wife Redford seemed to balance. If not for the scandals, she might still be premier today, and a successful one at that.

Although Redford certainly contributed to the demise of the PCs, she was far from entirely responsible. The decline had begun long before her leadership collapsed. PC loyalists, caucus members, Cabinet ministers, and government confidants were in open conflict. Ministers were routinely arrogant toward party volunteers. They wouldn't listen to the advice of campaigners and those on the ground. They shared a fundamental delusion that no matter how open and bitter their own fights became, no matter how vigorously ministers stabbed each other in the back in almost full public view, the public would still continue to accept them because the PCs were the natural governing party. They couldn't imagine losing to any opposition — especially a left-wing one. The PCs considered Wildrose their only possible rival and believed that even that threat had been eliminated after the Wildrose floor crossings on December 17, 2014. That powerful delusion would only accelerate the PC defeat.

Little was learned from Alison Redford's revivalist election win and her subsequent fall from grace. Redford's descent was interpreted more as a personal stumble than as a party or government failing, but indeed it was all three. This failure to recognize the party's internal weakness was a massive miscalculation by the party brass. In fact, the seeds of the dynasty's downfall were sown years before.

The party had misinterpreted the electorate's 2012 rejection of Wildrose as an eternal turn to the Tories. In fact, it was a momentary flashpoint for the people's doubts over the Wildrose Party's competency to govern. Voters scurried back to the PCs, but not without concern over the old regime. Within two years the PC government had run through three more premiers, painting indelible images of a party riven by betrayal and instability. By the time the 2015 election began, the PCs had constructed a nearly perfect campaign — for Rachel Notley.

CHAPTER 5

BORN TO RUN

The victories of Rachel Notley and then Justin Trudeau sparked talk of family dynasties and their role in Canadian politics. Name recognition certainly played a part in their courting and then securing nominations. Obviously, if the name is respected, the voter will be interested in version 2.0. But the candidate should be sharp from the start, because he or she will always be compared to version 1.0. In Rachel Notley's case the comparison has been highly favourable, because she has the charisma, wit, enthusiasm, and compassion of her dad. With Justin Trudeau, part of the appeal is his difference from his dad. While he does share his father's charisma, he does not have Pierre's brittle brilliance. Yet even that has worked in Justin Trudeau's favour, because his intelligence has been vastly underestimated. On the campaign trail he proved himself as formidable as, but very distinct from, the founder of this family tradition.

While the two Trudeaus are the first Canadian parent-child prime ministers, there have been many examples of parents, siblings, children, spouses, and other relatives who have won federal, provincial, and municipal elections. Notley's father was, of course, the highly respected Alberta NDP politician Grant Notley. Although he became leader of the Official Opposition, he never became premier. In British Columbia, both W.A.C. Bennett and then his son, William R. Bennett, were successful premiers. In Prince Edward Island, the father-son premiers were Joe Ghiz and, later, Robert.

There are numerous other examples on Canada's political landscape. Recently, Toronto's Ford brothers, Rob and Doug, have figured prominently, at least in the media. Their father, Doug Ford, Sr., was an Ontario MPP. The late Rob Ford was both a city councillor and mayor of Toronto; his brother Doug Ford, Jr., also became a Toronto councillor. Their nephew, Michael Ford, was a Toronto school-board trustee who won the July 2016 by-election for the ward seat left vacant by his uncle Rob's death.

If a politician is particularly successful, his or her supporters hope the magic can continue with the next family candidate. Preston Manning, son of former Alberta Social Credit Premier Ernest Manning, opted for a unique and even more ambitious job than that of his father. He devised and led a federal right-of-centre movement called the Reform Party, aiming for the prime minister's office but never unseating Liberal leader Jean Chrétien. Yet his party ultimately spawned the Conservative Party and Prime Minister Stephen Harper.

Nova Scotia conservative Peter MacKay followed his father Elmer into the Progressive Conservative Party. MacKay senior was a Cabinet minister under Brian Mulroney, while MacKay junior, as head of the federal PCs, played a critical role, with Harper, in uniting the right under the Conservative banner.

The late Jack Layton followed his father, Robert, and his grandfather Gilbert into politics. Gilbert was a minister in the Quebec Union Nationale government of Maurice Duplessis, while Robert was a minister under Prime Minister Brian Mulroney. Jack chose the NDP rather than his dad's PCs and seriously challenged Conservative Prime Minister Stephen Harper. Mike Layton, Jack's son, became a Toronto city councillor.

Former prime minister Paul Martin Jr. followed the political path of his father, Paul Martin Sr., who failed to secure the Liberal Party leadership after three hard tries. Paul Jr. finally succeeded and fulfilled the family ambition of occupying 24 Sussex Drive.

The pressure to forge a political career is enormous for the children of high-profile politicians. Some, however, choose to forgo it completely, precisely because of that or because they know how politics consumes absolutely any family time. Peter Lougheed's son Joe was once again being pressured to run for the leadership of his father's party, the Alberta PCs.

It's likely no coincidence that both Notley and Trudeau are working on a new political paradigm that would make politics more family-friendly; they know what a life in politics can do to people, how suddenly it can rob a child of a beloved parent. For Rachel Notley, both politics and then a plane crash took away her father. Despite the immense personal pain that she and the rest of her family endured, Rachel chose to carry on his tradition.

RACHEL NOTLEY IS a natural-born runner, both in sneakers and on the campaign trail. She started running to help her quit smoking. The political skills were learned in childhood, acquired from duty-bound parents determined to make a change. Both had clear and ambitious goals: social democracy for her dad, Grant Notley; social justice for her mom, Sandy Notley. The goals elegantly intertwined, sewing political and personal beliefs into a tapestry of family and community calling. Rachel's parents were hard-working dynamos who were too often separated by duty. Each understood that personal constancy would keep them together even as political missions would separate them.

Rachel Notley was born in Edmonton on April 17, 1964. She would be followed by two brothers, Paul, a lawyer and tutor at Alberta's Athabasca University, and Stephen, a cartoonist and video game designer.

Rachel's mother, Sandra Wilkinson, was from Concord, Massachusetts, and her father, Walter Grant Notley, from a farm family in Didsbury, eighty-five kilometres north of Calgary. Sandra Wilkinson Notley was a staunch Anglican and social activist. She registered African-American voters in the segregated U.S. South. Her sense of mission took her to Nicaragua and South Africa. After coming to Canada, originally to see a friend, she became interested in the New Democrats and they in her; one, Grant Notley, took a particular interest in her. She brought her experience with international poverty and injustice to what she saw as a receptive and motivated group. "Sandy's American social gospel background grounded her," says Laurent Jeff Dubois, a long-time friend of Rachel's parents and former NDP candidate. "Her theology helped frame her sense of social justice."

Rachel recalls wistfully her childhood in Fairview, the heart of Peace River Country in Alberta's northwest. Her mother was often alone raising the three children while her dad was campaigning throughout the province. "She did have strong social justice values, but she was actually quite conservative on a social basis. Dad and I used to debate her quite regularly on some of her archaic ideas.

"The Wildrose would love this, but she was left of many democratic socialists in terms of many of her economic views of the world. She was very smart and very compelling in terms of making her case on it. My mom really put her money where her mouth was in terms of the way she lived and the way she spent money. She donated her money and she donated her time to causes she chose to support. She never bought an outfit from anywhere but a thrift store. She donated all this money to typically Third World development causes through the church. She met Desmond Tutu because she was part of the anti-apartheid campaign. She was in Nicaragua after the Sandinistas won the election."

And yet Sandy Notley was very much in her children's lives. "She took the time. I didn't agree with her on all things, but she was very heartfelt. She was a liberation theologist and her view of democratic socialism and the teachings of Jesus and [how] they overlap was something she would talk about. Because she was very religious; very religious. Mom took all of us to church every Sunday."

Today, Rachel "sometimes" goes to church, "but not the same way."

In time, Rachel learned from her mom how persistence and compassion could change community; from her dad, she would understand that diligence and passion would change politics.

"Both of them played a big role," Rachel says.

"My dad obviously, by way of example. The legislature was six hours south so we didn't see him as much. But certainly, by example. Not only were his values obviously instilled but also his work ethic and his willingness to go up against the odds. It was sort of a celebrated quality, quite frankly. He'd say, 'Oh, the odds are against us even more! Great! It's going to make it even better!' So, he really did have quite an incredible work ethic. He was somebody who just drove through adversity in a big way.

"I was talking to the Girl Guides, who were [visiting] the legislature, and [asking them] whether they were comfortable public speakers. And I was telling them about how I used to break into a cold sweat over public speaking. I didn't like it, and I really had to get used to it and practise. It wasn't until my late twenties that I was actually someone whom I would describe as not breaking into a cold sweat when I speak in public.

"What got me to that point was the fact that my parents used to tell me, and their friends would tell me, how my dad, who was renowned by the time I was old enough to really know him, was known as a brilliant public speaker. He had actually been horrified at being a public speaker and would have to practise for hours and hours in the mirror, over and over. He'd memorize his speeches and practise jokes, and just had to put in hours and hours and hours. Because he was actually a very shy person and it wasn't his thing. He was just not one of those people who could get up and charm a room. But he ended up being seen as a brilliant public speaker because he just practised until he got it right. So that was my example."

Grant Notley attended the University of Alberta, a breeding ground for activist politicians of all ideological stripes, including former prime minister Joe Clark; Reform Party and eventual Official Opposition leader Preston Manning; Laurence Decore, mayor of Edmonton and afterward the provincial Liberal leader; and before them, PC founder and then premier Peter Lougheed. Grant Notley was a vocal New Democrat in a lively setting that spun off successful politicians with remarkable regularity.

Long-time Liberal stalwart Darryl Raymaker was a first-year law student with Notley, and the two became friends. "He invited me to a CCF [Co-operative Commonwealth Federation] meeting," recalls Raymaker. "It was a motley crew at the university, and we had potluck dinner. The guest speaker was Neil Reimer, who went on to run. From our talks, Grant must have thought I was a potential ally. At the end of Reimer's talk, Grant asked all of us to join in a circle, clasp hands, and then he led us in a resounding rendition of 'Solidarity Forever.' By then, I concluded that I was perhaps a little too mainstream for Notley and slipped out of the meeting. But Grant was a really nice fellow."

Notley had recognized in Raymaker another hardy soul seeking change. While not as left as Notley, Raymaker did go on to become a robust Liberal, running provincially in 1967, and federally in 1979, 1980, and 1984. He was president of the federal Liberal Party from 1980 to 1983.

Grant Notley often felt like a minority of one, even though his party already had much deeper roots in the province than most Albertans realized. The United Farmers of Alberta, a progressive agrarian party, governed the province from 1921 to 1935. Some UFA members and like-minded followers met in Calgary in 1932 to form the Co-operative Commonwealth Federation. The CCF went through various upheavals and degrees of electoral success, both provincial and federal, before agreeing with the Canadian Labour Congress in 1961 to form the federal New Democratic Party.

A year later, the NDP's Alberta offshoot was organized under the leadership of Neil Reimer of the Oilworkers International Union. There was a small but encouraging success in 1966, when lawyer Garth Turcott won a provincial by-election in the southern riding of Pincher Creek-Crowsnest. He would lose a year later in the general election that saw Social Credit win its ninth victory.

But the political winds were shifting in Alberta. The Progressive Conservatives, under dynamic new leader Peter Lougheed, won six seats and became the Official Opposition. Although few people realized it then, the province was heading for one of the seismic spasms that turn Alberta politics inside-out after a long stretch of one-party rule.

Grant Notley had a fierce desire to be in the thick of it. He ran in two elections and lost both before taking over the NDP leadership in 1968. A year later a by-election beckoned, where he was again defeated. The breakthrough finally came in 1971, when Notley energized his faltering party by winning Spirit River-Fairview. It seemed an anomaly, as Lougheed's PCs swept the tired old Social Credit from power. But Notley's surprising win would be only the first of four straight victories against the strongest organizing efforts the PCs could throw at him.

Social Credit didn't even run a candidate against him in 1975. The party hoped this would avert a vote split and allow the PC candidate to defeat him. "But Grant won with 50.1 per cent of the vote," says his biographer, Howard Leeson. "In elections after that, he did very well."[1]

Family friends knew that Notley's remarkable skills and ability to inspire followers were only half the story of his success. Sandy Notley was the other half. "Sandy was the constant," Jeff Dubois recalls. "She was the consummate pillar. Without her support and encouragement, Grant couldn't have done what he did."

Grant Notley used his precarious foothold to become the provincial conscience for the powerless. His name alone came to symbolize integrity in politics. There was something about his singular passion for social justice, untouched by malice toward his opponents, that inspired admiration, even among staunch conservatives.

Randy Dawson was just getting started on his long path to PC strategist when he found himself face to face with Grant Notley at a forum in Peace River Country. Dawson had been driving Ged Baldwin, the respected, long-term federal Conservative MP, around his riding as he campaigned once again for his seat.

Notley looked at Dawson, grinned, and asked, "How can you be a PC so young?" Both chuckled, but then Notley said, "Ged is a highly respectable man. He's a good candidate."

Dawson still speaks admiringly of Rachel's father: "I liked Grant Notley and I respected him."

Notley believed that working for the public good was the highest calling on Earth. Even his political enemies were reluctantly moved by the sight of him constantly tilting at the Tory windmills.

For the New Democrats, money was hard to come by. The party survived by work, grit, and tight fiscal discipline. "Grant was so frugal," recalls Dubois. "We used to kid him about being cheap. But what he and Sandy did on so little! God bless her for stretching the dollar, adding more water to the proverbial soup and just making it all possible."

Dubois recalls Notley "travelling the countryside toiling day after night, taking all those hard roads to the towns and the halls bringing his message. Then one of us would pass the hat and hope there was enough to carry on another day." The young politician rarely paused for breath. He tried to make it home to his young family every second weekend, but often failed.

For the family, Dubois says, "Sandy gave all of them a sense of calm throughout the rough waters. Everybody made a big investment for the party, but she made the biggest. With Sandy's strong social conscience, she deeply felt that what Grant was doing would make a far better world. She was the backbone and she was integral in the workings of the party."

After his first victory, the Notleys moved their young family from Edmonton to the riding town of Fairview. In 1976, they settled the family in a home they built on a small ranch near Dunvegan. There they experienced the invigorating solitude of grass and hills and country vistas.

Anyone who has spent time in Peace Country knows it's a breathtaking land of limitless dreams.

Sandy Notley told the children stories of Grant's work, often encasing them in parables of the good man righting wrongs. "I remember being five and her describing what my father did from stories — Robin Hood, The Prince and the Pauper," Rachel told the *Edmonton Journal*'s Alan Kellogg.[2]

When he was home, Grant tackled ranch chores, making way for even more stories. "One time Grant said he had to leave early because he had some fencing to do on the ranch," recalls Dubois. "So, he parked just above an embankment and got out to dig the holes for the posts. But in his haste he left the truck in gear. It suddenly started to roll, picked up steam, and rushed down hitting trees, before scattering into the neighbour's quarter section."

Rachel, who was working with her dad, remembers the '68 Dodge truck and its three-on-a-tree gearshift that took an impromptu ride into NDP lore. In an interview with Dean Bennett of the Canadian Press, Rachel recalled that her dad "winched it out without any repairs, made my mom drive it for the next three years."[3]

Dubois says he never heard a word of complaint from Sandy, nor did he ever hear Grant raise his voice. "He was so strong and principled. And he always plugged into Sandy for energy, inspiration, and encouragement. She was the one who asked me to run for the NDP in St. Paul." The 1971 provincial election saw Dubois, a local businessman, mount a strong challenge, but he couldn't stop the PC sweep.

"I always saw Rachel with her mom, but not with her dad, as he was so often on the road campaigning. Sandy and Grant's roles were distinct but equal," recalls Dubois.

Sandy took Rachel to her first demonstration at the age of ten, in Edmonton. Many protest marches to the provincial capital building start just south of the High Level Bridge that spans the North Saskatchewan River, connecting the University of Alberta district to the legislature area. For kids and seniors it can be a daunting and seemingly endless slog. "She took me on some anti-war demonstration. I honestly can't even remember what it was," Notley told Bennett.[4] But she did recall its effect and three things specifically: it was long, loud, and effective. "There was the energy of people coming together to try to change things. A [protest] letter is easily dismissed. Five hundred people marching together is less so."

Dubois remembers Sandy Notley as strong willed, independent, quick witted, engaging, and smart. "She was knowledgeable and approachable, and could speak to anything. Nothing was regurgitated."

Many of her mother's qualities seemed to have settled naturally on the daughter, as did some of the father's, she told Kellogg. "From my dad, I got more of a sense of the strength of will than the politics. He had this phenomenal hard work ethic, this steely-eyed determination. It was: Don't talk about it, just do it."[5]

She turned into a feisty teenager who would challenge both her dad and other NDP heroes. While all the national NDP greats such as Tommy Douglas and David Lewis made their way to Alberta, Rachel the kid wasn't always impressed. She told Graham Thomson about her now-embarrassing encounter with former national NDP leader Ed Broadbent. "I met him at some event; he smiled and introduced himself and shook my hand, and I said, 'Oh, you have that same fake politician smile as my father.' Just horrible, right? I was just your standard obnoxious twelve- or thirteen-year-old."[6]

After high school Rachel moved to Paris as an *au pair*. She lived in the elite seventh arrondissement, the home of Parisian nobility, the French National Assembly, the Eiffel Tower, the Musée d'Orsay, and the Musée Rodin. For an impressionable social activist and a proud prairie farm kid, Paris was a powerful experience. Her boss was a woman in a wheelchair whose husband worked with UNESCO. She took kindly to her Canadian employee and wanted her to have an easy start. Notley recalled that when she made her first dinner for her employer, "she asked for macaroni and cheese. So, naturally, I asked where the box of Kraft Dinner was. She was appalled. But she was patient."[7]

Armed with a working knowledge of French and a desire to make a difference, Rachel returned to the Peace Country and enrolled at Grande Prairie Regional College, a less expensive option to the big-city universities. She would also be close to her mom.

"I still remember my first essay that I had to write in undergrad at Grande Prairie College. I'd never written a thoughtful university essay before, and I was trying to figure out what to do. I'd been kind of a hapless, yet reasonable student, but I didn't try very hard. So I came home and said I don't know what to write for the political science paper. Mom

[went] down to her library and [came] up with this stack of books this big," and Notley spreads her arms wide. "There's everything about Central American politics, and the intervention of the U.S., and the arguments about the Nicaraguan revolution and yadda, yadda, yadda. There's stuff about Fidel Castro, and it's all just big." Notley holds her hands a foot apart and then assumes her mother's gentle but firm voice. "She says, 'Now read these books, and this is what your thesis should be.' And blah, blah, blah. So I read all these books, and then we talked about it. Afterward, I was very excited because I got a perfect mark on my paper. I'm like, 'Oh, wow. I do kind of understand this stuff.'"

For lucky young college students, parents are there to help fund, advise, and argue with. If Notley senior had temporarily forgotten his daughter's fearlessness and wit, he would soon be reminded. She went to a speech Grant was giving in Grande Prairie, and listened attentively as he condemned poverty in Canada's breadbasket. "I waited until it was question time, stood up, and identified myself as a student who was living on nothing but crackers that week. He waited until the room emptied, and was, of course, mad. So what does he do? He gives me a $20 bill! What a guy." Notley laughed as she recounted the tale to Kellogg.[8] Others, knowing it was the father's daughter, could barely contain their guffaws.

Grant Notley's NDP caucus doubled in the November 1982 provincial election. Ray Martin's victory in Edmonton-Norwood made the New Democrats an Official Opposition of two. They were the only party standing when Lougheed's Progressive Conservatives carried the province with seventy-five of seventy-nine seats. (Two former Social Crediters, Ray Speaker and Walt Buck, left their party and won as independents.)

Notley and Martin would scold and cajole the PCs, whose solid phalanx of caucus members spilled from every corner of the legislature. Somehow, the very puniness of the NDP magnified both Notley's persona and his message of economic and social justice. Lougheed wisely told his MLAs to treat the New Democrats with respect, partly because they could so easily look like bullies, but also because he had developed a sincere personal regard for Notley, even when his opponent blasted both Ottawa and the Alberta government for hurting the whole country with their epic feud over the 1980 National Energy Program. On that one, however, most Albertans sided with Lougheed.

By 1982, Rachel was at the University of Alberta in Edmonton, a twenty-year-old undergraduate working on a BA in political science. On the night of October 19, 1984, she recalled later, "we had a huge party. At around 4:00 a.m. I got a call from Tom Sigurdson [Notley's executive assistant] that there had been a plane crash and that I should go home."[9]

Hours earlier, wanting to spend time with his family after another arduous week, Grant had grabbed a last-minute seat on the familiar twin-engine run from Edmonton to his northern riding. The Wapiti Aviation flight fought fog and snow as the pilot searched for the lights of the High Prairie airport. The Piper suddenly grazed the tree-tops and crashed down a dark hillside. Notley and five other passengers perished while four survived, including the pilot and Alberta housing minister Larry Shaben.

Rachel's brothers were at the family home, but their mother had not yet arrived. By pure coincidence, the RCMP were driving her home after her car had stalled near Whitecourt. The Mounties knew about the crash but turned off the car radio so she wouldn't hear the news before joining her family. The CBC's Byron Christopher had broken the story before the Notleys were notified, later citing Notley's importance as a public figure as the rationale.

Rachel Notley, now at home, was worried but still hopeful. "It was serious news, of course, but my dad had been in a couple of plane mishaps before. And he had survived a terrible car crash, hitting an elk, walking out of a bubble with the rest of the car totalled."[10]

When Ray Martin called, the news was devastating. Rachel would now have to break it to her mom. In a sense, though, Sandy already knew something was terribly wrong. The Mounties' silence seemed to engulf the car with grief.

Dubois vividly recalls Notley's funeral, and especially the emotional reaction of then-premier Lougheed. "I had a clear side view of the premier," he says. "He was shaken. Tears welled in his eyes and dropped on his cheeks. He clenched his jaw, the way he did when he was overcome. I looked around me, and was startled as the tears just streamed down his face." The depth of his affection and admiration for Notley was on public display. It's more than three decades since Grant Notley perished, but for Dubois it's as if Sandy Notley has just called. "It overcomes you, even today."

Later, the legislature honoured Notley in a poignant ceremony. "It was a very tough time for me and all of us," recalls Martin, who stood beside Grant's empty chair. "The sergeant-at-arms was Oscar Lacombe, who always had a very regimental bearing. I can tell you, when Oscar marched over toward me and saluted Grant's empty seat, I nearly lost it. So did we all."[11]

Albertans everywhere were powerfully moved. Lougheed ran one of the most dominant and respected governments in Canada, but Albertans didn't believe it should be unwatched or unopposed. In Notley they'd found a trusted voice for their doubts about oil industry dominance, government deals with the industry, wealth inequity, and many other issues.

A 1985 by-election to fill Notley's vacant seat saw New Democrat Jim Gurnett win handily. When the province went to the polls a year later, the NDP under new leader Martin captured an historic 30 percent of the popular vote and sixteen of eighty-three ridings. While Notley's former assistant Tom Sigurdson won, Notley's old riding finally fell to the PCs. It would remain with them until New Democrat Margaret McCuaig-Boyd regained the riding, now called Dunvegan-Central Peace-Notley, thirty years later.

The New Democrats again became the Official Opposition and would retain that title and the sixteen seats in the 1989 election. But their popular vote dropped two points to 26 percent as the Liberals climbed. Although they captured only eight seats, they had 28 percent of the vote.

Then the 1993 election decimated the New Democrats. Their popular vote dropped to 11 percent and they won not a single seat. The Liberals became the Official Opposition, jumping from eight to thirty-two seats, capturing 40 percent of the popular vote. The Progressive Conservatives shed eight seats but still slid comfortably into power with fifty-one seats on 44 percent popularity. Premier Ralph Klein, the populist ex-Calgary mayor, was more than ready to take on an old rival, the popular ex-Edmonton mayor, Liberal leader Laurence Decore. Completely lost in the political fray was any whiff of the NDP dream. It would wander in the wilderness for a decade.

Martin resigned as leader, replaced for a short time by Ross Harvey, a one-term federal MP. Then Pam Barrett, a tiny dynamo, took over the party. She had been a researcher for Grant Notley and later decided to run in the 1986 election. She chose Edmonton-Highlands, considered unwinnable due to its popular PC incumbent and Cabinet minister, David King. Barrett upset them all and won. She would keep her seat until the

1993 NDP collapse. Back again in 1997, this time as the new NDP leader, Barrett was victorious, along with her Edmonton-Strathcona colleague Raj Pannu. He would retain that seat until 2008, when a woman named Rachel Notley would succeed him.

Barrett remained leader until a bizarre incident overtook her in 2000. While lying in the dentist's chair, she had an out-of-body experience. The woman known as "Mighty Mouse" for her feisty approach to politics and life abruptly quit her political post. As the spiritual beckoned, Barrett chose tranquility and reflection. Eight years later she died of cancer.

Raj Pannu took Barrett's job, and a popular Edmonton councillor, Brian Mason, won her riding in the 2001 election. Three years later Pannu stepped down as leader, with Mason taking the torch just in time for the 2004 election. The NDP doubled its caucus to four, with Ray Martin rolling back in alongside rookie David Eggen. Ominously, though, the NDP popular vote dropped to 10 percent, a point lower than the party's 1993 wipeout. It slipped to under 9 percent in the 2008 election. Only two New Democrats made it to the legislature, Mason and newcomer Notley. In the 2012 election they again doubled the caucus, bringing back Eggen and adding rookie Deron Bilous.

And yet, the NDP was going nowhere. The party routinely won a few seats because support was heavily concentrated in Edmonton, but it was chronically unable to break out of the capital. To most Albertans it had become a fringe party, often useful in opposition, but no candidate for government. Even the boldest New Democrats wouldn't have dared to suggest that within three years they would crush the PCs.

But then, there was Rachel Notley, custodian of a name still so evocative that in 2008, the very year she entered the legislature, her father was named one of Alberta's ten greatest citizens of all time in a project conducted by the *Calgary Herald*. Not far behind Peter Lougheed, Grant Notley won a large share of the vote, mostly from southern Albertans, who weren't represented by a New Democrat and never imagined they would be.

"The *Herald*'s poll amazes me," said Ray Martin at the time. "Politicians are soon forgotten, generally, and he died a long time ago. The fact that he's remembered says a tremendous amount about his contribution."[12]

It also said something about discontent with the PCs that would only grow over the coming years. A hunger for change was developing, along with a yearning for leaders who could better represent modern Alberta. The impulse helped bring Naheed Nenshi to the Calgary mayor's office in 2010. The NDP, meanwhile, had always been led, from Notley to Brian Mason, by principled and skilled leaders who never sold out to the government. They stayed themselves. Although a minor party, it seemed, the NDP was always sharply defined in the minds of Albertans.

Rachel Notley was in the legislature, gaining experience, at exactly the crucial moment. By 2014 she had become a sharp and appealing MLA with a humorous way of voicing NDP outrage. She and Mason punched far above their weight, as the sportscasters like to say, but eventually he began to appear tired. A highly skilled politician, and certainly the wittiest in Alberta, he had never managed to grow the party outside Edmonton. He decided to step down as leader while staying on as an MLA. As Notley considered her future, she also reflected on how much leadership matters in Canadian campaigns. She needed to decide if she could overcome her own uncertainties just as her father had when he practised and practised before every speech, whether on a podium in a forum or beside a cowpie in a field. "My parents taught me that an NDPer in Alberta has to work three times harder than any other politician to earn votes. It's a lesson I won't forget."[13]

Was she ready? Did she have what it takes?

In the years after her father's death, Rachel Notley had finished her University of Alberta B.A. with Honours, and then had moved to Toronto and enrolled at Osgoode Hall Law School. Keeping close to her roots, she became a student in Osgoode's poverty law program with Parkdale Community Legal Services. She also took time to form an Osgoode NDP club, actively backing Dave Barrett, the former B.C. NDP premier, for the 1989 federal leadership. It was, as too many leadership contests become, a battle of earnest, principled people smothering good intentions with bitter backbiting and betrayals. The duelling platforms featured the wrenching truth of Canada: the alienation of the West versus the solitude of Quebec. That Notley favoured Barrett spoke more to the politics of geography than gender. Yet the eventual victor, Audrey McLaughlin, was an Ontario-born Yukon MP who became the first woman to lead a prominent federal party.

Notley returned to Alberta, articled with Edmonton labour lawyer Bob Blakely, and was hired by the Alberta Union of Provincial Employees to help injured workers win proper compensation. But British Columbia beckoned under its NDP government, led by Mike Harcourt, and in 1994 Notley moved to Vancouver as a health and safety officer for the Health Sciences Association of British Columbia. She spent a year seconded to Attorney General Ujjal Dosanjh's department as a ministerial assistant, where she contributed to one of the most important pieces of legislation in the country: granting same-sex couples equal rights in family law.

"She was very politically savvy," Dosanjh told the *Globe and Mail* columnist Gary Mason. "She was bright but not impulsive. Everyone knew she was Grant's daughter. She had great political smarts. She was a wonderful sounding board. And just really, really likeable."[14]

Notley resumed her Health Sciences Association job, now armed with on-the-ground government experience.[15] With her considerable skills and strong background, she was selected to represent the B.C. labour movement in negotiations to rewrite workplace health and safety laws for the entire province.

Her former boss, Dosanjh, went on to become B.C. premier from 2000 to 2001, when the NDP went down to defeat. In 2004 Dosanjh dramatically switched political allegiances to run federally as a Liberal. Under Prime Minister Paul Martin, Dosanjh served as minister of health until the Liberals lost to Stephen Harper's Conservatives.

While she was in British Columbia, Rachel's beloved mother fell ill with cancer. She had remarried, to Alan Kreutzer, and was only fifty-nine when she died in 1998. Sandy Notley Kreutzer had continued her deep Christian commitment to social justice after Grant's death. She remained in Fairview, where she was an active Anglican who taught in her local parish and wrote and edited for the *Anglican Magazine*. She also contributed to a number of Anglican committees such as the Consultation for Peace and Disarmament, the Primate's World Relief and Development Fund Committee, and the National Consultation on Human Rights. In 1988 she ventured to Tanzania and volunteered for the Inter-Church Coalition on Africa. She received the Anglican Award of Merit in 1994.[16]

The spirit of her parents would embolden Rachel as she continued with NDP volunteering, campaigning, and strategizing on election committees. During one Alberta election campaign she worked closely with another committed social and political activist, Lou Arab. But it was not love at first sight. "Did Notley, who sat on a relevant committee, directly fire itinerant organizer and ex-Haligonian Arab years ago or not? At any rate, a serious reconciliation clearly followed," wrote Alan Kellogg.[17] Notley soon found in Arab a kindred spirit, and the two would share their deep commitment to social justice and political change. They would marry and share much more, especially their beloved children, Ethan and Sophie.

NOTLEY ENJOYED HER time in British Columbia, where she experienced first-hand the power of government to pass legislation that improves people's lives. She learned that the most effective way to make a difference is by working collaboratively with a diverse team of stakeholders. What resulted were laws that were not only fair, but improved, and in many instances, saved lives. Notley was thriving in British Columbia as her professional and political lives merged so fluidly. She continued to volunteer, with Vancouver Community College as a board member, and with "Moms on the Move," which advocates for special-needs children and youth.

But she missed the province of her own youth, and when she and Lou began a family they looked home to Alberta. That's where they wanted to raise their children. By 2002 they were back in Edmonton, where Lou became communications director for the NDP provincial caucus of two. Notley and Arab were like every other modern young family: juggling kids, career, and couple-time. Lou kept the permanent paycheque while Rachel cared for their baby and toddler, working under contract with unions and universities. There was tutoring at Athabasca University, teaching at MacEwan University, contracting with the National Union of Public and General Employees, and later, working as a labour relations officer with the United Nurses of Alberta. She continued volunteering, always managing to find time for such groups as Friends of Medicare and the Strathcona Community League. It was the see-saw life that so many women experience as they try to balance being a loving mother and partner while keeping some semblance of their hard-earned professional standing. It's a daunting feat that can only flourish when the marriage is a union of equals, especially when the man changes diapers and makes dinner. Lou Arab appears to have mastered that role. "He's very involved and supportive," says a close family friend.

"Luckily, my husband has been the cook for a long time, before I became the premier," says Notley. "I'm the laundry person. On Sunday I still do most of the laundry." And then she laughs, "Because if he gets to them, the clothes are done."

The pull of politics never left her. When the children grew into grade school, Pannu, the valued NDP MLA, decided it was time to step down. His Edmonton-Strathcona riding encompassed the University of Alberta and its attendant hospital, a strong base for burgeoning left-wing politicians. Notley was arguably the most prepared of them all, nurtured from birth to be a social democrat and political crusader. The opening in her own riding gave Notley and Arab little choice. They would have preferred waiting another four years, but the opportunity wouldn't hit pause. She had to seek the nomination. Little did she imagine that she would be acclaimed; nor did she imagine that she would receive the added bonus of having Jack Layton in the audience when she accepted the nomination. The federal NDP leader was a hero to Notley, and she was as distraught as so many other Canadians when Layton succumbed to cancer on August 22, 2011. As leader of the Official Opposition, his popularity put him closer to the prime minister's chair than any federal New Democrat before him.

For Notley, it was time to put her politics into action. "You can deal with each issue individually over and over again, or you can change the law — once. I grew up with this, and as hard as things can get, it can be a rewarding life," she told Alan Kellogg as she prepared for her first electoral run.[18]

An integral part of that preparation was family. How would she and Lou maintain their close-knit life with their children, relatives, and friends? With their busy personal commitments, could they manage a strong election run? They were determined to do it with help from their personal circle and their professional circle — most of whom were the same people. The couple distributed chores. He cooked; she campaigned. He managed her public relations; she managed her public speaking. They talked, strategized, played with the kids, took them to school, picked them up, went to their concerts, and simply listened. Most of all they tried to keep the life that they treasured grounded and strong, even as the pressure of the election intensified.

"She was warm and reached out to people. She didn't wait for them to come to her. I knew she was a unique politician who was going places," recalls committed New Democrat Roy Piepenburg. He knew her father well and had campaigned for the party throughout his many years in Alberta. The long-time social activist and now-retired civil servant was beyond upbeat. "I was as excited about Rachel as I had been about her dad; I think even more so. I knew she would win the riding."

As the 2008 election campaign wrapped up, Notley easily kept the NDP seat and joined colleague Mason to again form a two-person caucus. Then it hit her. No matter her background, no amount of family heft could disguise the stark reality: Notley was a parliamentary novice. She would need more than adrenalin to keep her nerves in check. Thankfully, she had the perfect corrective in Brian Mason. He'd learned his politics in the municipal birdbath of city hall where feathers splash and spray. From the University of Alberta to bus driver to city councillor to MLA to NDP leader, Mason was a man of passionate conviction and enviable experience.

Notley was in good hands, but in her early legislative days she didn't want to be the lone New Democrat to counter the House noise. Even as she presented a cloak of confidence, Notley was overwhelmed. She relied on Mason whenever the House was in session. "When she was first elected and I got up to go to the bathroom in the legislature one time, she dug her fingernails into my arm and said, 'Please don't leave me here.'"[19]

Her anxiety would soon subside as she learned the lay of the legislature and absorbed her many files. She had always been a quick study. Of the twenty-four PC Cabinet positions, her rookie role was to cover twelve. Mason took the other half, including the heavier portfolios. It was grinding work as Notley tracked the legislative labyrinth of truth and obfuscation. Yet she soon demonstrated that she could hold her own. Her watch was Aboriginal relations, advanced education, agriculture, children and youth services, culture, education, employment and immigration, environment, justice, seniors, sustainable resource development, and tourism.

With her workload on steroids, Notley was at maximum capacity. Or so she thought. But only a month after the election, one of her part-time office staffers, a young woman, pulled off an audacious piece of theatre. She and another Greenpeace enthusiast stealthily made their way to the ceiling of the Shaw Conference Centre in Edmonton, where Premier Ed Stelmach was to speak. As he talked, they slowly descended in harnesses and released a banner that said, "Stelmach: The Best Premier Oil Money

Can Buy." The protestors were quickly stopped and soon identified, and when the woman's employer became known, Notley was promptly grilled.

Her labour-law expertise and experience quickly kicked in. "It was something that I didn't find out about until after she had done it," Notley told reporters. "It's a personnel matter, and so it's something I'm going to discuss with her in person and not through the media."[20]

In the background, many New Democrats were convulsed with laughter. They thought it was the best stunt they'd ever seen. And one had to wonder: had it happened thirty years earlier, could that young woman floating down from the rafters have been Rachel Notley?

Notley's growing skill as a politician was evident as she handled the legislature's question period, as well as speeches throughout her riding and the province. "What she did in opposition was amazing," says a long-time family friend. "She was holding the government's feet to the fire in her role." In the 2012 election she was re-elected to her Edmonton-Strathcona riding with 62 percent of the vote, the highest for any MLA of any party.

Two years later Mason stepped down as leader. Notley had flourished under his mentorship and soon decided to run for the post. So too did fellow MLA David Eggen and union leader Rod Loyola. On October 18, 2014, she won with 70 percent of the vote on the first ballot, becoming the second Notley to hold the job. As he passed the mantle of hope to Notley, Mason recalled her early anxiety and then proclaimed: "Look at her now. She's developed into an articulate and passionate politician, a parliamentarian and a very, very effective communicator."[21] Within six heady and heavy years, Notley had grown from an anxious neophyte to the accomplished legislator. In his pride, Mason added: "I think our party is going to go from better to great."

THERE WERE OVER three hundred exuberant New Democrats waiting for Notley as she strode to the podium. But her message was addressed far beyond the ballroom of Edmonton's Sutton Place Hotel; it was a speech intended for the province as a whole. "Let's leave the parties of the past behind," Notley said. "This time, let's not forget history. Let's not repeat history. Let's make history." It was a message that would be heard many times over, and it would resonate with Albertans when they went to the polls less than seven months later.

But the question on the minds of those who remembered her father was asked by the CBC's Kim Trynacity. What would her dad think as his daughter now assumed his legendary role? "Obviously he would be proud and certainly I want to build on the work that he did," Notley replied, and then astutely acknowledged those things that "others have done, and that Brian Mason has done to present to Albertans a party that will really represent their interests first."[22] It was a considered but caring reply. Notley knew the hard work so many had given to their dream of an NDP government. She would need their support and that of many more Albertans to achieve the elusive goal.

But her dad's personal sacrifice and that of the Notley family were very much evident the next day. It was the thirtieth anniversary of her father's fatal flight. At the memorial in Edmonton Notley reminded everyone that the champions of change are not one, but the many who get involved. "We as a movement are not about one person. We are not about the last leader, the current leader, the next leader," she said. "I'm very excited about what is to come. I think there will be another breakthrough. And it will not be because of one person."[23]

When Piepenburg first saw and heard Notley, he thought, "This is a politician who is going places. She's dynamic, friendly, honest, and knowledgeable. Most of all she's trustworthy. She's the right person to lead as all of us work for change." Piepenburg was ready to knock on doors, as always, this time perhaps even more excited than he had been for another Notley all those decades ago.

While she focused on her new responsibilities as NDP leader, Notley never forgot her first shadow portfolios. She was furious when then premier Jim Prentice cut the child and youth advocate Del Graff's budget by $275,000. Deaths of children in care seemed to appear with alarming frequency, and Graff's department needed the funding and independence to investigate what was happening. Notley vowed to give Graff what his office needed to do its job and protect vulnerable children.

To keep up her spirits and her stamina, as well as her resolve to never smoke again, Notley ran. She would continue running, and on the evening of May 5, 2015, she would win. Her brother Stephen was skeptical until election night. As he waited with the family in the Weston Hotel, wrote *Maclean's* columnist Colby Cosh, Stephen finally asked his sister, "OK, so, you do have, like, several different speeches lined up for all the different outcomes that might transpire here?"[24]

Rachel told her brother she had just one. "And I thought to myself, 'Huh. I guess she's pretty sure this is happening,'" Stephen said.

Rachel Notley now knew what was going to happen. All the polls had predicted her victory, and as her initial shock faded she focused on what must be done. But her victory evening was for those who couldn't share this moment in history, especially her mom and dad.

"Tonight, I also want to say that I'm also thinking about my mother and father. I know my mother would be completely over the moon about this. I think my dad would too," she told the ecstatic throng. "I'm sorry he couldn't see this. This really was his life's work, but I can say this: I know how proud he'd be of the province we all love."[25]

As for ninety-year-old Roy Piepenburg, his joy over seeing his life's dream realized was elegantly simple: "This is a rebirth of Alberta."

The next day, Rachel Notley put on her sneakers and went out to run.

CHAPTER 6

THE PURPLE PRELUDE

Every generation wants a leader it can recognize. We don't know who it is until we hear and see the person who touches the times. In Calgary, Naheed Nenshi became that face when he spoke not just to urban youth, but to people of all ages who felt that city politics had become barren, distant, cold, and lacking in any inspirational vision. When he was elected in 2010 the same longing was already abroad in the land, waiting to attach itself to leaders on the provincial and federal stages. Ultimately, the premier and the prime minister were in some way heirs of the mayor.

Just as the election of the NDP in 2015 would give lie to the claim that Alberta is eternally conservative, the election of Nenshi shattered stereotypes, drawing international notice and making the young university professor famous. He was, and is, a political phenomenon who has transcended his city and even his country — a fact that irks some of his detractors at home. It took a rare new political talent, and a tremendous amount of skillful political work, to make this happen.

But the ground was already prepared for him by his predecessors in city hall, in the same way that the actions of the PCs had helped to pave the way for Notley and the NDP. Change was overdue in a vibrant, dynamic young city that had been ruled by a traditional government more concerned with potholes and taxes than any kind of wider civic vision. Nenshi's ascent signalled a generational upheaval that was waiting to happen on the provincial level and even nationally. It blew apart old distinctions of left and right, and drew young voters into a vision of collaboration and community action. Nenshi's victory would be a powerful early signal of the electorate's discontent with the traditional, hidebound way of governing, with its reliance on cronyism and an eternal alliance with business elites.

The PCs of the day, still ruled by Premier Ed Stelmach, could have used the warning to reform and save themselves. But they thought it was all just a stupid mistake.

IN THE SPRING and summer of 2010, Nenshi, then thirty-eight, was trying to get Calgarians' attention. The professor at Mount Royal University first wanted to find a mayoral candidate he could back with enthusiasm in the race to replace retiring three-term mayor Dave Bronconnier. But Nenshi couldn't convince anyone who he felt was promising enough to run. So he thought he might do it himself.

Nenshi spent a gut-wrenching three months deciding whether to take the plunge. "I knew Calgary was ripe for a real, in-depth, thoughtful conversation about who we wanted to be," he said. But Nenshi wasn't sure who should lead that discussion. He wasn't interesting in running simply to elevate the tone. He'd already tried that when he ran unsuccessfully for city council in 2004. He was in it to win, and fully intended to start with a "winning strategy — I had to cut through the clutter."

On Tuesday, just after the Victoria Day long weekend, he went out for dinner with two close advisers, where they chewed on pizza and politics. Was he going to run or not? Finally, Nenshi was "in." On Thursday morning, May 27, 2010, he broke the news on Twitter and Facebook. Then he held interviews. There was no press conference or scrum. "We had to execute our strategy and work our tails off," Nenshi said.

He attended the summer council meetings, live-tweeting them all. Anyone who voluntarily sits through such meetings during a Calgary summer deserves a prize. But would it be the mayor's chair? "I had to be in third place by the end of the summer. I knew how to win after that."

He was an expert in non-profits, had a high profile in the arts, and wrote a popular column on civic affairs for the *Calgary Herald*. He'd even run unsuccessfully for city council. It was a decent record to make a run for ward councillor, but nearly everyone thought he was deluded to believe he could be mayor. His reception was tepid, even after he announced his run. One political columnist even declined his friendly invitation to lunch (and deeply regretted it later). Just about everyone who heard of the professor's ambition thought he was getting way ahead of himself. Like Notley and Trudeau later — both written off as underdogs who had little hope of winning — he was to prove them wrong.

A deeper look at his record shows that Nenshi was already very accomplished. He was a promising young marketing professor at Mount Royal University, with a resumé highlighted by a Harvard University Master of Public Policy degree, a position with global marketers McKinsey and Company, as well as United Nations work, and his own consulting firm, Ascend Group.

He had returned to Calgary in 2001 to be with his family. His parents had immigrated to Canada from Tanzania in 1971, and within a year the family had moved to Calgary. Devout Ismaili Muslims, the Nenshis taught their children the importance of giving back. "My parents stressed that no matter what we had, there was someone who had less, and that it was our duty to give back in whatever way we could," his sister Shaheen Nenshi Nathoo told Marcello Di Cintio, writing for *Readers Digest Canada*.[1]

Nenshi's academic work centred on civic engagement, and by 2009 he was actively "trying to recruit people to run for office." In April 2010 he incorporated his academic research into a TEDx Calgary talk and showed how communities had become segregated by age, ethnicity, and income. When his talk was posted on YouTube, it became widely popular and broadened the discussions he was already having with students, friends, and potential candidates. While breaking down the myths about politics to those he canvassed, he uncovered one essential fact. The reason people said they didn't get involved or volunteer in civic politics was simple: "Nobody asked me."

The people who dismissed Nenshi usually weren't aware of this deep and detailed political work in his past. They thought he was just an ambitious neophyte, when in fact he was the most sophisticated candidate by far.

Early in the campaign Nenshi was already clicking with a small group of people who recognize political talent. Former premier Ralph Klein, who'd also been mayor of Calgary, liked him from the start. Klein approved of Nenshi's roots in Calgary's working-class east side. "My advice to any-one running for mayor," he said, "is look east of Centre Street, physically and philosophically."

For Klein, the strategy was simple: "I pressed the flesh and went to the people." So did Nenshi, working the grassroots, going "anywhere where people gathered in the community." Nenshi and his campaigners showed up at the summer folk festival, river pathways, community parks, and grocery store parking lots. They got themselves invited to residences, housing com-plexes, and shelters like Awo Taan Healing Lodge, which uses Aboriginal traditions to help abused women and their families. It was a favoured char-ity for Klein and his wife, Colleen, who is very proud of her Métis roots. "When Naheed Nenshi came to Awo Taan, he was the only candidate to do so. That said a lot about him," continued Klein. "Colleen and I both voted for him. He even reminds me of me," Klein laughed, remembering wist-fully his first time running as an underdog for Calgary mayor.

Nenshi wanted to get people, in his words, "hyper-engaged." There were coffee parties to provoke discussion. Toward the end of his campaign, Nenshi remembered, was his final coffee invitation to a house in Ramsey, just east of the Calgary Stampede grounds, where the tiny home filled with so many supporters that they spilled out onto the lawn and beyond.

That wasn't how the campaign began. "Our strategy was to do a slow, slow, slow build over the summer," said Nenshi in an interview. He sim-ply ignored the old adage of no politics in the summer because no one is paying attention. "You get the hyper-engaged people, who are paying attention, interested."

By the end of the summer fifteen candidates were in the race, with two clear front-runners: then-city councillor Ric McIver and popular former TV news host Barb Higgins. Both were considered establishment candidates. McIver led the polls, with Higgins second. Far behind them in third place was Nenshi, followed by a cluster of hopefuls.

When Higgins first announced her candidacy on July 28, 2010, Nenshi was delighted. He needed someone between him and front-runner McIver. "It played out to be a very beautiful thing. We've got one who's been around for nine years and one who's never been to a council meet-ing. So what do you want? Something in between, someone who knows what they're doing but is not part of the system," Nenshi said.

A Leger poll released in mid-September for the *Calgary Herald* and CTV showed McIver leading with 43 percent, followed by Higgins at 28 percent and Nenshi with 8 percent. That, too, was exactly where Nenshi wanted to be.

Nenshi, like Notley and Trudeau after him, proved popular on the campaign trail. Voters rushed to meet these candidates and get their pictures and post their selfies. While all three used social media to their advantage, they mainly engaged in the most important political activity, meeting and then listening to the voters. Unlike Prentice and Harper, Notley and Trudeau weren't reluctant to wade into the crowds and convince them where to park their votes. Nenshi became something of a rock star as people stopped to talk and flash their cellphones. But Nenshi also went to people in the halls and living rooms and coffee shops. He was very careful not to leave out groups that were used to being ignored. He identified and courted the forgotten. Nenshi's strong community support helped him rocket up the middle in a three-way race, which is exactly what Notley and Trudeau would do.

Nenshi's campaign began to be noticed because it was, in terms of Calgary politics, completely unprecedented. Convinced that people really wanted to talk about the city's future, he and his team developed a program of "Twelve Better Ideas." The campaign distributed a detailed explanation of each idea, along with a short statement that summarized the main point being argued. For example, "Calgary Transit should be the preferred choice not the last choice." For each idea, the campaign posted video and audio podcasts. Those who wanted more information could read the accompanying research paper, complete with footnotes for further exploration. "Any one of those twelve better ideas contained more words in it than the combined platforms of all my opponents. Citizens actually read them — that's the shocking part," says Nenshi.

Essentially, Nenshi provided voters with everything from quick soundbites to academic-level policy discussions for twelve subjects. There had never been anything like this escalating level of quality and detail in a civic election campaign. Even voters who didn't read much of the material began to see Nenshi as a serious, credible candidate.

Nenshi himself was finding his thinking confirmed — people really were willing to engage and discuss their city and its future. Volunteers were starting to come to him, including one who, unbeknownst to Nenshi, gave his campaign a huge boost right at the start.

Nenshi kicked off his run with a fourteen-minute speech. A man named Gordon McDowell recorded the talk and uploaded it to YouTube. By the end of that week the Nenshi video had more hits than other candidates were getting for their pitches. Nenshi had no idea who the amateur videographer was, but McDowell soon showed up and volunteered to help on the campaign. Nenshi asked to see the numbers for the video. "Gordon showed that the vast majority who stopped to watch it, watched it to the very end. That told me that people were willing to engage much more deeply than politicians give them credit for." Some people on the campaign thought that was because of Nenshi himself — his profile was growing, and people were curious about him. But to Nenshi, it proved his theory that people were deeply interested in ideas and policy.

After the two front-runners declined to debate Nenshi, McDowell scored again. He went through video from many other multi-candidate debates, Nenshi told Kate Torgovnick, "and he spliced the three of us into a YouTube video. Citizens could watch, so they could compare and contrast. He created a virtual debate."[2]

People were concerned about health, safety, education, the environment, and Calgary's future. Nenshi called it the "purple revolution," because the majority of citizens were neither Liberal red nor Tory blue. "They're purple," he said. "This was not just about change, but about connecting with people and stripping out the partisanship. People are pragmatic." Even today Nenshi always finds something purple to wear, whether shirt, tie, socks, or shoelaces, to reflect the pragmatic politics that govern the city. "They always say, 'Are you liberal or conservative?' and I say, 'I wear purple every day. It's neither red nor blue' — and that is very much on purpose."

Nenshi's approach was far different from the classic civic horse-trading that characterized Bronconnier's council style. In those days, someone always owed someone else, so contentious issues were settled through votes carefully orchestrated behind the scenes. Favours were exchanged, and the successful mayor knew where he stood. (Unfortunately, in Calgary there have been no women mayors.) Both Bronconnier and Al Duerr before him were liberals as well as deal-makers, and both were responsible for the direction of Calgary's rapid growth. Bronconnier was enormously successful at getting vital projects built in an era when rapid growth followed a decade of cost-cutting. But there were sharp divisions on council, especially with McIver, who was determined to win the mayor's chair.

Nenshi called for a more collaborative approach to civic engagement. His philosophy of pragmatic politics stems from his belief that people are smart and will do the right thing when given the relevant information. "There is an enormous amount of expertise in the community in regular everyday people that I need to be able to tap into," he says. For Nenshi, it wasn't about a brand of progressive politics or being left-wing or right-wing. "The left hates me as much as the far right, which people sometimes forget," he says. Instead, it's about what Nenshi calls "politics in full sentences." It means going out to the people and saying, "Let's treat you with respect."

In Nenshi's view, it's a mistake to say that once people vote they become engaged citizens. Rather, they get involved and engaged first, and then they vote. That means that successful politicians must work even harder between elections to keep people excited about their community. "Then they come back and vote. The key is to get excited about something."

Many weekends, Nenshi easily puts three hundred kilometres on his odometer as he travels from place to place within the city, attending events and talking to people, participating where he's asked. "Our big rule is the old political adage: Go to people where they live. Don't expect them to come to you," he says. "Many people live online and they form real communities online." Nenshi treated those communities as he did the others he could travel to by transit or car — he engaged and led discussions. Those conversations nurtured new ones and generated more interest, especially among young people who wanted information. "Because of social media, the millennials are the most informed generation. They choose to be unbelievably well informed," he adds. Where other political hopefuls had ignored the youth who lived on social media, Nenshi courted them.

There's one important initial goal in a political campaign: get someone's phone number. The general rule in politics is that one name and number in a database is worth four or five votes, because that person talks to others who aren't in the candidate's files. Social media change that rule. "Millennials are hyper-engaged," notes Nenshi. So their support on social media might mean several hundred votes through "likes" on a Facebook page, or a blog post or an Instagram photo. As Facebook friends weigh in, the conversation expands, and if the candidate can convince them, the "likes" can translate into votes at the polls.

Few of those potential numbers register with traditional pollsters. Millennials generally don't have landlines, but they do own cellphones whose precious minutes they're loath to waste on a pollster's call. Telephone polls survey those with landlines, leaving out important demographics. They often exclude millennials and those speaking English as a second language, citizens that Nenshi knew how to target in his multi-faceted campaign.

Getting out the vote meant more than going through the traditional phone database. Emails were sent reminding supporters of the election date as well as poll locations and transportation choices. Reminders through Facebook, Twitter, and messaging aren't costly but get the critical information to voters.

Although well behind in the polls for most of the campaign, Nenshi always led his rivals on the social media sites favoured by millennials. That's where he had first announced his campaign. His number of Facebook "likes," at twelve thousand, was nearly three times that of McIver or Higgins. "We used social media like a telephone. They used it like television. That made the difference," Nenshi's campaign manager, and now the mayor's chief of staff, Chima Nkemdirim told Marcello Di Cintio.[3]

Nenshi's rise in the polls was only surprising to those who didn't understand his larger strategy of being "way, way, way behind in third place." His 8 percent in early polls, he said, "was also eight times what anybody else behind me had. It was exactly what I wanted." He talked about the old adage in Alberta politics that voting decisions are made over the Thanksgiving dinner table. "And it absolutely happened."

There were other clues too that a deep undercurrent was building.

Nenshi was standing on the bridge near the Victoria LRT (Light Rapid Transit) station, handing out flyers to fans on their way to the Calgary Flames hockey game in the Saddledome. A young man in his Flames shirt walked past and then rushed back to take a selfie with the candidate. He told Nenshi that he had gone away to university but was back just for the Thanksgiving weekend and was excited because he could vote. Nenshi asked when he planned to do that, as the advance polls closed that very day. The student was flying back to university right after Thanksgiving, and the election was just a week away on the following Monday.

"No problem," said the student, who added that he planned to vote the next day.

"But there are no advance polls on Thanksgiving Day," Nenshi told him. Nenshi continues: "He looked at his dad, dropped his bag, ran to city hall, voted in the advance poll, and then ran back so he could still make the hockey game. I went, 'Whoa,' as I was talking to his dad. That was when I knew something was really, really changing."

There was a final poll released on the Wednesday before the election, but Nenshi wasn't waiting for the overnight *Calgary Herald* online edition. He had a 6:00 a.m. CBC Radio *Eyeopener* interview. His sister, however, had stayed awake. She excitedly phoned his campaign strategist, Stephen Carter, and told him that the candidates were now in a virtual three-way tie.

Nenshi was elated: "I had always said the traditional polling was underestimating me by five points, as it wasn't getting people for whom English is a second language, and young people with cellphones. So if there was a three-way tie, mathematically at that point we knew we had won. But you never know until you're standing there on election night and you're watching the results coming in."

Which was exactly what Nenshi did, waiting on a stage at a Calgary nightspot for the campaign after-party, staring at the TV screens to see if there would even be one, greeting and thanking everyone coming up. The room was blazing hot and blaring loud, and Nenshi tried to guess from the TV–body language of those being interviewed whether he was losing or winning. All his scrutineers were at the individual polls, phoning in their unofficial results to the staff at his small campaign office; the staff were texting their numbers to Nenshi's friend. The problem was that his friend, who needs a scooter to move about, couldn't pass close enough through the crowd to get Nenshi's attention — since Nenshi was still trying to decode the results from the facial expressions on the screen.

"When the race tightened up on the TV screen, I knew I was going to win, so I turned and saw my friend who's sitting about fifteen feet away on his scooter. 'I'm going to win. What am I going to say?' I mouthed. A little puzzled, my friend looked at me on the stage and pointed to his phone, mouthing back, 'I know. Haven't you been getting the numbers?'" Nenshi grinned, "Nooo," and had barely a few minutes to compose his speech before the crowd started roaring for their new mayor.

Klein anticipated the Nenshi victory. "He came up the middle, and that's not surprising. He's a good man, well educated, well spoken, and articulate in every sense of the word. Nenshi brings a new face, a new tone, and a new style to civic politics," said the man who did exactly the same to Calgary politics thirty years before. Klein also saw in Nenshi a man who could remain mayor for as long as he wished by listening, staying open minded, and taking time to make up his mind on critical issues. "He's personable and likes to talk to people. If that doesn't change, we will have a very good mayor for as long as he wants to do that. Communicating is the greatest asset a mayor can have. And listening."

Nenshi's massive upset prompted Calgary Progressive Conservative MLA Kyle Fawcett to tweet: "Nenshi ... BIG mistake Calgary."[4]

The only mistake was Fawcett's reckless comment, for which he later apologized. His condescending attitude toward Nenshi, shared by many PCs, only emphasized how out of touch the provincial government was becoming. They never seemed to grasp that a Nenshi-style uprising could migrate to the provincial stage. Five years later it finally did, as Fawcett himself was defeated by New Democrat Craig Coolahan.

When 53 percent of Calgary voters went to the polls on October 18, 2010, they posted the largest turnout in the forty years since the city started calculating the numbers. Nenshi earned twenty-eight thousand more votes than his closest competitor.

He became the first Muslim mayor of a large North American city. His win was fuelled by a wave of volunteers, who reflected the city's grow-ing million-plus faces — a mix of diverse ethnicities, ages, and incomes. He had excited young people who were tech-savvy, well educated, and liberal, especially on the deep social issues like LGBTQ rights, women's right to choose, as well as pay equity and homelessness. Nenshi was dynamic, charismatic, and quick on his feet. He attracted global interest. The Americans, in particular, seemed amazed at the election of a Muslim mayor, just as they were, nearly six years later, when London, England, elected Sadiq Khan as its first Muslim mayor.

Nenshi has three times been asked to attend the prestigious World Economic Forum in Davos, Switzerland, including 2016, where he was both a presenter and a panel moderator. The forum named him a Young Global Leader. On his forty-third birthday, Nenshi was awarded the 2014 World Mayor Prize. Every two years the prize goes to a "mayor who has made outstanding contributions to his/her community and has developed a vision for urban living and working that is relevant to towns and cities across the world."[5] It is given by the London-based City Mayor's Foundation, a philanthropic think tank on urban affairs. Calling Nenshi "the most admired mayor of any large Canadian city," the award cited his use of both social media and old-fashioned on-the-ground politics to win the 2010 mayor's chair: "He is an urban visionary who doesn't neglect the nitty-gritty of local government. For many in North America and indeed Europe, Mayor Nenshi is a role model for decisive management, inclusivity and forward planning." The award noted Nenshi's "strong leadership during disasters," including the devastating Alberta flood of 2013 as well as a massive power outage in the city's downtown.

When the flood hit, the mayor was in the air, on the ground, on radio, TV, Twitter, Facebook, and everywhere that people congregated. After a state of emergency was declared, he moved from the Emergency Operations Centre to evacuated communities, to the water-treatment plant, and to empty homes littered with soaked and muddied belongings.

One of Nenshi's widespread warnings ran across the airwaves as the "Darwin" quote: "I can't believe I actually have to say this, but I'm going to say it. The river is closed. You cannot boat on the river. I have a large number of nouns that I can use to describe the people I saw in a canoe on the Bow River today. I am not allowed to use any of them. I can tell you, however, that I have been told that despite the state of local emergency, I'm not allowed to invoke the Darwin law."[6]

NENSHI'S POPULARITY, WHICH began among Calgary's millennials, reflected a changing province and country. Edmonton had already elected a woman mayor in 1989 — Jan Reimer, who served until 1995. Later, Edmonton elected its first Jewish mayor, Stephen Mandel, in 2004. With Nenshi's win in 2010, the two big-city mayors in the province showed the world what collaboration, community, diversity, and mutual respect are all about. When Mandel with his wife, Lynn, travelled to Calgary to celebrate Shabbat, the Jewish Sabbath, at the Reform Temple B'nai Tikvah,

Mayor Nenshi was with them. The two mayors gave the sermon, and the synagogue was transfixed as people prayed, listened, and watched how the world should be. Nenshi travelled to Edmonton to join Mandel at the Al Rashid Mosque's seventy-fifth anniversary. Nenshi has been active at community-wide fund-raisers for the Beth Tzedec congregation and other houses of faith throughout the city, as has Mandel in Edmonton.

Both Mandel and Nenshi are strong supporters of LGBTQ rights, and Nenshi has followed Mandel's lead by participating in the city's gay pride parades and activities since taking office. Mandel also started the Mayor's Pride Breakfast to raise funds for the gay youth leadership retreat, Camp fYrefly.

After Mandel stepped down in the fall of 2013, three councillors ran for his coveted chair: Karen Leibovici, Kerry Diotte, and Don Iveson, as well as three other candidates. On the evening of October 21, 2013, Edmonton elected another dynamic, intelligent, savvy mayor, the thirty-four-year-old Iveson, who won with an overwhelming 62 percent.

Like Nenshi, Iveson went to the online community and posted on his blog, Facebook, and Twitter, as well as loading videos on YouTube. He held a Reddit question and answer. "Social media is still an emerging thing and no doubt it played a role in connecting, certainly with users who are heavily online, and to be able to do rapid response there was really handy," Iveson told Slav Kornik of Global News.[7]

Again, as with Nenshi, Iveson's online followers multiplied, reflecting his growing appeal. On election night he had 10,000 Twitter followers; the next morning, that had morphed to 15,000. His closest competitors each amassed far fewer, with 5,400 Twitter followers for Diotte and 3,600 for Leibovici.

Iveson also had a solid ground game, with hundreds of volunteers who worked especially hard in neighbourhoods with young families. He and his team knocked on doors throughout the summer and fall, contacting voters from the northeast to the southwest.

There was no such thing as a robocall in this election: "Everything we did, we did with human beings," campaign manager Chris Henderson told *Edmonton Journal* columnist Paula Simons.[8]

Simons astutely summarized Iveson's campaign: "That disciplined, carefully timed mix of old and new strategies, delivered a stunning victory Monday night."[9]

BOTH MAYORS HAVE made social media work for them and their cities, as their tweets range from the political to the personal. By March 12,
2016, Iveson, (@doniveson) had 77,100 followers and had posted 15,100
tweets, while Nenshi (@nenshi) had 286,000 followers and 45,400
tweets. Both Iveson and Nenshi stress that social media are simply one
facet of a campaign, and that talking with citizens face to face is far
more important during the election and afterwards. The ground game is
crucial in reaching out to voters, having a conversation, and laying the
foundation of the campaign.

"Social media is critical as a good broadcast tool, but not as a listening
tool," emphasizes Iveson. "It's still evolving as a listening tool."

Henderson, a strategist with Edmonton-based Calder Bateman
Communications, adds that social media also act as a volunteer recruitment tool and set the tone for the campaign. "You can lose a campaign
on social media, but you can't win one there," he adds perceptively. Social
media have also become a receptacle for the angry and intolerant who
use the Web, especially Twitter, to vent their vitriol. As Henderson puts it,
"There's so much noise, it can be useless."

Iveson's election, like that of Nenshi, signalled that the youth vote isn't
a chimera and that politicians need to realize that millennials are voting if
they hope to catch the wave of victory.

But they mustn't forget the older demographic, either. The polling
done for Iveson has convinced him that he needs to attend to the opinions of all demographics. "Certainly in our research, the younger an
Edmontonian is, the stronger my support is. But in all my research the
spread wasn't as big as you would think. I won boomers by almost as
much as I won millennnials, and boomers still turn out way more fre-
quently than millennials do." As he noted, he didn't see the huge surge in
millennial turnout for the Edmonton election that occurred in Calgary
2010, which was even more hotly contested.

Iveson has found that young people prefer a "post-partisan allegiance
that is more issues-focused," and are more likely to be engaged by an
election campaign that concentrates on the environment, economics, as
well as balance and quality of life. At the civic level, millennial issues are
centred on their local communities emphasizing available and affordable
housing and transit, as well as work and entrepreneurial opportunities.

Like Nenshi, Iveson feels that pragmatic politics is "what the public expects. I think they've had enough of being a card-carrying member of one school of thought. The world has become too complicated for that." Those kinds of confrontational positions are far too divisive, and the complexity of modern concerns, such as interjurisdictional, environmental, and indigenous issues, requires more creative political approaches. "There's no playbook for that, and voters are looking for your attitudes and your aptitudes when they decide whom to support," says Iveson.

When it comes to the tough calls, voters need inspired decision-makers and people they can trust. "They want to know where you stand on issues that are important to them. By trying to reduce that to the polarity of a single political platform ... politics is becoming too complex for that."

Iveson and Nenshi teamed up to lobby for their cities and create partnerships, using, in Iveson's words, "the political capital" of a combined Edmonton and Calgary. "Seize the capacity that exists," says Iveson, to develop a long-term strategy. There's a range of social issues that could benefit from a collaborative effort in such things as public health, mental-health intervention, low-cost housing, and job creation, all leading to an improved quality of life for the vulnerable.

NENSHI AND IVESON share a focus on social issues and a desire to engage with the widest possible spectrum of voters, qualities they appreciate in Notley's NDP government. Nenshi is particularly impressed with the premier's pragmatic side. "That's why people voted for her in the election," he says. She is the fifth Alberta premier he's dealt with since becoming mayor in 2010. Over that chaotic period there have also been eight municipal affairs ministers. Since Notley arrived, Nenshi feels, the city's relationship with both the provincial and federal governments "has never been better, precisely because they invite us into the conversation," even if they disagree.

"When Don Iveson and I went to present to [the NDP] Cabinet — that is the first time anybody has presented to Cabinet. They just don't do that. The fact that they were willing to let us into the room doesn't mean they're going to give us everything we want. But the fact that we're able to have that discussion is very, very good. I'm always nervous, and I'm waiting for the other shoe to drop to betray me really badly. It hasn't happened yet."

Nenshi feels that Notley's style goes beyond strict party politics. "It's about really connecting with people and stripping out the partisanship. It's getting beyond that by being pragmatic and practical with people. When Ralph Klein was at his best, this is what you saw."

Toronto swept in change the same year Nenshi arrived on the scene, with the election of Mayor Rob Ford. Although these events couldn't be less similar, they both represented a reaction to what had gone before. Calgarians had grown weary of the horse-trading, pot-holes and taxes agenda of a combative, sharply divided city council and wanted someone new, who represented Calgary's future — a candidate with vision and ideas to match. That they found in Nenshi, a mayor in whom they saw themselves.

Toronto, too, was reacting to age-old civic politics where downtown elites had ruled the metropolitan city while the suburbs continued to grow even as their influence diminished. In 2010 the suburbs responded with a dramatic takeover of city hall by electing Rob Ford. Like Nenshi, the late mayor also caught global attention, although, sadly, Ford did so for entirely different reasons.

To some Torontonians, Nenshi seemed to be representing the wrong city. "There's been a very *Freaky Friday*-esque feeling among Toronto's leftist downtown types, ever since Calgary got the mayor they thought Toronto deserved," wrote *Postmedia* columnist Lauren Strapagiel in May 2013.[10] This notion hints at an old Ontario stereotype that always offends Albertans — Calgary is a redneck city, so how could it possibly deserve Nenshi? In fact, the election just showed how young, dynamic, and progressive Calgary had been for a long while.

Nenshi is far from perfect. He can sometimes speak before he thinks, a penchant that has pulled him from his perch a few times. He fell into a kerfuffle with well-known Calgary builder and philanthropist Cal Wenzel that saw Wenzel sue Nenshi for $6 million for defamation. Nenshi apologized and the suit was dropped, with each paying his respective court fees.

Then there was the anti-Uber YouTube rant that was downloaded around the continent. Unbeknownst to the social-media-savvy mayor, every word he said to the Boston cab driver was being recorded, including his calling the CEO a "dick."

"I apologize to Travis Kalanick, CEO of Uber, and his employees for my being, well, a jerk," Nenshi later posted on his blog. "One should be the same person in private as in public and I take full responsibility for my interaction with others."[11]

Nenshi certainly is himself, no matter what. When he won the 2014 World Mayor prize, he said: "All I try to do, as you all know, is be very authentic, be real with people and focus on working hard, on making this community a better place — just like everyone else in the community."[12]

That attitude, offered to a public hungry for change, won him a second election and a large measure of renown. Eventually, the same forces and qualities would bring Rachel Notley — and then Justin Trudeau — to office.

CHAPTER 7

BIG DREAMS IN BAD TIMES

Rachel Notley hasn't stopped running since her historic win. "There was no sitting around at home. It was the next day and I was in the office. We just started at eight o'clock in the morning and went until ten o'clock at night. And the next day, we did the same thing and on into the next days, over and over. There was a whole list of things that had to be dealt with."

Nearly ten days before her victory, Notley asked Brian Topp, her director of tour and communications, to chair a transition team and prepare for what her latest poll predicted. The team also included John Heaney, long-time top toiler with the B.C. NDP, and Anne McGrath, former national director of the federal NDP. McGrath came with plenty of Alberta credentials, both as an NDP candidate and as an activist. She had run for the Alberta NDP leadership in 1995, finishing just behind the victor, former MP Ross Harvey. She also has strong personal ties to the province, with two of her adult children calling Alberta home. In January 2016 McGrath would become Notley's deputy chief of staff, and in late June the premier's principal secretary.

Notley's chief of staff would soon be Topp, one of the most experienced New Democrats in the country. He had worked with former Saskatchewan NDP premier Roy Romanow as well as the late federal NDP leader, Jack Layton. In addition to co-running numerous federal NDP campaigns, Topp had also campaigned for the federal leadership, coming in second to Thomas Mulcair.

His experience was vast with incoming NDP governments that had faced similar trials of transition: in British Columbia, Saskatchewan, Manitoba, and Nova Scotia. When the Alberta New Democrats assumed power, they had at their disposal the brain trust of NDP governments past and present.

"I don't think most Albertans I saw during the campaign believed the PCs were going to fall until the day they did," said Topp. "This culture was so used to the idea that a PC victory was inevitable. People so believed that, [yet] our duty was to consider the possibility of doing a transition. We called in all the work that had been done in every transition team in the NDP universe in the preceding twenty years. We piled all that stuff in a room. We read and distilled into a 'Do List' for the Alberta NDP, and ended up with a synopsis of the best work of all the transitions.

"It became our bible of things to do. One of the nice things was that we were able to download all the institutional wisdom of governing New Democrats. We didn't make the mistake of overthinking it. This was not a luxury we were ever going to have. We had a checklist of what had to be done. Canadian provinces are mostly structured in the same way. By having a really good road map, the job became doable."

Topp's team took a meticulous and sequential approach to what they faced. One of the earliest decisions was how to deal with a senior public service that had worked under only one party for nearly forty-four years. "We were going to do the dirtiest, rottenest thing we could to the Alberta public service," Topp says, laughing, and then gets very serious. "We made the right choice. We wanted to work with them and wanted their best work." It was a respectful as well as astute approach, especially since much of the civil service likely voted New Democrat in the party's sweep of Edmonton. That would likely not be true, however, of the hand-picked top Tory bureaucrats.

To start, Topp talked with Alberta's senior civil servant, Richard Dicerni, deputy minister of the Executive Council. A widely respected veteran federal bureaucrat, with an avuncular manner that belies his impressive range of experience, Dicerni had been hired out of retirement by Jim Prentice. He would remain with the NDP government for nearly a year as it transitioned from Tory rule.

"We knew Richard Dicerni pretty well. He had worked in the past with the NDP and was well known with the [federal] Liberal government.

He was extraordinary," said Topp. "We said, 'We want you to stay,' and he said, 'Really?' One of the best things Premier Prentice did was bring in Dicerni to rebuild the public service. We worked together in the tradition of public service."

Topp's admiration for their commitment and for Dicerni is clear. "The professional public service has risen to an extraordinary challenge and done an amazing job. Serving a reform-minded government, and a different government in Alberta, hasn't been seen in a long time."

Notley was impressed with Dicerni's grip on government and his attention to detail. "The next morning [when] we met, he said: 'Here are the fifteen bombs that are about to go off and need to be addressed now, and that you have to deal with.' He gave advice on that stuff and we just got to work." For Notley and her team, there was no time to even consider the enormity of her victory, just the vast landscape along the rock-strewn road ahead.

Notley's platform for the 2015 Alberta election was written before she had any idea her party would win. The farthest thing from NDP minds was suddenly being faced with keeping a multitude of promises — until May 6, when Alberta woke to an altered reality, and the new governing party faced a gargantuan task. She had won a majority on an election platform that championed change.

This platform was shock treatment for a province that had been ruled by conservatives of one design or another since 1935. Entitled "Leadership for What Matters,"[1] the plan contained a formula for the most abrupt, radical change the province had ever seen. It was nothing less than government engineering of a new economy, through a shift from non-renewable resources to green industries that either didn't exist or were still in corporate infancy. Notley proposed major changes to tax and social policy; an aggressive climate-change plan that would be Canada's most advanced, following years of PC waffling that had left Alberta an environmental outcast; gender balance in politics and society; a higher minimum wage; a new and more respectful relationship with First Nations; and a great deal more besides. All this would require government action and intervention on a scale that most Albertans, through the long decades of conservative rule, never conceived possible.

Voters had found Notley very appealing during the campaign. A great many were more enthusiastic about her platform than conservatives would ever concede. But swing voters were also pushed toward her by their disgust with the long-running PCs. She seemed to be a safe protest vote. Many who finally decided to vote NDP likely hadn't read the platform document — or if they had, didn't imagine that Notley would ever get a chance to implement her strategy.

But she would, and very quickly.

AT FIRST, THERE was some hope for economic recovery that could give the new premier the fiscal cushion she needed. On election day the price of West Texas Intermediate crude oil, the measure that matters most to Alberta's petroleum industry, seemed to be stabilizing above US$60 per barrel for the first time in months. Some forecasters were saying it would average US$63 for the rest of the year. That estimate was US$40 per barrel below boom-time pricing, but still a level the government could adjust to if the price persisted.

It did not persist. By the end of 2015 prices had crashed again, into the range of US$30 per barrel. At this level of fiscal stress, Alberta budget numbers become so contorted that they actually showed the province owing money to the oil and gas industry, rather than collecting royalties from it. This wasn't a real-world concern ("No damn way we'll be paying them," said one government official), but the accounting anomaly illustrated a fiscal crisis so severe that even numbers could be bent, like light waves by gravity. Jim Prentice, at his most pessimistic, hadn't envisaged a crash this dramatic.

The economy seemed to call for government caution, but Notley decided to forge ahead with nearly every element of her plan. Like many a leader before her, including most Alberta premiers, she chose to interpret her mandate as approval of the entire platform, even something she didn't specifically mention during the campaign — a general carbon tax that would cost consumers $3 billion a year.

There was indeed a loyal and lively political market for such measures, especially in urban Alberta. The province's environmental lobby is as active as any in Canada, and in a sense it had won the election. Thousands of relatively new migrants to Alberta weren't stuck in the traditional conservative mind-set. Many of these people were overjoyed at the PC defeat. Notley felt she would betray those constituencies, as well as her own ardent caucus, if she stalled on major elements of the platform, most especially action on climate change. Delay could also mean she'd never get the chance to reform anything. It would take years, not months, for the system she envisaged to start spinning off abundant green jobs. If she couldn't demonstrate significant economic progress by the next election in 2019, that could be the end of the NDP government.

The enormity of her challenges was obvious even before she was sworn in.

LESS THAN TWELVE hours after the final results were in, the PCs at the legislature were busy destroying documents they chose to define as irrelevant, creating an unforgettable image of a dynasty in panicked flight from its own history. Notley wasn't yet the premier and had no executive authority, but she decreed an end to the shredding — to no avail.

While that was happening, she had to quickly create a government that only a few weeks earlier nobody had imagined would exist. She relied heavily on imported talent, something her PC predecessors had also done. Yet that would bring criticism, even though the PC culture had incubated only conservative travellers for the elite political positions.

"There used to be a political culture in Alberta where you did not speak truth to power, because the power had been in for so long that you would be punished," Notley said. Anyone even related to someone who challenged the political status quo or questioned government decisions was often ostracized. People who weren't conservative, but wanted to be involved in government, often left for opportunities outside. Some of those former Albertans would return to join Notley's government, like Anne McGrath.

While Notley had the cream of NDP Canada at her disposal, she also wanted many senior civil servants to remain in their jobs, most notably Dicerni. Even this move won her no praise from conservatives, however. Double standards ran loose everywhere. When former premier Alison Redford brought in key aides from Ontario there was some muted grumbling but little active hostility. The incredible anger toward Notley appointees, often verging on hatred, had little to do with their address of origin. It was because they were New Democrats.

NOTLEY QUICKLY CONVENED her caucus, which would ultimately be 47 percent female. Women held twenty-five of the NDP's fifty-four legislature seats, giving her caucus the highest percentage of women in Canadian history. The NDP caucus was also comparatively young, both in experience and age, with just four returning MLAs and a high quota of members in their twenties and thirties. It was a refreshing representation of the province's diversity. But criticism came instantly. New Democrat MLAs were derided as amateurs with little knowledge and less experience, no match for the deep experience of the departing PCs.

Long forgotten was the fact that the first PC government, which took office in 1971 under Peter Lougheed, was less experienced than Notley's crew. Lougheed had six returning MLAs to Notley's four, but three of hers had more cumulative experience than Lougheed's entire little corps. Brian Mason had been in the legislature since 2000; Notley since 2008, David Eggen from 2004 to 2008 and then from 2012; and Deron Bilous since 2012. The rest of the caucus were rookies, but ready to work and learn. The argument that the NDP had no government experience was absurd on the face of it, especially when only one party had governed for all those years. But the very people who excoriated the New Democrats for lack of experience were positively apoplectic when they brought in people who had experience.

The case for NDP incompetence had another side, equally partisan and dubious; they didn't just lack experience in government, but in work and life itself. The reality was that NDP MLAs had a wider range of experience than the departing PCs, who in later years were mostly from the business world. The New Democrats ran the gamut of provincial occupations, including electrician, geologist, pulp mill worker, bus driver, airline attendant, small business owner, yoga instructor, psychologist, IT specialist, doctor, lawyer, nurse, teacher, professor, union worker, social worker, writer, editor, journalist, sales worker, student, restaurant manager, and real estate broker. One MLA soon gained experience no other Alberta politician had ever achieved;

Calgary's Stephanie McLean gave birth to a baby boy four days after Notley named her to Cabinet, the first MLA to do so while in office.

Most people who lived in Alberta on election day had not been born when the PCs took over in 1971. More than half the population was under forty. There was so little understanding of provincial regime change that for some the prospect induced something close to panic. It took a voice from an unexpected quarter — an original Lougheed MLA and Cabinet minister, David King — to set this familiar Canadian experience in context for Albertans. King had once lost his own seat, and hence his Cabinet post, to the late NDP dynamo Pam Barrett, but remained magnanimous about it all.

King wrote in the *Calgary Herald*:

> [The first Lougheed Cabinet had no one] who had ever managed more than 25 people; there was no one who had ever been responsible to others ... for a budget....
> I can remember the caucus being disparaged because of the vocations represented in it....
>
> There are at least three things wrong with this kind of criticism. First, it is essentially undemocratic. Democracy is not government by philosopher kings, or technocratic elites, or monetizing self-selected elites. Democracy is government by a representative cross-section of the entire community, and I argue the current NDP caucus is more representative of the community as a whole than was the recent PC slate.
>
> Indeed, given the world we foresee, a gender-balanced caucus that includes a software development project manager, an applications engineer, a hydrologist, a communications professional, an oncologist, a former public services commissioner, some nurses and other health-care workers, some union leaders, some teachers and a couple of psychologists — as well as a number of students — may well be more representative of Alberta today than was my first caucus 44 years ago. It certainly has as much potential to provide an excellent Cabinet.[2]

Finally, King argued that because so much change had been stalled for so long, "the incoming government is going to have to wrench Alberta in a different direction, which many of the province's reputational leaders — and the former government — would have been unable to do."

This remarkable defence from a long-time Progressive Conservative served to blunt some of the immediate criticism about inexperience, but Notley would never be free of frequent reproach from the opposition as well as the more alarming attacks from the shadier zones of social media.

With a solid transition team, Notley appointed a twelve-member Cabinet, herself included, the fewest since Social Credit took office in 1935. Representing a much smaller population that was still primarily rural, William Aberhart's first Cabinet contained eight ministers, while his successor, Ernest Manning had nine. By 1971, the Cabinet had jumped to twenty-one under Harry Strom. Lougheed's brand new PCs made it twenty-two.

Notley opted for the less-is-more approach with added responsibilities for each portfolio, relying on the experienced — and doubtlessly relieved — civil servants who kept their jobs, just as too many people in the private sector were losing theirs. Notley would also need the time to determine who within her caucus could successfully carry future Cabinet duties.

Topp recalls a similar government faced with a difficult economic situation, that of Roy Romanow in Saskatchewan. "We adopted Romanow's small Cabinet model," he says, adding that the newly elected caucus had "some great candidates to be ministers. They've proven it in their performance from a standing start. They demonstrated they were more than capable. And then we had the normalization of Cabinet earlier this year."

Notley increased her Cabinet by one in the fall of 2015, and then added seven more the following February, for a total of nineteen ministers. Gender parity was critical in the Cabinet makeup, another first for Alberta and Canada. Later, on November 5, 2015, a victorious Prime Minister Justin Trudeau would do the same when he appointed an equal number of women to men in Cabinet.

One woman who failed to make Notley's Cabinet was Calgary MLA Deborah Drever, a twenty-six-year-old Mount Royal University student, whose past on social media jumped out to bite her. Years earlier, Drever had posed for an indie album cover as a terrified woman about to be sexually assaulted by a man with a menacing bottle. "The photo I appeared in was in poor taste and I apologize for its offensive content. It is not a photo I would appear in today," she said in a May 15, 2015, release.[3]

She later revealed to the *Calgary Herald* that a boyfriend had asked her to pose for the album cover. "When we did the photo shoot, they told me they wanted to save me from an attack. The name of it was *Fear of Attack*, so the premise of it was supposed to be them saving me.

"Obviously, the picture did not show that. I did not feel comfortable with that picture, and I actually asked the band if we could do a reshoot [because] it was not representing my values in any way. And I got a straight 'no.' They were going to put it out to press and that's what they did. This was something I regretted then, and something I regret now, because it doesn't represent who I am in any way."[4]

The resulting uproar left the new MLA distraught, but her time for contrition had only begun. When two words — "gay boyz" — appeared on her Instagram account, in reference to Prentice and one of his ministers, Ric McIver, the clear homophobic slur was too much. Notley suspended her from caucus but would review the suspension if Drever worked hard on issues of homophobia and violence against women. Drever briefly became a top national mention on Twitter and other social media. The damaging uproar convinced many Albertans that the NDP caucus was dangerously inexperienced and irresponsible.

But Drever wasn't finished. She took Notley's advice to heart by researching a bill to allow victims of violence to break a residency lease without penalty. With plenty of help from the New Democrats, especially government house leader Brian Mason, her bill was drafted and introduced. It passed with unanimous all-party support. In early 2016 Drever was invited to rejoin the NDP caucus, but it will probably be years, if ever, before she escapes attacks from those who believe no NDP offence can ever be forgiven, especially from a woman.

WITH HER CABINET in place and her caucus in tow, Notley set about changing the course of her province during a dire economic storm. "We are facing an unprecedented dip in the struggle with respect to our economy," she said. "I think we're making the right decisions for the economy.

I think there will be bumps in the road. But I think our climate-change leadership plan is going to do profound game-changing things for this economy. It's not just about protecting the environment, which it's also doing, which is really awesome. But it is also about some game-changing things about economic diversification and restructuring the way our economy works, and preparing us and repositioning us for greater levels of diversification." With such huge change, Notley also emphasized that "diversification is not something that happens overnight, and that's the other thing that we have to keep in mind."

Before Notley's government was eight months old, it had introduced a complete climate-change policy that included the $3 billion annual carbon tax, to take effect January 1, 2017. The New Democrats had doubled the existing carbon price on large oil sands emitters, to $30 per tonne, and announced an accelerated plan to phase out coal-fired electricity plants throughout the province. They made good on their vow to examine energy royalties paid to the government, a subject that always inflames passions in Alberta and provokes heated opposition from the oil and gas industry.

All this happened as the oil-price crash was plunging the province into the worst provincial recession in thirty years. The year 2016 began in brutal fashion for Alberta workers. By March, over 120,000 people in petroleum and related industries had lost their jobs, raising the unemployment rate above the national average for the first time since 1986.

Notley made the case that diversification to a greener economy would rescue the province from the price straitjacket that renders revenues so wildly unpredictable. She noted, too, that Alberta was the only province or state in North America without an energy efficiency program to encourage people to conserve. She argued that the province had fallen so far in national and international opinion that it had become impossible to win approval for bitumen-carrying pipelines. The NDP believed that without a serious climate-change policy the oil sands would die, because no government would accept Alberta's bitumen. Alberta had become "an outlier," in Notley's delicate phrase. The more accurate word was "pariah." U.S. President Barack Obama had almost casually rejected the Keystone XL pipeline to the southern United States. The Northern Gateway pipeline appeared irrevocably stalled, to the point that Notley at first saw no point in lobbying for it. She later seemed to see some hope when talk of an alternative B.C. port began and she discussed this prospect with the Trudeau Cabinet in April 2016. But in late June, the Federal Court of Appeal quashed the former approval and admonished the Harper Government for not adequately addressing affected First Nations' communities.

Notley had hopes for the Energy East pipeline to Saint John, New Brunswick, but the project was running into serious protests, most notably from all eighty-three mayors in the Montreal area. The Trans Mountain expansion to Burnaby, B.C., had hit a solid wall of B.C. activism — even though it was to follow a right-of-way already used for decades.

Opinion had shifted steadily against the oil sands for years, and much of the opposition came from the NDP itself. Many NDP MLAs had been active in protests. Shannon Phillips, the province's new environment minister, co-wrote the introduction to a 2004 book called *An Action a Day Keeps Global Capitalism Away*. It encouraged "radical cheerleading," with verses like "The rich get richer / While the earth gets sicker / So kiss the back of my butt...!"[5] Her co-writer was Mike Hudema, an Alberta Greenpeace activist who is ardently opposed to the oil sands. Now she was introducing new laws for the province.

But the NDP, with its heavy union support, had never been inherently opposed to industrial development. The oil sands certainly qualify as industry; they also spin off a great many union jobs. While pushing hard for environmental gains and a slower pace of development, the party never advocated shutting down the oil sands or shutting in the bitumen. Rather, the NDP always believed that bitumen should be refined in Alberta and shipped elsewhere as acceptable finished product. In this they had an ally in former premier Peter Lougheed, who was cool about the Keystone pipeline because, as he told CBC Radio's *The Current,* he felt the economy would benefit more if "we process the bitumen from the oil sands in Alberta, and that would create a lot of jobs and job activity."[6]

Former Conservative prime minister Stephen Harper and the various former PC premiers had failed to get major new pipelines built, whether Kinder Morgan, Energy East, or Northern Gateway. Governments completely faithful to the status quo energy industry couldn't connect with those who had too much to lose. First Nations, environmentalists, and landowners along the routes didn't trust the governments, the energy companies, or reviews by the National Energy Board, which had long

merely ensured that projects complied with technical rules before bringing down the inevitable rubber stamp. Environmental concerns had been
diminished or ignored. First Nations were paid little more than lip service
with a smattering of local jobs, a bit of revenue sharing, and perhaps a
little funding for a few job-sharing schemes. Their patience wore thin,
especially as rivers were fouled and the people fell ill. Then, suddenly,
aggressive activism began to seriously stall huge national projects. Notley
and other New Democrats had warned for years that this would happen.

For several decades energy companies had enjoyed virtual carte
blanche in Alberta's oil sands. The province had allowed unfettered
development and paid little attention to the rising environmental and
social alarms. Infrastructure was deteriorating, and contruction of hospitals, highways, schools, and housing was falling far behind boom-time
needs. In a 2006 interview for *Policy Options*, Lougheed warned the PC
governments of the need to decelerate the rampant oil sands growth. "I
was just up there on a trip, just helicoptering around, and it is just a moon-
scape. It is wrong, in my judgment, a major wrong, and I keep trying to
see who the beneficiaries are. Not the people in Red Deer, because everything they have got is costing more."[7] In early 2008 Lougheed told Anna
Maria Tremonti of CBC Radio's *The Current* that "they should have never
allowed so many of these projects to go ahead at the same time."[8]

Lougheed found himself in the position of many an elder statesman:
revered but ignored. If the most respected politician in the history of the
province wasn't heeded, there was little likelihood that First Nations and
environmentalists would be. Blocked from the board rooms of government and industry, they took their battle beyond the borders of the province and the country, where they were heard very loud and clear.

New York Times reporter Ian Austen spoke with a worried investor
who acknowledged that "environmentalists had won the debate on
Keystone XL as well as various other pipeline plans. 'I don't know how the
issue got away, but it's obvious now that it did,' he said."[9]

For too long the province's elite either ignored the environmental
storm, in hopes it would pass, or responded with Band-Aid policies
designed for public relations impact rather than real results. A full
climate-change policy was promised by the PCs as early as 2008 but still
hadn't appeared when they were defeated in 2015. Meanwhile, oil sands

expansion created a boom that swamped small communities with oil field workers, traffic, drugs, and escalating costs.

For many Albertans, the visible symbols of the oil boom raced along the main highways of the energy corridor — the Queen Elizabeth II Highway from Calgary to Edmonton, and Highway 63 connecting Edmonton to Fort McMurray. These routes became congested ribbons of road rage. Highway 63 was nicknamed the Highway of Death after thousands of collisions and scores of fatalities. Any day on both Highway 63 and the QE II, there were tankers, triple transport trucks, oil field services vehicles, packed buses, SUVs, camp trailers, immense flat-bed trucks carrying oversize machinery and camp housing, as well as all manner of super-hero pickups bought by tradespeople earning wages as outsized as their rides. Oil scouts were often the highway speed champions, as they raced between fields to spy on the discoveries of rival companies. So acute was the need for labour that some companies ran their own air services to ferry workers in weekly, or even daily, from the big cities.

The strangest victim of all was the provincial government itself. The boom created the demand for new schools, roads, and hospitals, all of which had to be built in a blazing economy with Canada's highest labour costs. After more than a decade of surpluses, the province began, in 2008–09, to book one deficit after another. The PCs were running the oddest of operations, a broke government surrounded by a wealthy economy. To many Albertans — especially New Democrats, but also Liberals like former party leader Kevin Taft — that could only mean money was being siphoned off by wealthy interests. Taft's 2012 book, *Follow the Money*, was a damning critique of PC flat-tax and resource policy. "We're leaving way too much wealth on the table," he told the *Calgary Herald*'s Darcy Henton.[10]

Think tanks like the Canada West Foundation offered viable ideas for the province to become an environmental leader in innovative technologies and alternative energy sources in such books as *Alberta's Energy Legacy*.[11] But advice was ignored if it didn't contribute to the one conversation the PC governments would hear: billions of dollars in oil sands expansion.

Notley and the NDP deeply believed that the only way forward was through remaking Alberta's image. No longer an environmental laggard, the province would vault ahead of patchwork environmental measures to become a world leader on climate change. This wholesale economic transformation began amid the worst financial terrain any new government had tilled since Social Credit assumed power in 1935 during the Great Depression.

While it was enthusiastically applauded by many, the NDP's aggressive redesign unsettled the public. Many liked what the premier was doing but questioned whether she should be implementing so much so soon when people were anxious about job loss and rising public debt. Polls confirmed that by the end of January 2016 Notley's honeymoon was over.

Essentially, she had placed a massive political bet — that by the time her first term is done, the NDP will have diversified the traditional oil-based economy with green industries. The carbon tax would provide direct incentives to wind, solar, and other alternative energy innovations as well as accelerate the switch from coal-fired generation to natural gas. The jobs created would replace many of those lost in the oil patch collapse. At the same time the NDP, like any government, counts on the eternal wild card — oil prices — to come up aces one more time.

The gamble could work in the government's favour if the innovation that transformed Alberta's energy sector could be replicated in the alternative energy area. It had been Lougheed's new PC government, aided by the Liberals in Ottawa, that had provided massive incentives for developing the technology to capture the oil in the northern sands. Notley hopes to capitalize on the province's entrepreneurial culture, with its history of innovation that has generated so much success. Essentially, she's using the power of government to refocus that spirit on clean technologies and green energy sources. But it will take considerably more than idealistic policies to generate outside investment.

NOTLEY ALSO ACTED quickly on many other fronts after being sworn in on May 23, 2015. Ministers almost tripped over each other to make major announcements following the government's first throne speech, read June 15 by incoming Lieutenant Governor Lois Mitchell. Notley introduced two bills that covered quick-fix campaign promises. Bill 1 banned corporate and union donations to political parties, while Bill 2 increased corporate taxes for profitable businesses as well as progressive taxes for high-income earners. In addition, Finance Minister Joe Ceci tabled an interim supply bill of $18.5 billion for health, education, and human services. Critical departments had been rudderless after ex-premier Prentice announced rollbacks in his earlier budget. Ceci was guaranteeing funding until the NDP could work up its own budget for release in the fall of 2015.

There were other equally important things that Notley had to do as the new premier. One was to address the findings of the national Truth and Reconciliation Commission. As premier, she apologized on behalf of Alberta for the harrowing abuse suffered by First Nations and residential school survivors, as well as all of those whose pain had gone with them to the grave. The previous year, in the very same legislature where Notley spoke, PC MLA Pearl Calahasen told of her own abuse at the hands of nuns in residential school.

When I went to school, I was the smallest girl, and I had to go to residential school. Being small is really not as much of an advantage as overweight people think it's an advantage. It was not an advantage. It was not a good time. The nuns were very cruel. They used to pick on me because I was so tiny. Many times I was hit by a ruler; it was always across the back. I do have scars from that. But I did get through it. It was no fun. I was probably the least of those that were affected by physical abuse.

As the onion was peeled from some of the people's soul, you got to the inner core of that individual. The only way that we can heal is by making sure that people know and understand the kinds of things we've gone through.

It's not the end. It is the beginning. And it's up to us as people who make policies to ensure that we continue to do that, to make sure that other children do not get harmed in this way. It is a dark time in our history, actually, and it's up to us to make sure that we get things done in the right way so that we can begin to see that people who need to be healed get healed.[12]

At the end of her tearful account, the legislature gave Calahasen a standing ovation.

In the words of the Truth and Reconciliation Commission, indigenous people endured "cultural genocide" under the guise of education. Young children were brutally taken from their homes and transported to places of unspeakable darkness, where all manner of abuse was rampant. Youngsters were beaten, sexually abused, starved, and killed. It all happened under the federal residential school system, and there are an estimated 12,000 survivors in Alberta alone. Of the 139 residential schools across the country, 25 were in Alberta. When Notley spoke to the legislature on June 22, 2015, she gave an emotional apology to all who had endured the horrors.

"We were shocked and at times rendered speechless as we learned of the First Nation, Métis, and Inuit children forcibly removed from their homes, placed beyond the protection and love of their families. We felt deeply for the adults who shared their journey to come to terms with the broken child within."[13]

Then Notley promised a path to healing and reconciliation. "We want the First Nation, Métis, and Inuit people of Alberta to know that we deeply regret the profound harm and damage that occurred to generations of children forced to attend residential schools. Although the Province of Alberta did not establish the system, members of the government did not take a stand to stop it. For this silence we apologize."[14]

Siksika chief Vincent Yellow Old Woman was thankful for Notley's apology, as the Calgary Herald's Daryl Slade reported. "I was very moved and touched by the words the premier made. I spent nine years in a residential school. I know what it was like to be in a residential school. I endured all the abuse you can think of and I was a survivor." The chief thanked the Creator, his elders, and his prayers for survival, saying that was how he and others were able to survive. "They have moved forward in spite of what took place."[15]

After her historic apology on behalf of Albertans past and present, Notley called for a national inquiry into the missing and murdered Aboriginal women. She also promised to collaborate with indigenous communities to end violence against women and families. It was heartening for the abused and their families to hear the premier apologize and promise change. More than an emotional moment, which it certainly was, it was also an opportunity for government to try to heal those who were broken because of a racist federal policy that aimed at destroying a way of life.

Notley pledged better relationships with First Nations, Métis, and Inuit, mandating her Cabinet ministers to foster partnerships and strategies for working together. Alberta Minister of Aboriginal Relations Kathleen Ganley told the *Globe and Mail's* Carrie Tait that members of the government had met with a number of First Nations and Métis peoples. "What we're trying to do is build a trustful relationship," said Ganley,[16] who is also Alberta's minister of justice and solicitor-general. The minister stressed the importance of her team having an open mind and listening, rather than simply offering their opinions on what needs to be done. Notley and her ministers rarely make an important announcement without pointing out that they're standing on one of Alberta's four areas of treaty land.

THE PREMIER ALSO moved quickly to find competent people to analyze elements of her platform. In June she hired the former Bank of Canada governor and eminent economist, David Dodge, to develop priorities for infrastructure spending within a far-reaching capital plan. For too long, PC members and MLAs jockeyed for political influence as the government doled out dollars for constituency hospitals, highways, schools, and related development. It was an inefficient process where rewards were too often based on loyalty as much as need. Critical infrastructure projects, including maintenance, were delayed, ignored, or underfunded. Dodge would examine the province's economic prospects for the coming years, including labour availability, and present his findings to the government before its October 2015 budget.

The next high-powered appointment was University of Alberta economist Andrew Leach, who would chair a new climate-change strategy panel. This would be the engine of the province's environmental train. When Environment Minister Shannon Phillips announced Leach's role, she also unveiled a higher carbon price for industrial polluters. By 2017 heavy emitters must reduce greenhouse gas intensity by 20 percent, even as carbon levies double from $15 per tonne to $30. "We are serious about making progress," Phillips said.

The third appointment was Alberta Treasury Branches CEO Dave Mowat, who was asked to head a new royalty review. When Energy Minister Marg McCuaig-Boyd named Mowat, she left the membership of the panel and the method for holding this controversial inquiry to the new chair. The oil patch was especially nervous as images of ex-premier Ed Stelmach danced in corporate heads. His 2007 royalty reboot angered producers and alienated potential allies when respected economists and other informed consultants were largely ignored in the process. The industry was furious about the lack of consultation and input, and was wary of any repeat in 2015. Oil patch fears were considerably soothed when Peter Tertzakian, one of the most respected energy economists in the country, was added to the panel. He joined former deputy minister of finance Annette Trimbee and Beaverlodge Mayor Leona Hanson.

Then it was Labour Minister Lori Sigurdson's turn to take to the podium and proclaim that by October 1, 2015, the minimum wage would rise from $10.20 per hour to $11.20. By 2017 the hourly rate would hit $15. The corporate and small business sector, already extremely nervous about poor oil prices, tax hikes, and the royalty review, were almost united in opposition.

With all the change and uncertainty surrounding Notley's new government, the premier went to the oil sands investors and delivered a resounding speech, lauding the innovation and accomplishments of the industry. Notley gave a shout-out to the oil sands as a "tremendous asset" and invited investors to park their money in the province where the taxes and talent will always favour those willing to support the oil patch.

"We will maintain a warm welcome for investors and uphold their right to earn fair returns," Notley told the Stampede Investment Forum in Calgary on July 7, 2015. "So Alberta will continue to be a healthy place for private investment under our government. This definitely applies to energy. Expanding existing oil sands projects, establishing new ones and pioneering advanced technologies — all this requires spending on a large scale. Under our leadership, Alberta's abundant oil and gas reserves will remain wide open to investment."[17]

It was a reassuring tone to take in a community hard hit by sliding oil prices, shattered investment dreams, looming layoffs, and uncertainty about the new government. Notley faced constant attempts by the opposition parties to paint her government as anti–oil sands. Essentially, they accused her of trying to shut down the industry. Notley always denied it. She was even photographed wearing an "I love oil sands" T-shirt.

Yet the patch remained wary of all the policy shifts, royalty reviews, and uncertainty piled atop extremely low oil prices.

Notley started working on her basic pledge to Albertans — pipeline acceptance in return for climate-change action. She headed east to seek support for the Energy East pipeline, stopping to talk with Quebec premier Philippe Couillard before moving on to St. John's for the Council of the Federation meeting. Her quiet, consultative approach contrasted sharply with the combative style of Saskatchewan premier Brad Wall.

If will could break down the communication bottlenecks that have plagued Energy East proponents, the pipeline expansion would already have been approved. But individual interest and community concerns along its route have exasperated those who need to get western oil to tidewater Montreal Mayor Denis Coderre, with his eighty-two colleagues from municipalities around Montreal, completely rejected the Energy East pipeline even though the National Energy Board had barely begun its examination. That seemed especially ironic to pipeline proponents, given that in November 2015 Montreal dumped billions of litres of raw sewage into the St. Lawrence River.

Wildrose leader Brian Jean took his anger to Twitter. "You can't dump raw sewage, accept foreign tankers, benefit from equalization and then reject our pipelines," he said. "Montreal buys millions of barrels of foreign oil from dictatorships, but it is rejecting oil from their friends in Confederation — it's ridiculous."[18]

Saskatchewan's Wall, meanwhile, began to seem like part of the Alberta opposition. Facing an election against the provincial NDP, he started painting himself as the champion of the oil and gas industry, tacitly inviting Alberta's industry to pull up stakes and move one province over. After Notley met Quebec Premier Couillard, she suggested that her climate-change policy could help win approval from Quebec for the Energy East pipeline. Wall said: "I do not think any province in Canada should be holding up approval of a pipeline. I don't think they should be able to hold it up by saying, 'We don't think your policies are stringent enough,' or 'Maybe we don't like the way you price carbon' ... I think that's of great concern."[19] Wall would go on to another resounding victory on April 4, 2016.

Notley responded sharply: "I am not at all concerned with being perceived as a pushover. That has never been something that's been part of my dynamic." To the charge that she would hand pipeline authority to other provinces, she added: "Under no circumstances would I now or would I ever do such a thing, and it is really quite ridiculous to suggest it. All I'm acknowledging is that it's going to be helpful ... to be able to talk to people about genuine efforts you are making to be environmentally responsible."[20]

The difference in tone between Notley and Wall underscored an ideological separation, but arguably a gender one too, as Notley approached the nationally divisive issue with a more female attitude to negotiation. Her final salvo expressed the sharp difference: "Negotiations are about what you get at the other end. That's what I'm focused on now."[21] The larger political calculation was that many Canadians were fed up with the image of a cranky, wealthy Alberta whose climate-change views were holding back the entire country. Notley was trying to give the province a friendly, collaborative, mainstream face. Some Albertans thought this was a disastrous mistake: Notley should be fighting, not smiling. Many others, though, were comfortable with her approach and willing to give it time to work. In the end there would be only one test — would the pipelines be approved and built, or not?

In the meantime, Wall was on the high road to prairie popularity. "Maybe we need to have equalization payments start flowing through a pipeline in order to finally get one approved through Central Canada," he said[22] — echoing many western premiers before him, including the great Saskatchewan New Democrat Allan Blakeney, who once said Ottawa would never adopt a policy "that would impede the free flow of money to Central Canada." Notley and her finance minister, Joe Ceci, refused to play the highly sensitive equalization card, essentially saying the formula wouldn't be an issue until the terms are renewed in 2019. In arguing this, Notley is trying to turn down this emotional tap even while the equalization spigot remains fully open to Ontario and Quebec. Those two provinces alone receive billions of dollars annually through the system, fuelled in part by an estimated $15 to $20 billion from Alberta's economy. This, despite the fact that through good times and bad, whether in boom or recession, Alberta hasn't received an equalization payment since 1963. Albertans are well aware of the irony; the equalization billions flow indirectly from fossil fuel revenues to provinces that now throw up hurdles to new pipelines.

By early 2016 there was no doubt about whose message was resonating on issues from pipelines to equalization: Wall's approval rating in an Angus Reid Institute poll was 62 percent in Saskatchewan, the highest of any premier. Notley's provincial popularity was down to 33 percent. In Alberta's business community, some leaders joked bleakly that the province had the wrong premier.

Notley did score a small victory at the meeting of premiers — they finally approved the long-awaited Canadian Energy Strategy.[23] It acknowledged that pipelines "have the potential" to enhance energy security and ensure safe transport of oil and gas. All this was bundled with support for uncontroversial electricity transmission.

On the ground, though, it was apparent from Burnaby to Montreal that fierce local opposition could stall any pipeline. Provinces were moving with impunity into an area of clear federal authority. While those political leaders were anxious about their local problems, most Canadians were in favour of Energy East — 64 percent, according to another Angus Reid survey. Support was sky high in Alberta and Saskatchewan, and stood at a respectable 48 percent even in Quebec. Notley had reason to believe her quiet diplomacy might win more Canadians over.[24]

AS THE PREMIER tried to retool Alberta's image with premiers behind the scenes, her heavy hitters reimagined the province's future. David Dodge's summer job, before Finance Minister Ceci's October budget, was to consider Alberta's economic future with an eye to taking the politics out of infrastructure projects and inserting logic instead. Noting that oil-price volatility has more direct consequences on Alberta than any other jurisdiction across the country, Dodge described a borrowing philosophy that would finance the critical capital plan.

His report, included in the October 2015 Alberta budget, stated: "What is clearly evident is that the Government of Alberta has had a strong bias to under-provide for maintenance, refurbishment and normal replacement of capital." He concluded that there was "a backlog of deferred needs and a continued call on the capital budget to meet what are really operating expenditures." Dodge termed it a "biased procedure" leading to "an inefficient allocation of resources and, over time, higher costs to the taxpayer." Put more directly, he was calling out previous governments for not building enough, and also for failing to provide enough funding to run the facilities they did build. He argued for "long-term government financing that will both improve government services as well as improve the opportunity for economic development."[25]

Dodge's capital plan takes a counter-cyclical approach to infrastructure investment: that is, it's best to borrow during an economic downturn when the competition for capital, materials, and labour is low, causing costs to fall. "By following this policy of counter-cyclical budgeting, public debt can be sustained at a manageable level over long periods of time — rising somewhat during periods of weak private sector demand … and falling during periods of excess demand."

Deborah Yedlin, the *Calgary Herald* business columnist, noted that Dodge "makes the point — very strong, given it appears in boldface type — for governments to get off the treadmill of being singularly focused on tabling balanced budgets every year." It can blindside government and, in Dodge's view, "will exaggerate cyclical economic volatility and have a perverse impact on long run growth."[26]

The budget itself had been cobbled together under extreme pressure after the election. It was based in part on an assumption included in the final PC effort, which never passed. But this was no PC document. It came with much more generous spending on health care and education, stepped-up borrowing for building infrastructure, and a pledge not to lay off public sector workers. The result was a projected $6.1 billion deficit, the largest in the province's history. The province that had been debt free in 2005 would owe $36.6 billion by 2018. All this was based on the revenue that was expected to flow from an average West Texas oil price of US$50 per barrel. On budget day, October 27, 2015, the real-world price was just under US$43 — always a very bad omen in an Alberta budget. Within months the price would drop below US$30. Notley's aggressive spending plan was certainly defensible in David Dodge's Keynesian world, but in nearly every pocket of Alberta conservatism it was seen as a disaster. Notley's argument that Alberta was still in better fiscal shape than any other province, although factually correct, would not blunt the attacks from both Wildrose and the PCs.

In the spring of 2016 Notley brought down the NDP's first full budget that owed nothing to earlier calculations from the PC era. Economic conditions had worsened further, causing the NDP to project two years of deficits above $10 billion — all-time records for Alberta — as well as accumulated debt of $57 billion within three years. All three major ratings agencies downgraded the province's once-stellar AAA credit rating. The budget also unveiled details of the carbon tax to come. "We're going to come out the other side in 2017," said Finance Minister Joe Ceci, trying to sound optimistic, but few conservatives believed it.[27] By this time, the oil-price crash had directly or indirectly caused as many as 120,000 job losses. Several "unite the right" movements sprang up with the goal of rallying divided conservatives to defeat Notley in 2019.

FOR THE PREMIER, there was always a matter just as important as budgets. Her government had already heavily focused on the United Nations Climate Change Conference to be held in Paris at the end of November and early December 2015. Officials and politicians were rushing to produce a policy that would, they felt, allow Alberta to single-handedly change Alberta's world image from carbon villain to climate champion.

THE DAY PREMIER Notley unveiled her "Climate Leadership Plan," on November 22, 2015,[28] she was flanked by the province's energy, environment, and First Nations elite. Their backing was a major coup for Notley and the NDP. What followed was a strategy that Notley believed would ease forever the oppressive environmental anger toward Alberta. "Our goal is to become one of the world's most progressive and forward-looking energy producers," she said. "We are turning the page on the mistaken policies of the past, policies that have failed to provide the leadership our province needed."[29]

Notley's bold three-pronged plan featured a $3 billion carbon tax, oil sands emissions eventually capped at 100 megatonnes annually, and by 2030, a wholesale phase-out of coal-fired electricity, to be replaced by wind power and future innovative energy sources. While the strategy was touted as revenue neutral, Alberta households would feel a deepening revenue hole in their pockets of $470 annually by 2018 if they didn't reduce their 2015-style energy use. Funds from the carbon tax would be reinvested in Alberta for research into alternative energy and other green innovations. In addition, the cost to low-income Albertans would be eased by cash rebates.

On the eve of the Paris climate-change talks, Notley's strategy signalled a sea-change in Alberta's economic and environmental direction. This historic and radical plan for Alberta's brand was backed by three men who have seldom — if ever — stood together: Energy entrepreneur Murray Edwards, Greenpeace environmental activist Mike Hudema, and Treaty 6 Grand Chief Tony Alexis. In the end, it was a woman, Premier Notley, who assembled them all toward a common goal.

Speaking immediately after Notley, Edwards said: "On behalf of Canadian Natural Resources Ltd., my colleagues from Suncor, Cenovus, and Shell, we applaud Premier Notley for giving us … leadership on climate policy." He added that the plan allows the industry "greater predictability," as it "recognizes the need for a balance between the environment and the economy."[30]

Suncor CEO Steve Williams was eager to underscore Edwards's remarks, noting that Canada's oil patch, "one of the world's largest oil-producing regions," will become "a leader in addressing the climate change challenge."[31]

Treaty 6 Grand Chief Alexis called Notley's plan "historic" for the province, as "we are now in a place where industry, government and First Nations can move forward together on climate change."[32]

Greenpeace spokesperson Hudema noted that the "targets give an important signal to business, let the world know where Alberta is headed, and help ensure that direction leads to the reductions that science and equity demand."[33]

It was a remarkable display; oil patch barons pushed toward a position they'd once resisted, while First Nations and environmental champions leaned in toward them. The relief in the business community had a practical source: rather than imposing the whole climate-change burden on industry, the NDP proposed to spread it across the economy through the general carbon tax. Beyond that, there was also genuine recognition in the corporate world that it was time to come to terms with climate change. Shell, for one, had long championed "meaningful government-led carbon pricing mechanisms."[34]

Alberta's conservative opposition, ever adroit, actually tried to paint Notley and the NDP as oil patch sellouts. Wildrose leader Brian Jean told the legislature: "I don't work for big oil; I work for Albertans." He admonished the NDP for "standing up for big oil — what a shock." It was an unintentionally comical thunderclap that had the legislature laughing at the absurdity of Alberta's New Democrats in bed with "big oil."[35] Lost in the silliness was a different point made by Jean — Notley had never mentioned the carbon tax during her election campaign.

But opinion was evolving. In June 2016 former PC provincial treasurer Jim Dinning called Alberta's carbon levy "sound public policy." In an interview with the *Calgary Herald*'s James Wood, Dinning said, "If you want to induce … decision-makers who are in homes or in businesses to bend the curve on emissions in Alberta, sending a price signal, i.e. a carbon tax, is a smart thing to do. We, as conservatives, should stop dragging our knuckles on this issue."[36]

Prime Minister Justin Trudeau was delighted with Notley's lead, posting via @JustinTrudeau: "Congratulations @RachelNotley on unveiling Alberta's Climate Leadership Plan. A very positive step in the fight against climate change."[37]

Former U.S. vice-president and global environmentalist Al Gore praised Notley's climate-change action as "an inspiring addition to the legacy of leadership and forward thinking action by Canadian provinces to speed our transition to a low carbon economy. This is also another powerful signal — well-timed on the eve of the Paris negotiations — that humanity is beginning to win our struggle to solve the climate crisis."[38]

Alberta's image was indeed improving, a phenomenon that only seemed to further enrage the opposition.

When Notley travelled to Paris with the Canadian contingent, she was confident Alberta's action plan would bolster Trudeau's efforts to bring Canada back on the world stage as a climate innovator. In her view, the province was now a pacesetter rather than outlier.

That was also why Alberta had to ensure that it introduced a royalty structure that was fair and balanced for both the province and the oil patch. Dave Mowat's royalty review was delayed a number of times; when it finally delivered, on January 30, 2016, the reason for the postponements was obvious. Alberta's royalty regime was clearly proper for the times. Basically, it would stay intact.

"It is not the time to reach out and make a big money grab, because that is just not going to help Albertans," Notley explained, with Mowat at her side.[39] Notley did the right thing, even in the face of a campaign promise to find "a full and fair return to the people of Alberta." The New Democrats had long criticized the PCs for a royalty regime that they claimed favoured producers over the people of the province. For years NDP MLAs had alleged that the public was being ripped off. And yet, when the findings of the review presented the opposite, Notley accepted the outcome. She had the option of being consistent and wrong, or inconsistent and right. In the end she picked the course that fit the facts. The conservative parties' opposition crowed that the NDP had been wrong all along, as was their right. It was left to Greg Clark, the leader and only MLA of the Alberta Party, to take a more dignified and statesmanlike view. "It's good to have political leaders who gather the information and base decisions on facts, not rhetoric," he said.[40]

The Wildrose lambasted the government for the cost of doing the study, while in the end endorsing the findings. What the review revealed categorically was the high-cost reality of extracting marketable bitumen from the oil sands. Robert Skinner, an executive fellow at the University of Calgary, added that "the review process showed that the province is a high-cost jurisdiction and there is not much more to trim off the profits."[41]

When the province produced conventional oil and gas, even former premier Peter Lougheed instituted royalty reviews. It's a rational practice when prices are higher and costs are lower. In 2006 Lougheed was concerned Albertans were "not getting the royalty return that they should be getting with $75 oil. So it is a major, major federal and provincial issue."[42]

But by the fall of 2015 oil prices had crashed. Now the entire industry was at a crossroads as it reached for more innovative and cleaner technology, as well as lower costs of production and alternative sources of energy.

Alberta's energy industry is world renowned for its technological advances in extracting non-conventional oil and gas, which places it in a unique mindset for inventing greener and cleaner alternative energy. Innovation leading to sophisticated technology has been key to the industry over the last fifty years, but this kind of progress takes time, research, and plenty of money. If Alberta's new climate-action plan aligns government tax incentives with industry initiative, combined with environmental and First Nations guidance, there could be a golden future for Alberta energy. But as Notley worked through her first year, many Albertans remained unsettled and worried.

NOTLEY'S GREATEST STROKE of luck was the election of Prime Minister Justin Trudeau on October 19, 2015. In the context of Alberta policy, the alignment with the federal government is almost perfect. Trudeau believes the provinces and the country must have a strong climate-change policy before pipelines can get built. He also feels that the process must be more rigorous, and must include the climate-change impact of pipelines before they are approved by the National Energy Board. Notley finds herself more in tune with the federal Liberals than she likely would have been with Thomas Mulcair's NDP.

This is yet another dramatic shift for Albertans. The provincial government is rarely well aligned with any federal government, let alone a Liberal one. Notley seems more in sync with Trudeau than successive PC premiers were with former Conservative prime minister Stephen Harper. The new alliance is so novel that many conservatives simply conclude that Notley is being taken for a patsy, and the province will be betrayed in the end.

It's a sentiment that no Alberta premier can ignore. By early 2016, perhaps stung by allegations that she wasn't standing up for Alberta, Notley said sharply that Ottawa's new system for pipeline evaluations couldn't be allowed to stall approvals. Reform of the National Energy Board is necessary to regain public trust, she said, "but it still needs to be done in a timely way. We can't have it go on forever. We need a beginning and a middle and an end to the NEB process."[43]

She also responded testily when, on the eve of the Vancouver meeting on climate change with Trudeau and all the premiers, the province of Quebec filed for an injunction against Energy East. Despite the usual denials of the obvious, the filing was clearly timed for political effect. Notley used startling language in return: "I'm going to leave the gun in the holster until we're actually in the gunfight … in the meantime, I will simply keep my holster close at hand." She added: "If we are going to build this country we must get a pipeline to tidewater. We just need to grow up and ensure that we act like a twenty-first century energy producer."

Notley wanted the rest of the country to recognize that Alberta's climate-change policy had vaulted from virtual non-existence to national leadership. The NDP, like the PCs before them, were frustrated that Ontario and Quebec seemed fixated on local opposition when their populations showed relatively strong support for pipelines. She was trying to remove one significant problem — the perception that Alberta wasn't just a climate-change laggard, but almost a denier.

The climate plan did a remarkable job of transforming Canada's image at the Paris U.N. climate session. Because of it, the prime minister owes her one. "Canada is back, my good friends," Trudeau told the huge delegation, representing 150 global leaders. "We're here to help, to build an agreement that will do our children and grand-children proud."[44]

Nobody wanted a repeat of the 2009 disaster in Copenhagen, where both Quebec and Ontario said they would not carry higher carbon-reduction burdens for the sake of the rapid oil sands expansion favoured by the Harper government. Weak federal emission targets "are simply not in line with what we are doing as provinces," said Quebec Environment Minister Line Beauchamp, as reported by Kelly Cryderman for the *Calgary Herald*.[45] International environmental groups singled out Canada — and the oil sands — for negative attention.

Alberta's cozier relationship with Ottawa sharply contrasts with the contrarian attitude of the past. The province was, after all, the birthplace of Harperism, the direct heir of the Reform Party. Alberta's perceived intransigence annoyed other Canadians to the point where Alberta's recession seemed to spark hints of national *schadenfreude*.

But Alberta's cranky decade was not entirely typical. Many times in the past there have been moments when the province was a reasonable mediator and problem-solver. In a sense, Notley is returning the province to its earlier tradition.

The late premier Don Getty was considered, sometimes with amusement, the big guy who kept the others in check during the constitutional talks. When then-Newfoundland premier Clyde Wells was about to walk away from the Meech Lake talks, Getty blocked him at the door. Ralph Klein did the same thing at another interprovincial meeting, phoning in for hamburgers so no one could bolt for the exit claiming hunger. Two years after Ottawa brought in the National Energy Program, Peter Lougheed was working for a constitutional settlement with Quebec. The contrarian image that grew up around debate over the oil sands and pipelines is certainly deserved, but is in many ways atypical.

Notley has made the simple calculation that since Alberta was getting no pipelines approved by being cranky, it couldn't hurt to try being agreeable. But old-school Albertans are still deeply uneasy about the meshing of both style and substance with Ottawa.

FOR THOSE WHO reside in rural Alberta the uneasiness runs even deeper. Notley's government seems to have a disconnect with those who live outside the urban orbit. Beyond the city and its satellites is a province with a rural mindset filled with distrust of the urban power-brokers. Nowhere was this more evident than the controversy surrounding Bill 6, the Enhanced Protection for Farm and Ranch Workers Act.

On the surface the bill seemed a simple and fair act, designed to ensure that Alberta farm labourers enjoy the same occupational health and safety protection as their counterparts everywhere else in Canada. The Supreme Court of Canada had pronounced Alberta's lack of farm labour protection unlawful. But Alberta remained the only province where farm workers had no protection under law.

And yet the Notley government's brilliant display of collaboration with competing interests on climate change was nowhere evident with Bill 6. Despite the bill's honourable intention of ensuring worker safety, the debate around the bill went horribly awry. Farmers felt that an insensitive government was dictating who could help them and whom they could hire. Would family and friends who pop over to dig fence-post holes have to be covered by insurance? Would the bill mean that those same family members and friends who work together and exchange jobs, especially during labour-intensive and time-dependent seasons, are going to need costly extra coverage? Most small farmers exchange labour during, for example, harvesting or calving season. Farmers put their faith in neighbours rather than government. They ask God, not government, for their crops to come in free of blight and bugs, and undamaged by hail and snow. Not that He or She generally accedes to the request — but in the case of Bill 6 the Almighty might have been listening more carefully than the government.

And so the Bill 6 blunder became a symbol of an uncaring government threatening to destroy a storied way of life. Farmers and ranchers staged demonstrations throughout the province. When more than a thousand people arrived at the steps of the Alberta legislature to protest the bill's passage, Labour Minister Lori Sigurdson conceded that the government "could have done a better job communicating."[46]

And listening. That was the real problem. Dialogue hadn't simply broken down; it hadn't even begun. But one party was out in the fields, seemingly stoking the embers of discontent into flames. Wildrose fomented the Bill 6 blaze that engulfed the government, led by the loud and exuberant MLA Derek Fildebrandt, who often seems to be the Wildrose enforcer. He travelled throughout rural Alberta, organizing protests with already riled-up ranchers and farmers.

Energy Minister Marg McCuaig-Boyd, from the rural riding of Dunvegan-Central Peace-Notley, knew exactly what it's like to live on a farm, having participated in a family cow-calf operation for twenty-eight years. Another New Democrat, Debbie Jabbour from Peace River, told legislators that the day her family had to sell the farm she was bereft, because her children wouldn't share her farm experiences. That's why she was so bothered by those who claimed New Democrats had no understanding of farm life. "I am tired. I am tired of the rhetoric, the fearmongering, the half-truths we're hearing from the opposition, and I'm tired of the false accusations that I cannot possibly represent the farmers in my community unless I agree with your point of view."[47]

One of the most passionate addresses came from PC backbencher Richard Starke, a respected veterinarian representing the mostly rural riding of Vermilion-Lloydminster in east-central Alberta. He was bothered by the government's early bungling of Bill 6, but even more concerned about Wildrose's claims that played on rural distrust. "Has some of it been added to for political purposes?" he asked, before agreeing with Jabbour's remarks. "Quite frankly, it does us all as legislators a disservice … when we say more than what is there, when we distort what is really there, and when we talk about the intent differently."[48]

Starke also had worried that Wildrose was using Bill 6 as a contentious bridge in its efforts to unite the two conservative parties. "This is not an issue about parties. This is not an issue, as some have suggested, that will unite the right," Starke said forcefully. "This is an issue that should be uniting what's right."[49]

In the end the government passed Bill 6, but with crucial amendments that exclude children, relatives, and neighbours who help out but receive no pay. The amendment could easily have been written into the original bill before any of the blowback. The Wildrose reaction should have been forecast even before it helped seed the clouds for the eventual downpour.

Notley, who was no stranger to farm work herself, admitted the "missteps on Bill 6."

She also spoke with the *Calgary Herald*'s Darcy Henton. "We have to take responsibility ourselves for the fact that we created a certain amount of confusion in how we originally communicated and we allowed families to be in a position where they were worrying about what the impact of these changes would be on their family farm."[50]

The debacle was a cautionary tale for Notley and her government, even though the legislation was clearly necessary. Those within her inner circle certainly understand how a loud opposition that's particularly active on social media can undermine even the most humane legislation. It all could have been avoided if the government had used the same consultative methods with farmers and ranchers that it had with oil producers, environmentalists, and First Nations.

OFTEN IT'S THE apparently simple issues, not the more complex ones, that rise up to bite a government. Bill 6 should have been a quiet, routine matter. After all, Rachel Notley grew up on a ranch near Fairview, and her father never forgot his farm childhood near Didsbury in central Alberta.

Award-winning author and journalist Frank Dabbs, editor of the *Didsbury Review* newspaper, points to another Alberta anomaly. "Remember, Didsbury produced Grant Notley, but it also produced

Gordon Kesler of the Western Canada Concept Party." In February 1982 Kesler won the Didsbury-Olds by-election, running with the western separatist party, which he soon led. His victory was short-lived, however, when he lost in Highwood during the November 1982 election.

The offices of rural newspapers are always open for chats and coffee, and Dabbs loves to listen to the local buzz. He believes the province is beset by the sharpest rural-urban divide since its inception in 1905. "It's historic, in my view. The NDP doesn't understand and appears very naive about rural Alberta. The farm bill reflects that."

As rural Alberta started to empty into the cities, Social Credit premier Ernest Manning saw a growing gulf between the two cultures, one he ably bridged. So too did Peter Lougheed, who moved deftly over the divide by changing not only his suit but also his way of speaking. "Ya just done good," Lougheed once told a rural audience after another PC victory.

The NDP needs to do more than rely on its MLAs who grew up on the farm. "They have to sit down and listen to rural Alberta. They're not doing that. The question is, do they even care?" asks Dabbs.

From his vantage point, Dabbs doesn't see the right uniting quickly, because it's again being organized by urban insiders and MLAs. "There's no real rural understanding. So the rural MLAs will remain staunchly rural and mistrusting of urban views. Rural issues are distinct and very different." For those MLAs of all stripes who grew up on the farm and then moved to the cities, they should listen to those who never left.

THE NDP ALSO made a serious misstep when it tried to ban conservative gadfly Ezra Levant from news briefings. His ultra-right website www.therebel.media mounted a challenge to Notley and her government after he and his contributors were banned from government news conferences because they weren't considered a "journalistic source."

The next day, Notley's government backtracked, with her director of communications, Cheryl Oates, issuing a new statement. "We've heard a lot of feedback from Albertans and media over the course of the last two days and it's clear we made a mistake. The government has appointed former Western Canadian Bureau Chief for Canadian Press, Heather Boyd, to consult and give us recommendations on what the government's media policies should be. In the meantime, no one will be excluded from government media events."[51]

The NDP apparently believed that because many mainstream journalists didn't like *The Rebel* they would applaud its exclusion. But the point wasn't personal annoyance; it was the constitutional guarantee of "freedom of thought, belief, opinion and expression, including freedom of the press and other media of communication."[52] The language appears to give full rights to every form of new media, while refusing to define what is journalism and what is not. Columnists from one end of the country to the other, regardless of personal politics, backed Levant.

The Notley government's quick retraction prompted *National Post* columnist Jen Gerson to observe: "I can only imagine the Rebel Commander's disappointment when the NDP backtracked so entirely for its mistake on Wednesday. He seems to have bounced back alright, I'm happy to report. By mid-day, he was already promising to oppose the Boyd review, accusing Canadian Journalists for Free Expression of spinning for Notley and trashing the media 'industry cartel' on Twitter. Bless his heart."[53]

The episode carried an eerie echo of a celebrated Alberta case of the 1930s, when the Social Credit government passed a law it called the Accurate News and Information Act. It gave the Social Credit Board, as author and academic Ian Greene explains, "the power to prohibit the publication of a newspaper, force a newspaper to print corrections of articles that the board considered inaccurate and prohibit newspapers from publishing articles written by certain blacklisted persons."[54] Fines could total $1,000 day — an insane amount in the pit of the prairie Depression. At one point the government tried to jail an *Edmonton Journal* reporter. The *Journal* became the first non-U.S. paper to win a prestigious Pulitzer Prize, for "its leadership in the defense of the freedom of the press in the province of Alberta." Other Alberta newspapers, including the *Calgary Herald*, were awarded Pulitzer citations for fighting the Social Credit law.

Inevitably, the Supreme Court quashed the act. Chief Justice Lyman Duff wrote: "It is axiomatic that the practice of this right of free public discussion of public affairs, notwithstanding its incidental mischiefs is the breath of life for parliamentary institutions."[55]

The Notley government's dispute with Ezra Levant was a far cry from that case, but it was one of the weirder symptoms of high stress during a period of escalating change. Notley's first year in office was an over-whelming cascade of policy shifts, economic distress, and national polit-ical upheaval, all mixed in with no small measure of incidental mischiefs. But despite all this, she remained remarkably focused on her goals.

THE YEAR WOULD not end easily for Notley and the NDP, however. At the end of it, the fire came. It rode through the crisp boreal forest sur-rounding Fort McMurray, igniting a beast that devoured everything in its path and forcing 88,000 people to abandon their homes. There were har-rowing escapes as the fires consumed 229,000 hectares, demolishing over 2,400 structures in their fury. What Notley called "the ocean of fire" would not, however, take the city's hospital, schools, and most civic buildings.

Nor could the beast consume the soul of the city, its people, whose courage energized the country and triggered an outpouring of donations and support. Fort McMurray is a microcosm of Canada and, indeed, a place where many across the nation have come for secure work. They stay a short time or forever, and they reveal the grit and tenacity of both a community and a nation. Nowhere was this more evident than in fire chief Darby Allen, whose job encompasses the Regional Municipality of Wood Buffalo. A native of Birmingham, England, Allen emigrated to Canada in 1990, work-ing in Calgary before moving north and being named chief in 2013. His face wore the horror and fatigue that his firefighters endured as they worked endlessly to contain the fiery villain. To media touring the devastation with him on the bus, he said, "It was like a fire I've never seen before in my life, like a beast, like an animal."[56] To a tense nation on May 4, 2016, Allen stated, "We are here, and we are strong, and we will keep doing our job."

The other leader who kept doing her job was Notley. Just as Naheed Nenshi did during the devastating southern Alberta flood of 2013, Notley went to the community, to the evacuees, to the air waves, and to social media. There was no grandstanding or showboating. She was there to lead and inform. But she did not intrude. There were news briefings at least twice a day, with emergency officials, telling Albertans exactly what was happening and helping the area residents cope with the enormity of their emergency. One fatal crash killed two people escaping the fire

— including, tragically, the daughter of a deputy fire chief. All the others managed to reach safe havens.

"This city will emerge from this emergency with real structural resiliency and most of its critical infrastructure saved. It is a home you will return to and we're going to work together to get this job done," Notley said. "All of Alberta will have your back until this work has been completed. It is going to be made safe. It is a home you will return to."[57] With her voice sometimes breaking, Notley talked about the courage of the people and of the "heroic firefighters" who managed in the end to save so much of their city.

Throughout it all, Notley emerged as a worthy leader for the people of Fort McMurray, who had escaped with their courage and dignity even as they watched their material goods erupt in flames. They reminded the comfortable outside the inferno of the force that built both Fort McMurray and indeed the country, of the grit, tenacity, and compassion that make us all one nation.

This may have been a turning point in Notley's leadership. Even her enemies had to agree that she brought to the crisis a blend of compassion, dedication, and restrained common sense. Some politicians can't hide the fact that every big moment is all about them. Notley conveyed the sense that this crisis was all about everybody else.

AS THE CITIZENS of Fort McMurray awaited their time to head home, Notley praised their incredible courage amidst such catastrophe.

"The people of Fort McMurray have been profoundly patient, resilient, determined, and graceful under tremendous pressure," she told reporters. Notley explained to the evacuees that "people are going to react to the stress a little bit differently. They need to give each other room to react to it differently, but remain focused on that overriding goal of supporting each other and coming out of it stronger down the road."[58]

In a sense, Notley could have been speaking to all the citizens of Alberta, who each had his or her own response to the dramatic political change that had occurred in just over a year.

As she showed when she faced the roar of the wildfires, Notley's own grace under pressure never wavered. She proved to be a determined political chief, enabling what she believes must be done for the province to achieve a competitive and prosperous future beyond its decades-long dependence on fossil fuel. The sobering fact is that the world is searching for affordable energy alternatives. Until reliable and abundant substitutes emerge, oil and gas will still be used, but much more sensibly than in the past. Notley is preparing Alberta for that transition, but she often faces a tough provincial audience that hasn't grasped how a leader who believes the age of oil will end can also argue for pipelines. The rebuttal is simple but counterintuitive in a province used to breakneck expansion of the oil sands: oil and natural gas will still be needed, and that means pipelines, but the pace of growth will slow and eventually stall. Her policies promote environmental leadership alongside responsible energy production.

Even Saudi Arabia, awash in easy oil, is now planning for the eventual demise of fossil fuel. In April 2016 Saudi Deputy Crown Prince Mohammad Bin Salman "unveiled an aggressive plan to move away from oil revenues by 2010," reported Yadullah Hussain of the *Financial Post*.[59] Until then, however, "the Saudis are burning through their reserves before environmental policies limit demand and competitors erode market share."

Alberta's leading climate-change plan puts the province in the role of an environmental and energy leader. "Alberta's leadership is being noticed far beyond its borders," wrote Michael Bloomberg, the business mogul and former New York City mayor.[60] Notley brings her new Alberta directive to those in Canada that continue to import the real dirty oil from petro-dictators abroad who blatantly ignore all environmental consequences.

And she will use her more collaborative approach to see her plan through, buttressed by the support she has earned from her own nearly gender-equal caucus.

CHAPTER 8

MATH IS DIFFICULT

"I haven't done the math yet," declared the elated premier-elect, "but what I think is true is that we have elected the most women in any government caucus in the history of Canada. So that's kind of cool."[1]

With her collection of twenty-five female MLAs ranging from an ex-hippie to an ex-banker, Rachel Notley made former premier Jim Prentice regret that he ever said to her: "I know math is difficult" — the line that helped sink him in the party leaders' debate.

Forty-seven percent of the fifty-four elected New Democrats were women, bringing her new caucus the closest to gender parity of any government in Canada. She soon went on to establish another Alberta first by appointing an equal number of women and men to her twelve-person Cabinet.

When Liberal leader Justin Trudeau was elected prime minister on October 19, 2015, he followed her lead. His thirty-person Cabinet also featured an equal number of women and men. Asked why, he replied: "Because it's 2015." The comment brought global attention to the charismatic new prime minister. But his caucus, unlike Notley's, still wasn't close to gender parity. The Liberals elected fifty women, who made up just 27 percent of Trudeau's caucus.

On June 13, 2015, Ontario premier Kathleen Wynne shuffled her Cabinet to include 40 percent women. Importantly, she gave gender parity to her priorities committee, led by the premier, deputy-premier Deb Matthews, and Treasury Board president Liz Sandals.

Canadian leaders from ex-prime minister Brian Mulroney to Jim Prentice himself, who actively recruited female candidates and even brought a female opposition leader into his fold, have been eager to tilt their Cabinets toward gender balance. But that alone doesn't substantially change the tone of government. Women who lead primarily male-dominated caucuses, in fact, can often appear as combative as the men. The tone is very much an expression of the entire caucus culture. Even governments with a number of female ministers can continue to sound pretty much the same as any other.

Notley's crew is different. The strong female influence in her caucus quickly changed both the tone and substance at the very core of government. Many more women were hired for political roles. Ministers breezing by in legislature hallways often trail an all-female team behind. Condescension by male MLAs is distinctly out of fashion; with so many female colleagues, including the premier, they wouldn't dare. The legislature rings with declarations of female pride; for the first time, International Women's Day in 2016 was treated as a major event.

Notley's chief of staff, Brian Topp, says he very soon noticed a shift in style unlike anything he'd seen in his years with Saskatchewan and Ontario NDP governments. "There's a different discourse when you have gender-representative government. You get a more thoughtful government, a different tone in the team. Government spends more time working to align, as opposed to political teams, all male, which are more competitive, [where] players butt heads until someone comes out on top. It's a more thoughtful and more deliberative government." He notes that the female ministers are hardly "shrinking violets" in the legislature, but they work collaboratively in their own circle.

The premier is not one to make generalizations. Discussing the effect of gender parity in Cabinet, she quips, "I've never been around the Cabinet table where women were in the minority." Yet she does say that people "are more concerned about being respectful, more concerned about ensuring everybody is heard. That's certainly an ethos in our caucus. People are expected to treat each other with respect and talk about differences in a respectful way. That's a very organic expectation.… So that might be a function of there being more women. There's just so much diversity in our caucus. There's so much youth as well."

It's that diversity and range of experience that plays into a vibrant and innovative perspective on politics and decision making. Yet how all of that is reflected in government is "hard to say," adds Notley in an interview.

"I think, my own experience, whether it's a function of me or being a woman, is that people should be able to disagree and then come back and talk to each other about ways to resolve that disagreement without backing themselves into a corner on opposite sides of the room from which they will never depart. So we make decisions that way to some extent in government. We approach stakeholders that way to some extent.... We're not picking fights; we're not punishing people."

Notley has brought a new Alberta style to national disputes about climate change, pipelines, and equalization. This is partly a reaction to the pick-a-fight focus of earlier PC governments. The NDP calculates that Alberta needs to reboot its image, from national anachronism to international climate leader. But it's also arguable that Notley's approach flows from the gender shift. She doesn't face a caucus of disapproving males who want her to get out there and fight like a man. Rather, she's supported by female MLAs who prefer negotiated solutions to insults and shouting.

NOTLEY CAN BE sharp when pushed, but it's usually to tell the men to calm down. When Saskatchewan premier Brad Wall obliquely suggested she was giving Quebec a tacit provincial veto over pipelines, Notley said the charge was "ridiculous.... I am not at all concerned with being perceived as a pushover. That has never been something that's been part of my dynamic. I am saying that I understand that negotiations are not all about standing in a corner and having a tantrum. Negotiations are about what you get at the other end."[2]

Notley was clearly annoyed, though, when Quebec filed for an injunction to stall Energy East on March 1, 2016, the day before all premiers met Trudeau in Vancouver to discuss a national climate-change framework. But she put her ire on hold after being assured by Quebec officials that this wasn't a rejection of the pipeline itself. The premier was also silent about the B.C. government's startling criticism of Alberta in its 2016 throne speech that said: "Alberta has lost its focus. They expected their resource boom never to end, failed to diversify their economy, and lost control of government spending."[3] This appeared to be a calculated insult to Alberta (as well as to the grammatical rule of number agreement). It was certainly unprecedented for one province to criticize another in a throne speech. But Notley let it pass, keeping her eye on the much larger target of market access through British Columbia.

It's impossible to determine where the influence of gender begins and ends in all this, but there's no question that Notley feels freer to follow her instincts than many female leaders before her. The men in her caucus are supportive, obviously, but the real wind in her sails comes from Canada's largest female cheering section.

Canada remains a laggard in female representation across provinces and the federal government, but is gaining ground. After Trudeau's Cabinet was installed, the Inter-Parliamentary Union moved Canada to fourth place in the world for the number of women in national ministerial positions, tied with France and Liechtenstein. Canada was still behind first-place Finland, which has a ministerial contingent made up of 62.5 percent women, and Cabo Verde and Sweden, both of which are about 10 percent behind the leader. For Canada, however, fourth place was a huge leap forward from the twentieth position it formerly held, when our enlightened dominion had lagged behind Cuba, Guinea-Bissau, and Tanzania.[4]

The millennials who helped move Notley and Trudeau to victory stood on the shoulders of earlier women who clamoured, often fruitlessly, for an equal place in politics.

"Whatever women do they must do twice as well as men to be thought half as good. Luckily, it's not difficult," said the always-colourful Charlotte Whitton, longtime mayor of Ottawa in the mid-twentieth century.[5]

Many women who've successfully juggled family and work still can't imagine a life in politics. Rachel Notley knew the syndrome well from her own life with two children. Even before she took over as party leader she was determined to find strong female candidates. Indeed, this had long been an article of NDP faith. In the previous election in 2012, 45 percent of the party's candidates had been women. But very often an extra effort was needed to get their names on the ballot.

"It takes a little bit longer to talk women into running," Notley told the *Edmonton Journal*'s Mariam Ibrahim just before the election.[6] Many women who were approached believed they wouldn't be good candidates. Notley didn't stop asking, however, and her persistence paid off. She broke down myths and focused not just on the trials of running, but also on the rewards of winning and doing the job. She tried to show the prospective recruits how their personal and professional experiences would make them good politicians. "I've put a lot of thought into it," Notley said. "It comes down to how you approach recruitment. The path of least resistance is not equity, because my experience is I find men are more likely to say 'yes' earlier."

Notley was equally adamant about achieving gender parity in government. "We were very intentional about seeking women candidates. I don't apologize for that. It's always been my view if you want to increase diversity, increase representation, you can't just say things, because twenty-five years later it looks exactly the same. You have to say, 'We will have this many people from this group or that group.' You just have to do it; it won't happen otherwise, and that's what we did."

Notley never believed the larger public had a problem with women candidates, and the research clearly bears this out.[7] Voting patterns studied from the late twentieth century on reveal that Canadians don't discriminate between women and men candidates. They vote for the party they prefer regardless of gender. The major impediment to women's political aspirations today is not the voters but the parties that fail to nominate equal numbers of competent women.

"There is no problem with the electorate. The problem is elsewhere. The problem is with the parties and with their inability or unwillingness to make this a priority," Donna Dasko, former national chair of Equal Voice, told *Globe and Mail* columnist Jane Taber.[8]

Notley addressed head-on the gender bias in candidate selection: "I took ownership; we did intentionally do a few things differently to make sure we had more women candidates." Notley reasoned that if a balanced slate ran for office, then the NDP would "probably elect a balanced slate." The work that she put into recruitment was significant, and it paid off on election night. "It made it easier for me to make sure we had a balanced Cabinet," she said. "There were more to choose from."

Notley had explained to the women she hoped to recruit that notions of governing and leadership can be skewed by watching male politicians go at each other on TV news shows. "It's not about how well you debate or lecture, it's how well you listen; it's not about how well you lead, it's how many friends you have," Notley told the *Edmonton Journal*. "These are the things that make good candidates and they make good MLAs." She also said that women who don't think they should run should "get out of that construct of watching Tom Mulcair and Stephen Harper yell at each other on [CTV News] *Power Play*, and start thinking about what it looks like on an everyday basis as an elected official." That's the turning point where potential candidates "start to think, 'Oh yeah, I could actually do that.'"[9]

One of the biggest barriers women have to break through is their own biology. The fact that women bear children has been used as a way for society to prevent them from achieving their political potential. Until recently in Canada, far too many women have had to resist any inclination to run for political office because they plan to have children. A few promising male leaders also defer politics when their children are younger, but their hesitation doesn't begin to match the doubts women must deal with. If the capital is distant from the riding, they're even more likely to refuse. Partly for that reason, women have always been far more likely to enter civic politics in their town or city. Alberta's provincial election helped to shatter some of those precedents. Two MLAs were pregnant when they ran, and both were from Calgary, nearly a four-hour drive from the legislature.

Both were appointed to Cabinet in Notley's first mini-shuffle. Brandy Payne was named associate minister of health. Lawyer Stephanie McLean became minister of Service Alberta as well as minister of status of women just days before she gave birth to her first child.

"Having never had a child before and having never been a Cabinet minister before, these are things that will just sort of sort out as we go," McLean told reporters after her swearing-in as a minister.[10] It was an honest reply that any first-time mother could make. But she also had a boss, a mother herself, who understood and had her back.

There were other important legislative matters to sort out as well — in particular, parental leave. The MLAs weren't allowed to take it because they didn't contribute to employment insurance. Before McLean, no female MLA had needed parental leave, and few men thought much about it.

The premier vowed to change what she termed an "archaic" system. "We are looking at different ways to fix it. But we will fix it and we will make sure that [McLean] suffers no economic loss," Notley said.[11]

A baby about to be born waits for nothing, especially some silly law. McLean tweeted the birth of her son, Patrick Shane McLean-Bostock, a historic first for a sitting Alberta MLA. Notley tweeted "Congratulations" to McLean and her husband, Shane Bostock.[12] So did former PC premier Dave Hancock, who added: "Nothing reminds you more of why you are doing what you are doing than children (in my case grandchildren)."

There were precedents. In 1985 Quebec Cabinet minister Pauline Marois became the first Canadian minister to give birth while in office. She later became leader of the Parti Québécois and premier of Quebec. In 2001 British Columbia's Christy Clark had a child while serving as Cabinet minister. She too went on to become premier of her province. In 1987 Liberal Sheila Copps was the first federal MP to give birth. Federal MP Michelle Dockrill, a New Democrat, brought her seven-week baby from her house to the House of Commons in 1999, another first in Canada. Today, a common sight is McLean answering questions in the Alberta legislature while bouncing her baby gently in his sling.

Parents in politics face the same chores as parents in any profession, although the highly public nature of the job, along with the extremely long hours typical of ministerial posts, certainly poses unusual challenges. As work-life balance becomes a serious discussion in legislative bodies, it motivates government as an employer to realize that caring for the next generation shouldn't fall just into the hands of women. Child rearing should be the responsibility of both parents — and that task should be supported by employers and society at large. Laws instituting parental leave for a baby's birth are the start; employers should also offer suitable work hours so that parents can actually spend time with their children before school and in the evening. An on-site daycare at work should no longer be seen as a "progressive" extra; it should be viewed as simply humane, a standard feature. On the federal scene it took another woman, former speaker Jeanne Sauvé, to launch on-site daycare, called Children on the Hill, to serve MPs and all the others working in Parliament.

When parliament or the legislature is in session, debates and meetings can go into the evening hours, posing challenges not just for parents but all politicians. In Alberta, Notley's government changed the legislature hours to allow morning sittings and so free the evenings for those with family commitments.

Trying to create a work-life balance by making politics more family-friendly seemed a no-brainer, but there were those who found it hard to part with the old ways. Interim PC leader Ric McIver leapt to condemn the new notion. "All this talk about family-friendly is hogwash. This is a tough place to work, folks. There's not really much family-friendly around here. You can try to pretend there is but there isn't, and we all signed up for the tour of duty so we have no one to blame but ourselves."[13] McIver was walking, talking proof of how deeply disconnected from the public the PCs had become.

That type of thinking was exactly what Notley was trying to change even as she, like so many parents, worked within the reality of a pressing, and in this case political, life.

Just as there was nothing in place to help politicians trying to juggle their family and political obligations, there was also no playbook for their spouses. This is a particular problem for the spouses of political leaders, as each works within a tight and very public role.

"My husband and I have been partners," says Notley. "We really do work together on everything, ever since we've been together, and it will be our twentieth wedding anniversary coming up in 2017. We've had other challenges, and this is a challenge for sure. But we work through it and he believes as much or more in what we're doing and do. We both care very deeply about our family and about making sure our kids are well and do well. We're kind of on the same page on most of this, and it's different for sure. I'd like to be able to spend more time with my family than I do." And then, the premier's eyes tear up as her face reddens slightly. "So that's not a great part about it. Nonetheless, we're trying to work our way through. We do little things and we make time. We very clearly take time; and I don't let anyone touch it in my calendar. We make sure we have time to be together."

No matter how wrenching the realities of a life in politics can be, Notley is determined to continue breaking down barriers that in the past blocked far too many young parents, women in particular, from politics.

In Ottawa, Trudeau also has talked about making the House of Commons more family-friendly, initiating changes to sitting hours, calling votes earlier in the day, and ending Friday sittings. Many other measures could be taken. All law-making houses could use technology such as electronic voting and video-conferencing to open up the political tent.

Federal Minister of Environment and Climate Change Catherine McKenna made it clear that her family is as much a priority as her political job. She told her deputy minister, who also has a young family, not to book her between 5:30 p.m. and 8:00 p.m. "I have to set a tone from the start. I'm going to carve out time every single day where I'm going to go home," she told CBC Radio. "I'm happy to work long hours and I will work long hours, but I need to be home at dinner when I'm in town because we need to connect."[14]

McKenna is fortunate to be MP for Ottawa Centre. She has a short commute, certainly compared to an MP from British Columbia or Newfoundland and Labrador. She'll find it easier to work that balance. In the same interview, McKenna points out: "If we're going to attract not just women but people with families, young families particularly, we need to do things differently. I should be a role model." Members of Parliament and MLAs find themselves in a dilemma; while they work to improve the lives of children and families, they're forced to deprive their own. McKenna seems determined to break that cycle. "My kids mean everything to me," she said. "I'm in politics for them. It is going to be an absolute challenge but I think I can make it work."

Stephanie McLean has the same dream, but it will also be a challenge. Just before her child was born she said: "The job of an MLA or a minister, it's the kind of thing that you're always on deck. If you're sleeping, you're still the minister." *Edmonton Journal* columnist Graham Thomson dryly noted that as a parent-to-be, she apparently didn't yet realize that she would never sleep again.[15]

AS MORE WOMEN are elected to legislative bodies, both the tone and the substance change. "We've always said that more women in government will change the way government functions," says Mount Royal University Professor Lori Williams. "The electorate wanted change too. We now have more people with different sensibilities at the table and that brings different initiatives from within caucus."

While there's near–gender parity within the governing NDP caucus, it ends there. The Alberta Liberals and the upstart Alberta Party each has one

MLA, their male leaders. The shock, however, is the drop in the number of women sitting on the Wildrose and PC benches. As the Official Opposition, Wildrose elected only two women to its twenty-two-person caucus; the PCs have just one woman among nine MLAs. Both these parties had been led by women: former premier Alison Redford for the PCs, and Danielle Smith for Wildrose. After Smith crossed the floor to join Premier Jim Prentice and his PCs, Wildrose appointed Heather Forsyth as interim leader.

It's much easier to lead the NDP as a woman because of the party's receptivity to social issues. The neo-conservative Wildrose simply wants its leaders to be tough on fiscal and social issues. Perhaps because of that pressure, Smith allowed the "lake of fire" comment to burn her chance of becoming Wildrose premier of Alberta. Her denial of climate change on CBC Radio just before the 2012 election didn't help her with the Alberta electorate either. Yet Smith is a libertarian, fiscally conservative but quite liberal on many social issues, especially LGBTQ rights. Her party, however, didn't always agree with her.

It may still be that way if Wildrose MLA Derek Fildebrandt is represent-ative of the caucus. On March 1, 2016, Mike Morrison (@mikesbloggity) tweeted Derek Fildebrandt (@Dfildebrandt), "How's the Wildrose Party doing on those social issues. You guys going weigh in on them any time soon[?]" Here's what @Dfildebrandt tweeted on March 2, 2016: "Important issues, but in all honesty, social issues just didn't rank in the top 100 reasons I ran. I find these debates stale."[16] The comments don't mean he's hostile to the causes; just that Wildrose, still burning from the lake of fire, prefers to avoid them.

But response was quick, from both NDP and PC MLAs. Karen McPherson (@NDPKaren), stated, "If that's because you believe the issue to be resolved, it's not. LGBTQ youth are entitled to human rights."

Michael Connolly (@NDPMikeC) tweeted, "Homelessness, income inequality, interpartner violence, addictions, hate crimes, & LGBTQ rights are 'stale'?"

Veterinarian and PC MLA Richard Starke (@RichardStarke) minced no words in his tweet: "So … Homelessness? Support for vulnerable Albertans? Poverty reduction? Domestic violence? You find these 'stale'? Wow."

The PCs' only female caucus member, Sandra Jansen (@SANDRAYYCNW), tweeted: "'Social issues' encompass & affect a great deal of what we do. That you don't get this is mind-boggling!"

Professor Lori Williams cites the "tension" in the conservative move-ment, and nowhere is this more evident than in the utter contrast between the tweet by the Wildrose's Fildebrandt and the response from PCs Starke and Jansen. Wildrose leader Brian Jean has been adamant that his party is focused on fiscal issues rather than social concerns. "I've been very clear from the start, that's what our party is about. We are not about social issues nor do we want to tackle social issues."[17]

In the past, too many social issues, especially those that were con-sidered women's, were relegated to the back benches. Research has shown that when 15 percent of the elected representatives are women, the con-versation on so-called women's issues begins to change. There is a critical mass at 30 percent female representation, where sidelined issues come to the forefront, not as female but as societal concerns.[18] This is the figure that the Inter-Parliamentary Union targets as necessary for women's sus-tained influence. Abuse, neglect, intolerance, as well as jobs, pay, and tax inequity begin to be treated as general social issues rather than specialized female concerns.

Notley acted very quickly on some of these concerns. In September 2015 she increased funding for women's shelters by $15 million to $49 million. Alberta has one of the highest rates of domestic abuse in Canada, and the additional monies were targeted for counselling, as well as helping women and children transition from a shelter to a safe home.

Another important step against abuse was Bill 204, which allows domestic abuse victims to break leases without penalty, upon presentation of proof to landlords that they are in danger. (Bill 204 is the Residential Tenancies Safer Spaces for Victims of Domestic Violence Amendment Act.) As noted in the previous chapter, the bill was introduced by MLA Deborah Drever, who had been suspended from the NDP caucus over homophobic Instagram comments.

An abuse survivor, Drever spent her legislative exile studying intoler-ance and domestic abuse concerns. She settled on making a difference for women and children who were trying to flee abusive homes but were chained to a lease.

During the debate over Drever's Bill 204, New Democrat MLA Maria Fitzpatrick rose in the House to speak about her own horrific abuse at the hands of her husband. She made one of the most powerful and emotional member's statements ever heard in that chamber, one that had all MLAs, opposition included, locked in horrified silence, and then on their feet in sustained, unified applause.

> On September 5, 1972, five days after I was married, I realized that there was a problem but could not put my finger on it. Words were spoken, and I felt a shiver on my back and a knot in my stomach. I didn't know it then, but the trap was being set, and I was the game.
>
> The trap was released to some degree on Sunday, July 19, 1981, almost nine years later, when my daughters and I got on a Greyhound bus for a very difficult 62-hour journey across the country, ending in Yellowknife.
>
> The trap was finally broken in May of 1992, when I learned that my ex-husband was dead, and I could stop looking over my shoulder.
>
> My support for this bill comes from the middle of this experience in this trap, a trap that was intentionally or unintentionally supported by society. Silence, blame, guilt, and little-to-no support grew this injustice for decades, if not centuries.
>
> Three times I left with my kids, twice I went to shelters, twice I was forced to return or live on the street. Both times I returned, the violence got worse, and the threats, which he could have carried out at any time, became more frequent and more intimidating. Broken bones, black eyes, sexual assault, and two miscarriages as a result of this abuse were only some of the physical atrocities I had to endure.
>
> I did not have this kind of experience in my life before I was married, so I was not prepared for it, nor how I could protect my children and myself. I prayed. I asked God why this was happening to me. I'm a good person. I've never intentionally hurt anybody or anything in my life.
>
> Someone said to me: God helps those who help themselves. I figured I needed to do something, and I

did. I finally got away to a women's shelter and tried to figure out what to do and where to go. Suffice to say, this attempt was unsuccessful, as the limit at the shelter was two weeks, and I had nowhere to go. At the end of the two weeks, I was forced to return.

The next time I left, I was a little more prepared. I had contacted a lawyer before I left. I saved some money and then left again when I saw the chance to run. I met with the lawyer, but I couldn't get a court date for a month. The time in the shelter was only three weeks.

Again, I had to go back. There were no supports left after the shelter. This time, the abuse was so bad that I thought I would be killed, especially when I awoke from a very tentative sleep with a gun to the back of my head and the clicking sound of the hammer as the trigger was pulled. There were no bullets in the gun, and he laughed hysterically. He beat me. He raped me, and then he threatened that the next time, there would be bullets, and he would kill our daughters first to hurt me and then kill me.

I knew it would be just a matter of time before he followed through on these threats. I called the police as soon as I could, and he was arrested and then released on his own recognizance, and a restraining order was put in place.

I gathered whatever I could. I begged some friends and family for some money to get out of there, and I called the police 16 times in two weeks before he was arrested again, not so much for assaulting me, but because he broke the restraining order. This time, he was held in remand until the issue was settled in court.

In court, he was found guilty and sentenced to a year in jail, but this sentence was suspended, all but the days he'd spent in remand. He turned and, as he was leaving the courtroom, he said that he would kill me. I asked the judge how he could let him go. The judge said to me: "It's a marital issue. Get a divorce and leave." He proceeded, then, to give me a lecture on how much it was going to cost to keep him in jail.

When I returned to my house, he was there, holding my children and my mother-in-law at the point of a gun. At the end of a four-hour ordeal, his mother rose and asked God to help us, and he ran from the house. We spent a few more days barricaded in the house before we finally had the opportunity to get out and get on that bus and run for our lives.

This should never have happened to me, or these situations to anybody else. My children have been scarred for their lives, and I will be horrified if anybody in this Chamber votes against this bill.[19]

Nobody did. When Fitzpatrick finished her account, many MLAs of all parties were in tears. Every member rose for an extended standing ovation. The second reading of Bill 204 passed unanimously.

Without so many female colleagues standing behind her, Fitzpatrick likely would have found it more difficult to tell her intensely personal story of survival. Drever might never have been encouraged to introduce her bill. Fitzpatrick's speech was a signpost moment that showed how gender parity, combined with genuine female influence, can change political culture. "I commend Ms. Drever for her commitment to survivors of domestic violence," said Shannon Phillips, then minister for the status of women. "Bill 204 will help ensure that survivors of domestic violence are safe and have the support they need to maintain their independence."[20]

Fitzpatrick was talking to a legislature that had a status of women minister for the first time in nineteen years. Appropriately, the new ministry was fully in place on March 7, 2016, one day before International Women's Day.

In her announcement Premier Notley affirmed her campaign promise of promoting gender equality. "Working with the new Ministry of Status of Women, our government will include the voices of women in our policies, programs, and legislation. Our province will be richer as a result."[21]

Former premier Alison Redford had appointed an associate minister for families and community safety, Sandra Jansen, who had worked on family violence files. Notley's new ministry would have a broader range and much more impact as it dealt with the issues and challenges that were the direct result of gender inequality. In particular, its mandate would be "increasing women's economic security, leadership and democratic participation, while decreasing violence against women and girls."

For years there was no minister responsible for women's issues. There had once been an Advisory Council on Women's Issues, as well as a Women's Secretariat. Both were long gone. In the intervening years women's inequality in Alberta had deepened. When Shannon Phillips was director of policy analysis with the Alberta Federation of Labour, she pointed out: "We have quite high levels of economic inequality in this province despite our wealth and we do not have a ministry or a portfolio dedicated to women's issues."[22]

As the portfolio was being re-established, the logical choice for the initial responsibility was Phillips. The post, however, went to the woman about to give birth, Stephanie McLean. With a newborn son along with a newborn ministry, Minister McLean, with the premier's backing, had already embarked on changing attitudes as she moved to improve gender equality. To emphasize the push to make the legislature more family friendly, McLean brought her baby Patrick, wrapped in a sling around her chest, to the opening session. Appropriately, it was International Women's Day, March 8.

The province's gender wage gap is the highest in the country, with women earning just 63 percent of men's wages, according to the Parkland Institute, a think tank at the University of Alberta. "Women living in the province are among the most disadvantaged in Canada, facing higher income gaps, unpaid work gaps, and after-tax income gaps than women living anywhere else in the country," wrote Queen's University professor of law Kathleen Lahey, who is also a Queen's National Scholar.[23]

With a wry reference to former premier Ralph Klein's "Alberta Advantage," the Parkland Institute called its report "The Alberta Disadvantage: Gender, Taxation, and Income Inequality." Lahey explained that women's equality in the province has "markedly deteriorated" since 1995, without "effective pay equity or even employment equity laws." The reason was widespread gender discrimination "in employment, promotions, pay and job security." That economic reality is exactly what the new status of women minister wants to change through partnerships "with women and with ministries across government."

MINISTER MCLEAN ALSO hopes "to help eliminate violence against women." Increasing women's economic prospects while also erasing abuse are massive interconnected challenges. To stop abuse, society first has to wipe away attitudes that blame the victim rather than the abuser. There is so much to do in even reporting abuse and sexual assault. The courts can often do more damage to the victim.

One of the most bizarre recent cases arose in Alberta, during the trial of a Calgary man who was accused of sexually assaulting a nineteen-year-old woman over a bathroom sink while she was at a house party. Provincial Court Justice Robin Camp repeatedly called the woman "the accused," when in fact she was the key witness against the accused. As the *Calgary Herald*'s Daryl Slade reported, Judge Camp asked her, "When your ankles were held together by your jeans, your skinny jeans, why couldn't you just keep your knees together?" He also said, "Why didn't you just sink your bottom down into the basin so he couldn't penetrate you?"[24]

Judge Camp acquitted the man on September 9, 2014. The Crown notified the court of its intention to appeal on September 23, 2014. A CBC report on the case noted that in its written argument, submitted March 19, 2015, the Crown claimed that "Camp made legal errors, applied out-of-date stereotypes to the complainant, and transcribed all of Camp's eyebrow-raising comments about women, sex and rape."[25]

In the midst of all this — on June 26, 2015 — then-Conservative Justice Minister Peter MacKay appointed Camp to the federal court.[26]

On October 27, 2015, the Alberta Court of Appeal ordered a new trial. Writing for the court, Justice Brian O'Ferrall stated: "We are satisfied that the trial judge's comments throughout the proceedings and in his reasons gave rise to doubts about the trial judge's understanding of the law governing sexual assaults and in particular, the meaning of consent and restrictions on evidence of the complainant's sexual activity imposed by [Section 276 of the Criminal Code].

"We are also persuaded that sexual stereotypes and stereotypical myths, which have long since been discredited, may have found their way into the trial judge's judgment. There were also instances where the trial judge misapprehended the evidence."[27]

University of Calgary Associate Law Dean Alice Woolley and her colleague Professor Jennifer Koshan, along with Dalhousie University

Professors Elaine Craig and Jocelyn Downie, complained to the Canadian Judicial Council about "Justice Camp's sexist and disrespectful treatment of the complainant in the case and his disregard for the law applicable to sexual assault."[28]

Cristin Schmitz of *The Lawyers Weekly* reported that the legal academics also wrote to Alberta Justice Minister Kathleen Ganley as well as Canada's attorney general, Jody Wilson-Raybould, "asking the ministers to exercise their power."

The written complaints prompted the Canadian Judicial Council (CJC) to appoint a three-person panel to review the judge and his decision in the original sexual assault case. The Federal Court ordered the judge to handle no cases until the review was completed.

In a statement, Camp was contrite: "I have come to recognize that things that I said and attitudes I displayed during the trial of this matter, and in my decision, caused deep and significant pain to many people. My sincere apology goes out, in the first place, to the young woman who was the complainant in the matter.

"I also apologize to the women who experience feelings of anger, frustration and despair at hearing of these events. I am deeply troubled that things that I said would hurt the innocent. In this regard, I am speaking particularly to those who hesitate to come forward to report abuse of any kind and who are reluctant to give evidence about abuse, sexual or otherwise."[29] Camp said he would take gender-sensitivity counselling at his own expense.

Alberta Justice Minister Ganley noted she couldn't discuss the actual case, but explained she is "absolutely committed to ending any instances where sexual violence is excused or explained by blaming victims."[30] But on December 22, 2015, after consulting the NDP Cabinet, Ganley wrote to the CJC: "In my respectful opinion, the conduct of Justice Camp throughout the proceedings in *R. v. Wagar* was so manifestly and profoundly destructive of the concept of the impartiality, integrity and independence of the judicial role that public confidence has been sufficiently undermined to render Justice Camp incapable of executing his judicial office."[31]

On January 7, 2016, the CJC announced the creation of its inquiry. On July 4, 2016, the CJC posted its notice of response to the May 2 allegations. "Justice Camp agrees that he made insensitive and inappropriate comments during the *Wagar* trial," the statement said. "He has apologized generally and specifically. He intends to apologize at the Inquiry Committee hearing." The CJC noted that Justice Camp received counselling which "has given him a deeper understanding of the trauma faced by survivors of sexual assault and about the discriminatory history of assault law."

The statement also said Justice Camp hopes to remain a federal court judge. He "believes his training, counselling and this process as a whole have left him better equipped to judge cases with the empathy, wisdom and sensitivity to social context to which all judges aspire."[32] A public hearing examining the judge's conduct was scheduled for September 2016.

Cristin Schmitz pointed out that Wilson-Raybould didn't weigh in on Justice Camp because "as federal minister of justice, she will have to decide what to do if the CJC ultimately recommends Justice Camp's removal."[33] Schmitz also noted that Parliament alone has the right to remove a federally appointed judge, something it has never done. She added that in the CJC's forty-five years, this was only the seventh time that a justice minister (Ganley) "has exercised statutory authority to require a formal inquiry into alleged judicial misconduct."[34]

GANLEY'S INTERVENTION SIGNALLED the NDP's fierce determination not just to raise the economic standard of women, but to challenge discrimination and unfairness wherever it occurred. It extends far beyond this egregious case to many women's issues that have festered for years, including cyber-bullying and threats on social media.

Some of Notley's female ministers and politicians had very quickly become victims of such bullying and threats themselves. The Bill 6 imbroglio over farm safety played too well into the hands of violence-inciting basement bloggers. Alberta Energy Minister Marg McCuaig-Boyd spoke of the fear and cyber-bullying, as did her colleague Debbie Jabbour. "I, myself, was somewhat concerned to go home last week. I do know now what it's like to be cyber-bullied. I do know what it's like to have threats," McCuaig-Boyd told the legislature. "This past week we have received many calls — some in support, some not — but a climate has been created where people are afraid to speak." She urged all of her colleagues to put aside partisanship and work together. "We can dwell in the past for political reasons, or we can move forward for Albertans and for our constituents."[35]

The anger in the legislature over the farm safety legislation went beyond yelling and accusations of bullying to suggestions that the Wildrose was spreading discontent. A strong supporter of the bill, Liberal leader David Swann, decried the tone of the debate: "I was very unhappy with the politicization, the bullying, that went on, especially from the Wildrose caucus over this. I was very disappointed over the way they used this for political purposes."[36]

Wildrose leader Brian Jean vehemently denied Swann's remarks, saying, "The population has whipped the Wildrose into action."[37] But later, Jean had to go to social media himself to try and quell the escalating insults and threats toward the premier, some of which had appeared on his own Facebook comment section a few days earlier. "Over the last few days, I've seen far too many hateful and even violent social media posts directed toward our political opponents," wrote Jean on his Facebook page. "This needs to stop. These kinds of comments cross all bounds of respect and decency and have absolutely no place in our political discourse. This is not how Albertans behave."[38]

Security expert Neil LeMay told CBC News on December 12, 2015, that such threats are investigated. A former deputy chief of security for ex-premier Alison Redford, LeMay has had considerable experience investigating the authors of anonymous posts. He states that they are usually easy to find. "In the security industry we view most people who make threats as what we call 'howlers,' individuals who have no intention of carrying out their threats. The problem for law enforcement, though, is that among all these 'howlers' are what we call 'hunters.' Individuals who can pose a very real and significant danger to a public official."[39]

The premier's chief of staff, Brian Topp, calls the online abuse faced by Notley and her team "the worst I've ever seen. I've taken a close look at all of this as I've been concerned about it and how we operate as government." He's also concerned about those who seem "profoundly disturbed. Some of what they write makes you feel sorry for them and worry about the community around them. It speaks to the need for doing a better job on mental health issues." Topp differentiates those from the "thread among the populist right where some individuals engage in behaviour that rises where it should be of interest to the police. The RCMP, Edmonton and Calgary police services, and sheriffs are doing a good job to manage it. When we see crimes committed by these people, our task is to make sure law enforcement sees it, and then get out of the way to let them do their work." Topp worries that "we're heading for an uncurated political culture. The political discourse once framed in newspapers and curated by owners is no more."

In a sense, it's a social media range war where the vilest scoundrels meet at the online corral for a vicious shoot-out.

The premier tried to soften the madness erupting on social media. "I have a security unit. I'm told that none of what has occurred thus far with me is in any way, shape, or form out of the ordinary. I rely on them to do their job. I'm very confident that that's what's happened. I think it's a part of being premier in almost any day and age. It is what it is. Politics is politics; people have opinions."[40]

Notley looks at social media through the perspective of a politician who has never operated in a world without online commentary run rampant. As such, she sees a number of distinct impacts. "I think it's continuing to evolve. The notion of people being able to say things anonymously, I suppose, is a problem. I've never been in power before social media and so don't know what to compare it to. It brings about both a democratization of the process, as well as loosening up the rules a bit around how people engage with each other. It has both good and negative outcomes."

The premier continues: "From my perspective, even in the middle of Bill 6, I can count on half of one hand the number of times I have personally been presented with somebody who has been even remotely rude to me. When I'm travelling about or out, people are ambivalent or kind, since I've been elected, even with the economy being what it is, and our missteps on Bill 6, twice. I walk around my community and visit with neighbours and still do a lot of things I used to do before, so I don't know that what people are actually thinking is that different. I just think that we're seeing a different part of people, and a different part of society. I don't think it means that the collective approach is that different."

Most bullies are weak and fear face-to-face confrontation. That's the appeal of social media, where the online rumble allows the bully protective cover. It's a perfect forum for community cowards who prefer to hide their hateful rants in the darkness. It's the opposite of the legitimate critical debate that marks a vibrant democracy and respects those with opposing views.

Certainly, Notley was trying to cool the political cauldron of hate by downplaying the threats against her and equating them to those received by other politicians. She wanted to lower the temperature of the discourse — another more female approach to power. The late U.K. Prime Minister Margaret Thatcher was also noted for her skill in building bridges in order to push forward her agenda (although she could be fierce on the attack as well). No matter what devices female leaders use, however, they face vile sexual attacks on social media that powerful men never have to endure.

When comments of an unspeakably violent nature directed toward powerful women remain alive on credible sites, those prone to violence feel empowered. The consequences go beyond an endorsement of acts of violence, making recruitment of good women candidates more difficult. Women see the reality of bullying and the larger-scale abuse in modern politics. The legislatures that represent the pinnacle of democratic debate should not be a place where the cycle of abuse against women is routinely amplified. While it's hard to monitor social media action, whether on Facebook, Twitter, or Instagram, it's critical that elected politicians and their leaders do their utmost to break the cycle on any of their own feeds.

"We see nastiness that is directed at politicians all of the time, and they deal a lot with that. It's the level of the nastiness that's directed toward women, particularly the NDP in this case, that we find to be rather alarming. Not surprising, but certainly alarming," Melanee Thomas told CBC News.[41] The assistant professor of political science at the University of Calgary called the online sexual attacks "a whole class of crap that men in politics don't have to think about, much less address."

Michelle Bellefontaine of CBC News reported on Alberta Environment Minister Shannon Phillips receiving a despicable tweet from a coward who threatened to kick her in the face multiple times. Phillips said, "This is ridiculous. This is my work. This is my workplace, and there are some things that are just inappropriate."

Federal Environment Minister Catherine McKenna is also disgusted over similar Twitter violence that she faces as a woman. "No matter your political leanings, the vitriol unleashed against female politicians on @twitter is unacceptable," @cathmckenna tweeted. "Honestly, it sucks."

Federal Conservative MP Michelle Rempel strongly agreed, retweeting in caps @MichelleRempel, "YES. THIS."

New Democrat Deborah Drever, who had experienced particularly nasty online violence, invited her legislative colleagues to help stop the hate. Her member's statement on June 1, 2016, explained the extent of the harassment and how all high-profile women in political careers or others must endure such "hateful comments. They're nasty, gender-based, and demeaning. They are not constructive, and it's no wonder so many women fear choosing politics as their career. In no way do they provide a constructive conversation on policy or political action."[42]

Drever pointed out how quickly online hate escalates. "Name-calling, violent messages, rape, sexual assault, and even the threat of targeting family members are sent through online threats to feminists regularly." She asked all MLAs to "respect us and treat us with dignity and equality."

She received a standing ovation from MLAs of all parties.

Social media threats against women venture into dark alleys that no woman politician should have to walk. Rempel is consistently targeted because of her looks as well as her politics. As a politician, Rempel says she expects and can handle criticisms that result from her political beliefs. "I know there are going to be people that disagree with my political philosophy or say things to me that are sexist or even name calling, whatever. To me it's a different fear when you're actively threatening my person with violence," the Calgary MP told the *National Post*'s Ashley Csanady.[43]

But when the Twitter harassment turned criminal with appalling threats of violence, rape, and murder, Rempel went to the police. "It was really quite frightening, and the appropriate route was to take it to the RCMP," says Rempel. "It doesn't matter if somebody is making a threat to someone or proposing violence to someone to their face or in a different medium, it's still unacceptable."

For months Rempel endured the Twitter-torment quietly, and then the case went to court. One of the more active MPs on social media, Rempel kept the case and her personal feelings to herself. That's not surprising. Predators love to see the effects of their criminality on their victims, especially when those victims are high profile. The accused was convicted of criminal harassment and uttering threats.

MOST TWITTER CRITICISMS don't cross the 140-character limit into violence and criminality. What they do manage to trip over regularly is the clear line that separates civility from misogyny. It always seems open season on a woman politician, and especially her outward appearance.

Women in politics are subjected to such intense personal scrutiny that, given all the other hurdles to running, it's a wonder they don't give politics a pass. A woman's weight is tossed around the political court like a basketball. Her every wrinkle, whether on her clothes or face, receives more concentrated attention and commentary than the creases of a comparable man. Women are criticized for putting on weight, but men seldom are. Social media make it much worse.

Earlier, PC board member Jordan Lien posted an offensive tweet mocking the weight of Health Minister Sarah Hoffman. On June 1, 2015, Lien did apologize for his "insensitivity," but he should have known better. Men in politics should be the first to empathize with what women politicians have to go through. After all, they too can experience the sharp end of Twitter, though scarcely to such a piercing degree.

That's why the "suit experiment" devised by Coquitlam, B.C., Mayor Richard Stewart was so refreshing and revealing. When he ran for re-election in late 2014, Stewart decided to wear his off-the-rack, dark blue suit every single day until someone noticed. No one did. This continued for fifteen months, beyond the election season and far into his term as mayor.

Stewart pointed out the difference between the way he was perceived and the way a woman would be. "If a woman shows up to two all-candidates' meetings wearing the same outfit, she will receive emails. 'Your outfit looks frumpy.' 'What were you thinking with your hairdo.' That sort of thing," said Stewart to Tristin Hopper of the *National Post*.[44] Stewart had read about Karl Stefanovic, an Australian TV host who wore the same suit for a year. As the Coquitlam mayor's experiment dragged on beyond the election and then longer than a year, his suit somehow managed to get dry-cleaned only six times in the fifteen months. That in itself would tarnish a woman.

"All I'm looking for is that we end these inadvertent barriers that tend to keep women out of public life," Stewart told Hopper. "I think we need to get past that so that my daughters can be judged on how well they do their job rather than what they wore."

The suit experiment was refreshing progress from a front-page piece in the *Ottawa Citizen* in 1998. "Alexa McDonough, Call Your Dry-Cleaner," was the headline blazing below a picture of the former federal NDP leader. "The main point of this front-page column was that she had worn the same dress to two different events in the same week," wrote Queen's University political science professor Elizabeth Goodyear-Grant.[45]

In mid-June 2016, Premier Kathleen Wynne told *Globe and Mail* columnist Jane Taber that there is "so much pressure on women from the time we are little about the way we look." Taber noted, "It doesn't get any easier as a politician."

For women, the personal still remains political: *what they wear, how's their hair, and most of all, do they care?* Of course, with high-definition cameras and TV, all politicians want to look as presentable as they can. But for women, comments on their appearance too often go far beyond respectful suggestions. Make-over tips often mask blatant misogyny. Behind these comments is an attitude that women are only suitable for one thing: sex. Female politicians struggle to get their views considered, and social media, especially Twitter, constantly amplify the trivial and superficial. Many women in politics find themselves under the micro-scope for all the wrong reasons. Are they married or single, dating or not? Implicit is the question of whether they are available.

For the female politician, too little has changed since Agnes Macphail became the first woman elected to the House of Commons in 1921. "The misery of being under observation and being unduly criticized is what I remember most," Macphail wrote.[46] At one of her tormentors, Macphail hurled a comeback of Churchillian quality. When an MP asked, "Doesn't the honourable member wish she were a man?" she replied: "Doesn't the honourable gentleman wish *he* was?"[47]

With their personal lives under such scrutiny, it's no wonder marriages fail and some elected women forgo dating. "There are very few men who can stand the stress. There are very few men who could even date a female Cabinet minister. When you go into a room, you just take all the oxygen out. You're the one everyone wants to talk to," said Iona Campagnolo, a minister in Pierre Trudeau's Liberal government.[48]

AND YET, THERE is slow progress, accelerated by the breakthrough of Notley's caucus. The number of women in Canadian legislatures has increased, with Alberta now ranking third in the country thanks to the 47 percent female membership in the NDP caucus. The failure of the other parties, especially Wildrose and the defeated PCs, brought Alberta down to 32 percent overall. Ontario has 34.4 percent women in its legislature, while British Columbia tops all provinces with 36.4 percent female members. Significantly, all three provinces are led by women premiers.

Just a few years ago Canada had achieved gender parity among its provincial premiers, but with the resignation of some and the electoral defeat of others, only Ontario's Kathleen Wynne and British Columbia's Christy Clark were still in power when newcomer Notley became premier.

Only two provinces in Canada, Alberta and British Columbia, can claim two women premiers. Notley was the second elected female premier of Alberta, after Progressive Conservative Alison Redford, who won in 2011 and 2012. When Rita Johnston won the leadership of the governing B.C. Social Credit Party in July 1991, she automatically became the premier, the first woman to hold that position in Canada. In November that year Johnston and her party went down to defeat. In March 2011 Liberal leader Christy Clark became the second woman premier of British Columbia. She won a second term in 2013, although she lost her own riding and had to regain a seat in a by-election.

After Johnston's B.C. victory in 1991, Nellie Cournoyea of the Northwest Territories became the second woman premier in Canada that same year. She was followed by Prince Edward Island's Catherine Callbeck in 1993; the Yukon's Pat Duncan in 2000; Nunavut's Eva Aariak in 2008; and Newfoundland and Labrador's Kathy Dunderdale, first elected in 2010 and re-elected in 2011. Also elected in 2011 were British Columbia's Clark and Alberta's Redford; Quebec's Pauline Marois became premier in 2012 and Redford was re-elected the same year. Ontario's Kathleen Wynne won the leadership of the Ontario Liberal Party in 2013, automatically becoming premier. Clark was re-elected in British Columbia that same year, and Alberta's Notley won in 2015. As of 2016 there remain only four provinces in Canada that have yet to elect a woman premier: Nova Scotia, New Brunswick, Manitoba, and Saskatchewan. The notion that female leaders couldn't win was proved decisively wrong as voters across Canada showed they were ready to accept women as premiers. Indeed, Canada already had its first female prime minister, Kim Campbell, in 1993. All of the challenges and hard work of the women before them allowed new leaders like Notley to open the door of power, and push past the prejudice.

AS THE GENDER makeup of governments in Canada changes, the culture of government changes too. Formerly marginalized issues get attention, in part because the presence of more women in Canada's parliament and in provincial legislatures encourages female legislators to come forward with their ideas — and their stories.

The tender topic of abortion gets filtered through a powerfully female lens. In a tweet, NDP MLA Marie Renaud asked PC leadership hopeful Jason Kenney whether he was pro-choice or not. In a second tweet, Renaud revealed she had an abortion twenty years earlier and was thankful she was able to do so. The question was crucial because Kenney, as premier, would have direct power over abortion service that he didn't possess in Parliament, which sets the law but leaves health care delivery to the provinces. Kenney is widely assumed not to be pro-choice. When questioned, he routinely says that in twenty years as an MP he never gave a speech or presented a motion on abortion. Renaud's point was that strategic silence in the House of Commons could become action in the premier's office. This was quickly noted by many female PCs whose support Kenney will need.[49]

In another startling example of women feeling enabled to tell their stories, B.C. Premier Christy Clark revealed her harrowing escape from a childhood sexual assault. She was prompted by questions about her sudden support for an opposition Green Party bill to prevent sexual violence in British Columbia's post-secondary schools.

She was just thirteen and heading to her first job after school, Clark wrote in a June 9, 2016, column for Postmedia, when "a man suddenly jumped out, grabbed me, and pulled me out of sight into a deep copse of shrubs. When he pulled me down the little slope, it must have shifted him off balance. He loosened his grip for a moment, giving me a chance to wriggle away, clamber a few feet forward, and get out of the bush."[50]

And then she ran "like the wind," to her job — and silence. She told nobody — not at work, home, or school. In speaking to friends as she thought about telling her story, she said, it became clear to her that almost every woman had a similar experience, many far worse. "Our silence makes it easier for those who wish to harm us," she said. "We don't share our stories."

Clark's decision to speak challenged that impulse to secrecy. Victims of abuse can begin to feel empowered as they discard the shroud of silence. When a female premier speaks, with all the authority of her office behind her, the victims past and present finally have a voice. This shows how the numbers at the ballot box can change the will of the government at large to make such critical social issues primary government business.

Clark still regrets her silence. The thing that bothers her most about what happened, she concluded in her article, was "not knowing if the man who pulled me into the bushes kept going until he caught a girl who couldn't get away."

Clark's confession and her government's actions on sexual vio lence are significant, but such progressive actions remain some- what exceptional in Canadian politics. The words and deeds of many male-dominated governments (not to mention those of men outside of government) often show little real support for women who serve in gov- ernment. The reality is, it still isn't much easier for women to navigate the system once they get into government. Premier Wynne's reception in the Alberta legislature in May 2016 proved quite clearly that some men still have a hard time with women in power.

After an honoured guest is presented, the traditional legislative hos- pitality is to stand and applaud. Yet when Premier Wynne was warmly introduced to the legislature by Premier Notley on May 26, 2016, half of the Wildrose caucus did not offer the cordial greeting. Wildrose leader Brian Jean certainly knew about the generosity of Ontarians in the face of Fort McMurray's devastating fire. He experienced it firsthand. The prov- ince had sent firefighters, donations, and other aid to Jean's home city. Wynne herself had been gracious and sympathetic. If only for that reason, the whole legislature should have erupted in generous applause.

Instead, Wildrose allowed its most belligerent member, Derek Fildebrandt, to launch an inappropriate rebuke of Wynne and her prov- ince's finances while she watched from the gallery.

Many women thought there was a touch of sexism about this sight of an angry man shouting at one female premier while insulting another. This isn't wholly surprising since Wildrose itself is a classic case of gender imbalance; at that time the party had twenty male MLAs and only two females.

When the leader and half of his Wildrose caucus refused to extend common courtesy, they displayed a disturbing throwback to a past when women were an anomaly in government. It looked like an all-new episode of Notley-Nation-meets-*Mad-Men* Alberta style.

News of the Wildrose behaviour travelled quickly across the nation. "Instead of praise, Ms. Wynne was treated to an ugly, classless, partisan attack by the Wildrose Party and its lead pitbull, Derek Fildebrandt," wrote the *Globe and Mail*'s Gary Mason.[51]

In a statement to the Alberta legislature, interim PC leader Ric McIver said that "members who cannot bring themselves to live up to the most minimum levels of respect and courtesy for democracy, maybe ... ought to consider if this is really where they want to work."[52]

McIver's considered remarks and the Wildrose's ill-considered performance only reinforce the sharp divide between the two conservative parties. With Notley's New Democrats, there is no wavering on legislative protocol, regardless of political belief.

Until the Official Opposition's primarily male caucus works to grasp basic legislative decorum, perhaps Wildrose should use its day of embarrassment as a lesson and encourage enlightened female supporters to run for office. More women in the Wildrose caucus would lower the testosterone that sometimes appears to replace sensible leadership.

NOTLEY'S ELECTION LED to a change in both the tone as well as the direction of the debate over the province and its future. Her toppling of the PC dynasty prompted *Canadian Business* magazine to put Notley at the top of "The Power 50: Canada's Most Powerful Business People 2016."[53] It is the first time a woman has led the list and points to how important Notley's role is to Canada's as well as Alberta's economic performance and future. It was at just such a critical economic moment that former premier Peter Lougheed managed to forge a new role for Alberta in Canada. Notley will need Lougheed's fortitude and skill to manoeuvre the province out of its economic malaise and into a better place. But she'll do it with a far different style than any of her male predecessors.

CHAPTER 9

UNEASY ALLIES

After long decades of Progressive Conservative rule, there were many things Albertans had never imagined they'd see in the province's political life. One was the election of an NDP provincial government. Another was a friendly alliance between the NDP and a Liberal federal government led by a Trudeau. To Alberta's conservative traditionalists it seemed like a plot torn from a dystopian novel. And yet Albertans themselves effected the first change, and they played a significant role in the second. Of all the consequences, the most important was the new NDP-Liberal alignment on issues of major national importance.

AT THE MALL deep within Calgary's northeast Skyview riding, the parking lots were gridlocked but people kept swarming in on foot. Some were there Sunday shopping for fabrics, foods, spices, and sweets not always available at other big-box stores. But most were walking to the Magnolia Banquet Hall and its cordoned-off lot that was packed with more than a thousand Liberal supporters waving signs and chanting "Justin! Justin! Justin!" Inside the hall at least another thousand waited for the Liberal leader to speak, shake hands, and pose for selfies.

The enthusiasm was almost beyond memory for the federal Liberal Party in Calgary; it had last elected an MP from the city in 1968, in the first flush of original Trudeaumania. The city's reconciliation with the Liberals was temporary — the MP, Patrick Mahoney, lost his seat four years later, by 16,000 votes.

This crowd was a cross-section of Canada's history, diversity, and ethnic pride. When Trudeau appeared the crowd roared. That would continue for the next ninety minutes, broken by a joyous singing of "Happy Birthday." It was Xavier Trudeau's eighth birthday, and Trudeau held up his cellphone so his eldest son, with wife Sophie Grégoire Trudeau, could hear. It would also have been Xavier's late grandfather Pierre Elliott Trudeau's birthday. Canada was a day away from the national election on October 19, 2015, and Trudeau was still campaigning, in Edmonton, and then Calgary, before moving on to Vancouver for a final stop. A few wins in Alberta would provide cross-Canada political representation that had long eluded the national Liberals. Trudeau had worked hard to make it happen, with several campaign trips to the province, including three in Calgary.

"Alberta is important to me," the hoarse leader told the jubilant throng, as people pressed closer. "It matters deeply, and that's a message I've been delivering for years. I'm here to say it again on the last day before we vote. It's a message that I'm proud to deliver here with a big smile, as a Liberal, as a Trudeau and as a Quebecker."[1]

He was repeatedly interrupted when he said: "I know that it's time to bring this country together. So let me hear you: Alberta matters; Quebec matters; Canada matters." After urging the volunteers to get all voters to the polls the next day, he headed back inside the hall to talk with more supporters. But many people in the crowd outside didn't budge, hoping to get a final glimpse of the man. At the back of the building another crowd formed, as security guards gently urged them aside to allow Trudeau's bus to inch away from the door. Trudeau stood at the front window waving and smiling all the way to the closed-off street.

The welcome was a clear sign that something big was happening. This was the home of Prime Minister Stephen Harper, and the city had been so safe a Conservative haven that Harper rarely needed to campaign personally.

Trudeau got the kind of increasingly warm welcome Rachel Notley had received in Calgary leading up to the provincial election. Trudeau's Edmonton stop was just as jubilant and reminiscent of the late-campaign enthusiasm for Notley. Political blogger Dave Cournoyer conjured an earlier Trudeaumania triggered by Justin's father. Cournoyer compared "the energy" of the Justin Trudeau crowd to that of Notley's last large Edmonton push at the end of her provincial campaign.[2] Political scientist Duane Bratt, the chair of Mount Royal University's department of economics, justice, and policy studies, notes that "Notley and Trudeau ran similar campaigns in the sense that they were very positive campaigns. That was a striking feature."

Calgary Mayor Naheed Nenshi sensed the seismic political change about to roll through the province and country. "In the end, people saw Rachel Notley and went, 'she's pragmatic; she's going to try and do things differently and let's give her a chance.' In the federal election you saw something similar where people said, 'Justin Trudeau explains and he's been open. He's a straight-shooter.'"

Popular Conservative MP and former minister Michelle Rempel saw a similar phenomenon when she knocked on doors in her Calgary Nose Hill federal riding. She was getting an early start on the looming national race, right in the middle of the Alberta provincial campaign "I said we were with the federal Conservatives and I heard many people say, 'I'm so tired of politics. I want a fresh face.'" In the end, that change won the Alberta NDP an unprecedented fifteen of twenty-five Calgary seats.

By the federal election five months later, Rempel handily won her own riding and the province remained overwhelmingly Conservative, in part because many voters were unwilling to risk more change after the first months of a very different, highly activist new provincial government. But the Liberal victory count — two seats in Calgary, two more in Edmonton — was still a coup in Canada's conservative heartland.

While Trudeau was spending the election eve in Stephen Harper's political backyard, campaigning for Canada's future, Harper was indulging in a blast from the past. By choosing to spend his last large public event with Rob Ford and his brother Doug, Harper was betting that their appeal to the Conservative base might attract enough voters to tip crucial Toronto seats in his favour. He may also have decided to spend time with old friends, one of whom, Rob, was ill with stage four cancer and would pass away six months later on March 22, 2016. Yet Harper's final campaign days with the Fords seemed, on the surface, an act of desperation by a man staring defeat in the face.

Trudeau, like Notley, spent the election campaign working hard to reach out to new voters. At the same moment Harper and the Conservatives seemed to turn their backs on many Canadians they had courted before they held their majority. With Jason Kenney as the point man for relations with ethnic communities, the Conservatives had worked a minor political miracle by replacing the Liberals as the fallback party for many new Canadians. But in the 2015 election the party's empathy for issues important to various groups died a very public death.

Before the election writ was even dropped, Harper appeared to abandon the new Canadian vote by vehemently opposing Muslim women wearing the niqab during Canadian citizenship ceremonies. Calling the practice "rooted in a culture that is anti-women," Harper said it "was unacceptable to Canadians, unacceptable to Canadian women."[3]

Yet it was acceptable, and to one woman in particular, Zunera Ishaq. As a Muslim, she wanted to wear the niqab when she pledged her oath of citizenship, so she fought the federal ban. That sparked a nasty political squabble as Harper and his Conservatives argued for the ban. The Federal Court of Appeal decided in Ishaq's favour, which prompted the Conservative Cabinet to challenge the ruling at the Supreme Court while asking the Federal Court to stay its decision. The entire legal imbroglio ended after Trudeau's Liberal election victory.

During the election campaign, Harper also suggested that the Conservatives could introduce legislation banning the niqab within the federal civil service. When Justin Trudeau talked about a culture of fear and a backlash against Muslim women wearing the face-covering, he wasn't spouting rhetoric. There were troubling attacks on niqab-veiled women in Montreal and Toronto. Talking to Chris Hall, host of CBC Radio's *The House*, Trudeau said, "To the prime minister directly: Stop this before someone truly gets hurt. We've had women attacked in the streets for wearing hijabs and niqabs. This is not Canada."[4]

Another startling addition to the Conservative campaign was a plan to launch a "barbaric cultural practices" reporting system, soon dubbed the snitch line. This bizarre snitch pitch offended not only ethnics but many mainstream voters in a multicultural society that promotes equality with dignity. If the plan to report neighbours for dubious cultural traits was so critical to Canada, why wasn't it introduced and debated in Parliament when the Conservatives held power? The emphasis on the niqab, with a snitch line thrown in for bad measure, seemed to run completely against the trend of the Conservative Party's years of courting new Canadians. In an author interview, Kenney said, "I've never commented on the so-called snitch line. It was not my policy. In fact, the national campaign asked me to announce it and I told them I wouldn't. I didn't believe the message was suitable."[5]

In May 2015 the Conservatives introduced Bill C-24, which would give government the power to rescind the citizenship of Canadians convicted of terrorism. Civil rights groups immediately challenged the bill in court. Would marching in a demonstration against this or any other Canadian bill constitute terrorist activity? Would belonging to a non-establishment political party be considered a terrorist act? The concern was that a government could arbitrarily deport a Canadian citizen simply because that person literally marched to a different drum.

Both the Liberals and the NDP announced they would repeal the bill if they were elected. During the Munk Debate on Canada's foreign policy, at Toronto's Roy Thomson Hall on September 28, 2015, Harper accusatorily asked Trudeau, "Why would we not revoke the citizenship of people convicted of terrorist offences against this country?"[6]

A passionate Trudeau immediately shot back, declaring, "A Canadian is a Canadian is a Canadian. And you devalue the citizenship of every Canadian in this place and in this country when you break down and make it conditional for anyone. We have a rule of law in this country and you can't take away the citizenship because you don't like what someone's done. You can't do that."[7]

As Harper quizzed Trudeau, he began by stating that the bill was "put forward by a member of Parliament who is himself an immigrant, Mr. Devinder Shory."[8]

The bill not only irked civil rights groups, it also disturbed immigrants who weren't sure what it meant. Shory, who was up for re-election in the new Calgary Skyview riding that Trudeau himself visited on election eve, couldn't manage to explain it to voters. He didn't participate in an organized debate with others running for the seat, including Liberal Darshan Kang.

Many of the people who came to the Skyview rally in Calgary were furious about the bill, seeing it as an attack on immigrants. Kang told the *Calgary Herald*, "Everybody is hopping mad."[9] He said constituents were also upset by recent changes to immigration policy that capped the number of parents and grandparents who could come to Canada.

Kang defeated Shory in the election. Afterward, incumbent Conservative MP Deepak Obhrai told the *Calgary Herald* that he felt Bill C-24 was a factor in Shory's defeat. Obhrai, whose Calgary Forest Lawn riding abuts Kang's Skyview, had abstained from voting on Bill C-24 on its third reading.

"I did oppose Bill C-24 so it never became an issue in my riding," he said. "I am one of the very few. Now I can say it," said Obrai, adding that he was "taken to task" for doing so. "My immediate concern was on human rights issues. I do not believe any government has a right to take citizenship away. Anything that needs to be addressed for a crime should be applying equally to all Canadians."[10]

Obrahi was even more explicit in early April 2016, calling out his party for becoming an "elitist, white-only club."[11] The Conservatives had increased party membership fees to $25 and doubled the amount leadership hopefuls must put down, to $100,000. "When you put $100,000 for a leadership, you are only attracting the rich, and guess what, most of them [members of ethnic communities] would be, believe it or not, excellent candidates but again, the impression will be whites only," Obrahi told the *Huffington Post*'s Althia Raj. "And I'm the guy who worked my butt off to attract everybody and make the Conservatives a party for all."

Pitting citizens against each other by using immigration and ethnicity as emotional wedges in what should have been a mainstream election was extraordinarily ill-conceived for multicultural Canada. Political scientist Dr. Roger Gibbins, a professor emeritus with the University of Calgary and former CEO of the Canada West Foundation, watched the federal election with concern. "The Conservatives' niqab focus was so strange, because Conservatives had been courting the immigrant voter and doing so very effectively." He wondered "why they turned that around.... The Conservatives didn't have a good campaign, and Justin's contribution to the campaign was dramatic. He won that election."

It was a storyline that sounded very familiar to Alberta voters, who'd seen how government mistakes create the opening for a new leader.

Crushing defeat was hardly what Harper expected when he called the election on August 2, 2015, for October 19. Unlike the previous two election campaigns of thirty-seven days each, this one ran a full seventy-nine days. The extended campaign would allow the Conservatives to swamp the opposition with cash; they had a war chest of $69 million compared to $43 million for the Liberals and $30 million for the NDP.[12]

But the long campaign tried the voters' patience while allowing plenty of time for the Conservative mistakes to play out.

Naheed Nenshi, who as a former marketing professor knows the tactics of segmentation and targeting especially well, says that the federal Conservatives were traditionally strong on "hyper-message control." They were masters at micro-targeting, but in the 2015 federal election they became, in the mayor's view, "a great example of going too far. They have a solid base of 30 percent and they focused on that. It was enough in a competitive three-party race, but when the third party [the NDP] dropped off, it wasn't enough to win. If they wanted to win with 33 percent or 34 percent, that doesn't work anymore."

The bet by the Conservatives was that they would take the centre-right voters while the NDP and Liberals would split the centre-left. They were clearly expecting Justin Trudeau's first campaign as Liberal leader to be a disaster laden with bozo eruptions. Trudeau was "just not ready," the Tory ads said. This perfectly positioned Trudeau to impress people just by appearing routinely capable. But he did much more, showing surprising eloquence and conviction. Many voters decided he was indeed ready. Voters in the big cities began to abandon Thomas Mulcair's flat NDP campaign to back the Liberals.

Darryl Raymaker, former president of the national Liberal Party in Pierre Trudeau's day, had watched the young Trudeau grow into a serious politician. "The Harper government misjudged him. It became one of their profound convictions that he was a lightweight; not his father's son; not cerebral or enigmatic. Their expectations were so low, and it was all hubris on their part. It was a major miscalculation."

This reminded Raymaker of a very similar mistake that happened that spring in Alberta, when Jim Prentice appeared condescending toward Rachel Notley with his "math is difficult" line during the infamous television debate. "It was the same thing, the arrogance of power. All political parties make those mistakes, as do their leaders, eventually."

According to Michelle Rempel, "when the electorate wants change, there's not a lot you can do. In the federal election we were at the end of a ten-year mandate. Any leader of any party has a best-before date."

While Alberta remained a federal Conservative stronghold, Trudeau's persistence nonetheless bore fruit. He matched his father's seat count, with four. The new MPs were Kang of Calgary Skyview, Kent Hehr in Calgary Centre, Amarjeet Sohi in Edmonton Mill Woods, and Randy Boissonnault in Edmonton Centre. For the third time, NDP incumbent Linda Duncan was triumphant in Edmonton Strathcona. Because the NDP and the Liberals split the vote, the Conservatives were able to ride up the middle in several ridings. "In terms of Alberta, the Conservative support has really held from the fact that the Trudeau wave resulted in a split," MacEwan University Professor Chaldeans Mensah told Dean Bennett of the Canadian Press.[13]

The last time Alberta elected a Liberal MP had been 2004, when Edmonton returned its two incumbents: Anne McLellan and David Kilgour.

Trudeau's father won in 1968 with Mahoney in Calgary, Hu Harries in Edmonton, Allen Sulatycky in Rocky Mountain, and Bud Olson in Medicine Hat. They were all defeated the next time around, and Alberta didn't find any Liberal love to send to Ottawa until 1993, when Edmonton elected four Liberal MPs: Anne McLellan, John Loney, Judy Bethel, and David Kilgour, who had defected from the Progressive Conservatives to the Liberals in 1990.

"Edmonton is a little more generous toward Liberals, probably because the city is less dominated by the oil industry," says Raymaker. McLellan and Kilgour continued their run until 2006, although Kilgour relinquished his Liberal colours to sit as an independent in 2005.

Another famous Alberta floor-crosser from the Progressive Conservatives to the Liberals was Jack Horner, who became minister of industry, trade, and commerce in Trudeau's 1977 Cabinet. Horner lost that post when he went down to defeat in the 1979 election that pushed the short-term PC government of Albertan Joe Clark to victory.

The 1980s Liberal drought in Alberta was directly related to Pierre Trudeau's introduction of the National Energy Program on October 28, 1980. By attempting to make Canada self-sufficient in energy, the NEP tried to hold the Canadian price for oil and gas below the world price, while imposing federal taxes that Alberta considered unconstitutional. Alberta premier Peter Lougheed was furious and determined to fight Pierre Trudeau's paternalistic cash grab. The nation was already living through high inflation and interest rates, but Alberta suffered even more with massive unemployment. It was a time when the jobless just packed up their belongings and then walked away from unmanageable mortgages. In 1984 the new Progressive Conservative government of Brian Mulroney removed the NEP. By then the global recession had passed, and the gesture was interpreted as a political nod to Alberta.

Throughout the 2015 federal campaign, when there was a whiff of an NEP question, Justin Trudeau replied: "I will never use western resources to try to buy eastern votes."[14] Rachel Notley's chief of staff Brian Topp believes that Trudeau "is determined he will not end his prime ministership as estranged from western Canada as his father was." Topp notes that Justin Trudeau spent a lot of his life in British Columbia and knows western Canada quite well. "All evidence is that he is not going to lead his party to the kind of political results that his father did, so that there were essentially no Liberals elected in western Canada."

ON OCTOBER 19, 2015, when Justin Trudeau's Liberals won 184 out of 338 seats, over 69 percent of Canadians voted. It was the highest turnout since 1993, when another Liberal, Jean Chrétien, defeated Brian Mulroney's Conservatives. In 2015 many millennials were determined to make a change, and Statistics Canada bears this out. Voter turnout of those between ages eighteen and twenty-four rose 12 percentage points in 2015 from 2011.[15] For those between ages twenty-five and thirty-four, there was an 11 percent jump from the 2011 to the 2015 election.

"You were especially seeing younger people getting out to vote. You also saw that in Naheed Nenshi's election" in Calgary 2010, says Minister of Veterans Affairs Kent Hehr. For the federal election, notes Hehr, "there were two million new voters. We got the lion's share of the new voters who showed up. I sense social media had a role to play in that — getting two million more people engaged. But the Conservative vote didn't go down that much."

Harper at least retained his base, which remained at 30 percent. "It's not going anywhere," continues Hehr. "And I'd say a good 20 percent are socially conservative either on abortion or LGBTQ issues. So how they move on from this is fraught with peril. The federal Conservatives have the option — follow Stephen Harper or get back to the old PC Party that was slightly to the right of Liberals. Where do the Conservatives go with their base? How do they move from that base and still keep them in the tent?"

Rempel feels the Conservatives have a great opportunity to build, and discounts the social conservative criticism because "every party has extremists. That's not what defines our party. We voted to strike the marriage definition clause from the Conservative constitution by 90 percent. We don't discriminate on sexual orientation. There's lots of room for a centre role for us. The Liberals are far more progressive than they ever have been. I'm keen to see how that rolls out."

It will take the Conservatives more than a leadership contest to determine who they are and where they are going. "In truth, power was a devil's bargain for the Conservatives," notes *National Post* columnist Andrew Coyne. "They won government, but gave up much else: not only their principles, but their freedom, and ultimately their self-respect."[16]

From the big-tent politics of both Brian Mulroney and early Stephen Harper, the Conservatives lost their footing and found a false safety net in the politics of exclusion. Their future lies, as it has in the past, in the centre with a nod to the right. The Conservatives' May 2016 national convention was a welcome walk in that direction with their embrace of same-sex marriage.

Hehr agrees that the federal Liberals were more progressive than the federal New Democrats in the fall 2015 federal election, and more prepared. "When they said 'No' to deficit financing, how can you be any different than Stephen Harper's budget?" he wonders. "They had to form their platform early, because Trudeau was ahead early and it ultimately broke down. And Justin knocked it out of the park on the debate. He was young, dynamic, and thoughtful."

With a truly national mandate and MPs from every province and territory, Trudeau's win became an opportunity for him to work with all thirteen provincial and territorial leaders in the name of national unity — and with one in particular, Rachel Notley. "She is more simpatico with Trudeau's Liberals than any provincial or federal Conservative Party is, but the federal

Liberals have governed more by public-mood windsock than ideological purity," writes Curtis Gillespie for the *Canadian Business* cover story that put Notley at the top of "The Power 50: Canada's Most Powerful Business People 2016." Gillespie threw in this caution: "History suggests Trudeau will welcome Notley onto the bus or throw her under it, on a case-by-case basis."[17]

Gillespie's remark certainly resonated when Trudeau, using "cold, hard mathematics,"[18] selectively offered enhanced employment insurance benefits to many in Alberta, including Calgary, but left out laid-off workers residing in Edmonton and satellite communities. In early April 2016 Alberta Labour Minister Christina Gray told CBC Radio, "This arbitrary cutoff that they've imposed has left us with the situation where Edmonton actually has higher unemployment than some of the regions that were included elsewhere."[19]

Earlier in February Notley had asked Trudeau to ease the EI path for hard-hit Albertans suddenly jobless. He replied with empathy and historical understanding of the province's considerable contribution to the country's coffers. The expectation was that those who were abruptly terminated would find a prime minister who understood their pain. But not for those who worked in northern oil operations but lived in Edmonton. They were simply factored out of the extended EI equation since Edmonton's unemployment rate was lower on average than that of the rest of the province. The number is skewed only because the city also houses a robust provincial civil service as well as major post-secondary institutions.

By mid-May, as Trudeau visited Fort McMurray after the disastrous wildfire there, Ottawa relented. It would henceforth pay extended EI benefits in the Edmonton zone, as well as in southern Saskatchewan and the southern interior of British Columbia, which had also been excluded. The rationale for Alberta was that Edmonton now fit the statistical criteria, but there's no doubt that Notley's lobbying, and her strong relationship with the prime minister, helped win the concession.

Trudeau's temporary misstep over the enhanced EI benefits contrasts sharply with more harmonized efforts alongside Alberta on such issues as the environment and climate change.

"This new government seems to be essentially aligned with the government of Alberta on these issues, and we're engaged where we can see alignment and where we can get results," says Brian Topp. While he's relatively pleased with what they're hearing about committing to projects, Topp points out that "everything looks good in the first months of a government" before budgetary decisions and the like have to be made.

Topp also notes that when the New Democrats got into office, "we pursued a good neighbour policy with Prime Minister Harper. We reached out. Why not think of things we can agree on and see if we can move forward on some of them? We were starting on 'Where do we overlap and where can we work together?' That government was interested in infrastructure and interested in innovation. We had a pretty good conversation with the Harper team about energy competitiveness. We would have pursued that approach if that government had been re-elected. There appears to be more in common and more points of overlap and realignment with this new government than the previous one."

The Canadian ambassador to the United States at that time was Gary Doer, the former Manitoba NDP premier. "The Alberta premier, because of the economic strength even in tough times, has a pretty big megaphone nationally and with whoever is in government. She dealt with the former government and now with the new government. It's all about what Aretha Franklin sang — 'Respect'."

For the most part, Notley says that she and Trudeau get along well. "They were very happy with our climate-leadership plan, quite honestly. That gave them a lot to talk about in Paris. But more than that, we have good relationships. We have good relationships between officials and between political staff. And I've had a chance to have good conversations with the prime minister, and so far so good. I'm pleased with how it's been unfolding."

By naming Notley the most powerful business person in 2016, *Canadian Business* affirmed her critical role in the country's economic future. As Gillespie writes, "we're all at this crossroads together,"[20] and everyone is watching exactly how Notley manages. "Avoiding a pileup will depend on how she handles three things: oil and gas royalties, pipeline development and climate change action. The only problem is that she can't have all three proceed, or succeed, at the same time."

That's absolutely true. Notley has dealt with oil and gas royalties admirably by generally leaving the status quo and admitting that the NDP was wrong in its initial notions. Pipeline development will depend on both her and Trudeau's strong inter-personal and political skills with other premiers and national leaders, and will test the country's future as a nation undivided. Notley's climate-change action policy jump-started Trudeau's national endeavour and brought both the country and the province respect at the United Nations Climate Change Conference held in Paris from November 30 to December 15, 2015.

Notley points out that there's still some work around the royalty revamp that has to be finished, but "we're mostly there. It should not be particularly controversial." Since the principles are already established and much of that work is completed, Notley emphasized that the government is "going to make sure we stick to the issues around transparency and regular reporting."

Notley's climate-change initiative was instrumental to Trudeau's success at the United Nations Climate Change Conference. "The Alberta announcement takes away the biggest barrier Canada has had on climate action," Dale Marshall, national program manager at Toronto's Environmental Defence group, told Ian Austen of the *New York Times*.[21] Just days before the Paris conference, Austen wrote that "in less than a month, Canada has executed a complete about-face on global climate change," noting that the Trudeau government was "trying to make up for lost time." Austen added that Trudeau, with Alberta's New Democrats, "have now moved climate-change policy to the top of the country's political agenda." In particular, Austen singled out Notley's "sweeping new climate change plan," where her announcement included, "somewhat surprisingly," oil sands company CEOs standing alongside environmentalists.[22]

Notley's climate-change leadership plan is so critical that she's directly involved in all the crucial discussions. "Even though we've got a Cabinet committee that deals with it, and we've got a brilliant minister who's leading it, I'm still engaged at least twice a week because there are so many different pieces to it."

Notley acknowledged that "it's a very ambitious piece of work, but one I'm very proud of," especially since the plan pushes forward from what other governments have done. She also points to "the fact that we're getting this done with so much of industry working with us as partners."

The entire process allows Notley, her Cabinet, and related committees to "problem-solve and work through" the myriad pieces. "I think it's going to lay the groundwork for so much more positive opportunities, going forward. I feel pretty good about that, and from a business perspective, most business analysts agree it is the right decision."

Yet her goals can't be completed unless a pipeline gets approved. When it comes to transporting oil to tidewater, Notley has reason to be frustrated.

"The bottom line is that I don't get to make the decision on the pipeline," she states. "All I can do is advocate for it. So when you measure our success on it, the question becomes, 'How well are we advocating?' I have taken a very clear position that I don't believe that grandstanding for the sake of a headline is actually remotely connected to achieving success on it. I've been to enough of these meetings to know that if you can actually have an attentive, thoughtful conversation with these decision-makers you can get them to move. You can get them to the point where they will pick up the phone before they start thinking about doing something that will be problematic. You can get to the point where you modify the approach they're taking in order to keep the thing alive."

Notley points out that there are many ways provincial and federal leaders talk with each other "and make decisions based on the way they engage with each other. So you either have an intelligent, respectable, engaged relationship with those people, or you become a caricature of a spokesperson and you never actually talk effectively about how to reach a real outcome."

When there's a perception that opposing sides remain firm in their place, then solutions aren't possible. A mutual hate-on destroys any attempt at diplomacy and results. "The people who should be coming together to find a solution never do, because there's this narrative out there," continues Notley. "So nobody gets together to say 'No, actually there's lots of ways we can get together and make this work better.'"

Notley chooses talk over silence, diplomacy over disregard, conciliation over confrontation. Where there's a mountain of animosity, Notley grabs her political backpack and starts climbing. As a New Democrat, she's used to barricades that must be removed for dialogue to begin. Whether her climb is full of switchbacks with no end in sight matters less than the talk and the task at hand. She is convinced her approach has far more likelihood of success than that of the previous provincial and federal governments who seemed to be embroiled in dead-end debates over pipelines. She hopes her open dialogue with a Liberal regime will succeed where federal and provincial conservatives so abjectly failed.

"So that's the approach we're taking. I can't guarantee it's going to be successful," Notley explains. "There are legitimate and real political challenges across this country that impact on the pipeline. But I am absolutely convinced that the pipeline is in the best interests of the whole country. And I believe that the prime minister knows that. And I think more of my colleagues provincially are understanding more, and how much this impacts their bottom line too. And so we're just going to push it."

Notley feels that even if someone is critical of the New Democrats and their position on pipelines, "you still go in and talk to them. That is what we're doing. We are expanding the group of people that we are making our case to, across the country." She wants to win on the issue by talking about the merits of the pipeline. Her government's climate-change plan is critical to the pipeline discussion because, among other things, there is now a hard cap on oil sands emissions. The plan gives Notley and her colleagues more credibility and confidence as she broadens her discussions to environmentalists, First Nations, and other stakeholders who've been left out.

"What makes it very easy to do now is to say, 'Listen, this is a pipeline that's shipping product coming from a place where there is a cap. That cap is essentially one-third of what we were previously licensed to produce in terms of emissions,'" Notley adds. She always clarifies the meaning of emissions caps with respect to overall emissions, and the conversation begins. "So when you say that, you can get people to listen to you."

With two of her most ambitious plans either near the goal or at least within range, Notley's opportunity for the hat trick is beyond her immediate control. When it comes to the pipeline, Notley doesn't even have home ice. But she has a game strategy. And in the case of British Columbia, she has a strong bargaining position: a pipeline for a powerline. Notley was very explicit when she spoke from Fort McMurray about British Columbia's quest to sell its surplus electricity to Alberta.

"We're not necessarily going to have that much demand for that much electricity if we can't find someone to sell our product to. We have to get our product to other markets," Notley said. "That just has to happen. It's not separate."[23] The pipeline in particular that Notley wants expanded in British Columbia is Kinder Morgan's Trans Mountain project.

A day earlier, Energy Minister Marg McCuaig-Boyd was equally explicit about British Columbia's hope for the sale of excess electricity. In an email to *National Post* business columnist Claudia Cattaneo, McCuaig-Boyd said, "We'll do what's best for Albertans and Alberta's economy. We won't be buying more power if we can't get our resources to market."[24]

British Columbia premier Christy Clark wants $1 billion from Ottawa to upgrade BC Hydro's grid so its transformers can transport clean electricity to help Alberta "get off their coal habit." Yet if Clark doesn't see the merits of Notley's pipeline quest, there's no incentive for Notley to consider additional electricity from B.C. That's because "Alberta has abundant clean power sources of its own — wind power, solar and cheap natural gas," writes Cattaneo.[25]

Clark is not known for her camaraderie with Alberta premiers, whether Rachel Notley or the PCs' Alison Redford. In particular, the Clark government's throne speech in February 2016 featured an unprovoked attack against Alberta.[26]

Clark's Liberals were laying blame for Alberta's economic woes directly at the doorstop of the previous PC governments, while implying criticism of Albertans at large. That the immediate energy crash was precipitated by a brutal slash in global oil prices mattered not to Clark's government. Nor did the fact that Albertans always know a boom will end, although their soothsaying abilities fail to extend to the minds of Saudi Arabian oil sheikhs who control the output and hence, the price.

As for Notley, she is well aware of the ominous prophecy spoken by former Saudi oil minister Sheikh Zaki Yamani: "The Stone Age did not end for lack of stone, and the Oil Age will end long before the world runs out of oil."[27] Sheikh Yamani also forecast a dramatic drop in price alongside an oil glut.

This awareness underscores both Notley's ambitious plans for Alberta's economic diversification and the simultaneous climate-change strategy that makes Alberta's bitumen more palatable to pipeline critics. "The province has a more diversified petrochemical industry because Peter Lougheed wanted that to happen, and made sure it did," notes Topp. The province's diversification away from petroleum has indeed progressed. Oil and gas constituted 36 percent of the economy in the Ralph Klein era. By 2014 that had dropped to 26 percent. The B.C. premier, though, is unlikely to be swayed by Alberta statistics as she pushes both her hydro and liquid natural gas projects.

Notley has much more on her plate than worrying whether Clark will pounce on her. Every time the price of oil slides by US$1, the Alberta treasury loses $170 million in revenue. Oil topped US$106 per barrel in June 2014, and dramatically dropped below US$27 in February 2016. If that gap were maintained over a full year, the revenue loss would be $11.7 billion. The real-world losses are lower because the extremes are always temporary, but Notley's government still expects oil and gas revenues to be down 90 percent in 2016, to only $1.4 billion. Two years earlier, revenue had totalled nearly $10 billion.

Like the 1986 recession, the 2015–16 one was "directly triggered by the oil price drop. The duration and depth of today's downturn — 'lower for longer' — makes this recession unique," writes *Calgary Herald* columnist Chris Varcoe.[28] But it hasn't yet reached the carnage of 1982–83 where unemployment jumped to 11 percent, while the prime rate rocketed to 21 percent and the National Energy Program wove its own carpet of doom. By spring 2016 the price had climbed back to the US$50 range, but backed off and continued to seesaw into the fall.

That's especially harsh for to the more than 120,000 workers who have lost their jobs to the newest price rout and resulting recession. It's why everyone is watching exactly how Notley plays the most difficult economic hand an Alberta premier has drawn in more than a generation.

"Quite honestly, it's been a series of making a selection from a menu of bad options because we're in that situation right now," Notley stated to reporters. "But the … way we make those choices will continue to be driven by the values that we talked to Albertans about in the last election, which is supporting communities, supporting resilience and giving Albertans the tools to come through this and working together with partners — not by taking a situation and making it worse."[29]

For Notley to successfully complete her term and win another election, she knows exactly what she needs: a pipeline and higher oil prices.

Naturally, she hopes the recession will be history as oil prices rise and her economic diversification has spread the seeds of serious growth. All that will cut deep into Alberta's growing deficit, removing, with global luck, many of the recession's scars. "We'd like to be able to show reversal of that trend with respect to the budget," she states with determination.[30]

"Obviously, we'd like to make progress on the pipeline," she adds, clearly hoping her collaborative strategy interlaced with her climate-change plan successfully persuades those whom her predecessors ignored or incensed. Notley's climate initiative, with its carbon tax, is the centrepiece of her government. She is unequivocally committed to its success and absolutely considers it quid pro quo for a pipeline.

"On the chess board that's the big play," says Mount Royal University political analyst David Taras. "Her carbon tax is the largest piece. It changes the culture and changes the economy. For her it means we will no longer be seen as an international joke in environmental policy. We will be leaders in Canada. In exchange she hopefully changes the larger political culture and brings allies on board as she fights for the pipeline. In so doing, she's been extremely eloquent."

But everything still depends on federal Cabinet approval of major pipelines. Trudeau invited Notley to a Liberal Cabinet retreat late April in Alberta's Kananaskis Country. There she spoke about her climate plan alongside the need for a pipeline. Although there is still a remarkable alignment with Trudeau, some federal ministers, especially those from Central Canada, are nervous about the pipeline agenda. One thing Notley knew going in to the closed-door session was that her province's climate-change plan hadn't been absorbed by the federal Liberals. She did her best to explain that it's real, not for show, and it could be sold to their constituents.

Notley won't retreat from this because it's not just about Alberta. It's a critical component to a national climate-change strategy. No matter how incensed anyone at home gets about the carbon tax, this is the core of Notley's national strategy. The document she gave to every Cabinet member states this explicitly: "By taking strong and meaningful action on climate change, Alberta intends to improve its environmental reputation and gain national support for new pipeline infrastructure that will benefit the entire country."[31]

She received a friendly reception. Federal ministers appear to both respect and like her. They know too that she and Trudeau get along well. "They were really lovely in there," she said afterward.

THAT EPISODE WAS certainly far more amicable than the disastrous 2016 federal NDP convention held in Edmonton two weeks earlier, from April 8 to 10. In one wacky weekend the federal party managed to mangle itself into immobility by overthrowing its leader and annoying the most successful New Democrat in the country, Notley. The *Game of Thrones* take-down of Thomas Mulcair was humiliating to even the most hardened of politicos. *National Post* columnist Colby Cosh referred to "watching Tom Mulcair get ice-picked live in Edmonton,"[32] a wickedly apt reference to Leon Trotsky's elimination by a Stalin henchman.

The blood-letting began with the Leap Manifesto, whose intent is to eliminate fossil fuels. It encourages a dramatic economic move to renewable energy and transfer of ownership to community rather than private interests. It includes a moratorium on pipeline development and tanker traffic. Championed by author Naomi Klein and her husband, filmmaker Avi Lewis, Leap was a provocation unleashed in the heart of the country's oil patch. The intense regional hostility at the conference was underscored by the indifference of some delegates toward the tens of thousands of workers whose lives have been torn asunder by oil patch layoffs. At the same time, aerospace workers in Central Canada were offered the traditional NDP empathy. One angry Albertan told delegates that they care about workers, as long as they aren't from Alberta.

After the delegates had departed from the plains of Edmonton, Alberta Federation of Labour leader Gil McGowan blasted the Leap patrons. "I'm spitting angry. These downtown Toronto political dilettantes come to Alberta and track their garbage across our front lawn," he told CBC Radio's *Edmonton AM*. "They didn't give any thought to the political problems they're creating for the NDP in Alberta. They didn't give any credit for the work the Alberta government has been doing on climate change," which McGowan called "the best climate-change policies in the country, bar none."[33]

When McGowan said the Leap aficionados "just handed a big stick to the Wildrose and the PCs,"[34] the opposition parties were waiting in the wings, almost with glee at the national NDP arrogance and indifference to the one successful New Democrat government in the country.

Wildrose leader Brian Jean immediately called out "the radical anti-Alberta resolution that was passed today by the federal NDP."[35] In his release, he specifically attacked Notley who, he said, "sold her carbon tax, coal industry shutdown and a cap on oilsands development to Albertans with the promise that it would provide the credibility we need to get opponents of pipelines on board — that these policies would get 'social license.' Today, Premier Notley's social license experiment was put to the test and it failed. She wasn't able to get her own party's delegates, in her home city, to drop their opposition to getting Alberta's resources to market."

Notley was clearly annoyed with the Leap crew when she spoke to reporters. "The Government of Alberta repudiates the sections of that document that address energy infrastructure. These ideas will never form any part of our policy. They are naive, they are ill-informed, and they are tone-deaf."[36]

A day earlier, when she addressed the national NDP convention, Notley received a standing ovation. "We're not making a choice between the environment and the economy. We are building the economy," she told the delegates. "I'm asking you to leave here more persuaded than perhaps some of us have been, that it is possible for Canada to have a forest industry, to have an agriculture industry, a mining industry, and yes, an energy industry, while being world leaders on the environment."[37]

In her speech, Notley was clearly repudiating Mulcair's comments to CBC's Peter Mansbridge, in which the federal NDP leader promised to follow the wishes of his party if it passed a resolution to leave fossil fuel in the ground.

The crazy thing about the whole convention is that each of the big three NDP stars, former Ontario NDP leader Stephen Lewis, deposed federal leader Mulcair, and Alberta premier Notley, received rousing applause after a barn-burning speech where each completely refuted the other two. Lewis, father of Avi and a huge Leap supporter, was completely at odds with Notley. At least both knew what they believed in. Mulcair, seemingly dynamic at one point and hapless at the next, appeared unsure of what he stood for, except staying on as leader.

After welcoming Notley so warmly, the very next day the federal party voted to consider an agenda exactly opposite to what she was talking about, but completely simpatico with Stephen Lewis, Avi Lewis, and Naomi Klein. In the end the speeches revealed a national party utterly and perhaps irrevocably divided. A shaken Mulcair later hinted to Radio Canada's *Tout le monde en parle* that his defeat was somehow connected to the convention's Edmonton venue.[38]

Rather than looking to Alberta as the source of his downfall, Mulcair might consider instead the fate of Flora MacDonald, who ran for the federal Progressive Conservative leadership in 1976. As she surveyed the convention floor, a sea of supporters waved their "Flora" signs and wore their buttons proudly. She looked solid, but after the first ballot was counted, MacDonald was shattered when she finished sixth. All those promises were as thin as the hair of the retiring leader, Robert Stanfield, and her defeat became known as the Flora Syndrome.

The federal NDP rebuke of Rachel Notley and her government seems even more curious, since delegates knew that the only other NDP government in the country, that of Manitoba Premier Greg Selinger, was going down. It fell to Brian Pallister's PCs on April 19, 2016, leaving Notley the lone NDP premier in Canada.

Writing for CBC News, University of Calgary Haskayne School of Business professors Harrie Vredenburg and Tim Marchant argue convincingly that "well meaning activists ignore the unintentional consequence of their pipeline-blocking strategy. Global oil will simply be supplied by higher-carbon oil produced in less regulated markets and transported greater distances to customers. The result is more global GHG emissions instead of less."[39] Armed with her climate-change strategy, Notley deserved far better from the federal New Democrats. That they failed to endorse, if not embrace, how dramatically the province has shifted its focus to an environmental and economic plan that includes a carbon tax is an incongruity that speaks to much greater schisms in Canadian regional relations. It's also why Notley continues to address the "more moderate environmentalists" as she explains Alberta's quest for pipelines for its cleaner oil.

Gary Doer supports Notley's position on pipelines, especially since he approved two pipelines when premier of Manitoba. "Pipelines are more energy efficient and safer than rail. We're in the process of a long transition away from fossil fuels, but it's going to take time. In the interim, we need our fossil fuel mobility in the safest way."

Overall, Doer sees Notley "handling some tough situations very effectively." While it's still early in her tenure, Doer cites the way Notley dealt with "a difficult convention in her own city."

"The premier was very strong, determined, and principled, and there was no equivocation. She did not speak in ambiguities. I don't think pandering is in her DNA." With Doer's decades of experience as both a politician and a diplomat, he has dealt with a multitude of leaders. "The bottom line is that there are a lot of people who agree with Rachel Notley, and I'm one of them." He says unequivocally that Notley is "top-shelf in my view."

After the federal NDP convention, Notley's continued alignment with Trudeau seemed logical. The federal Liberals were elected on a mandate to rebuild the economy. When they consider what they can do to achieve that aim, to create the jobs and income that fuel the federal tax base, the immediate answer is resources. The biggest revenue generator is still oil and gas. Trudeau realizes that if his government pinches off Alberta's access to markets, it won't be able to do what he said it would do, and the economy will shrink.

Getting to a green economy will take a decade or more as technology is created and refined to make renewables the new generator. The great irony here is that oil and gas revenue will be used to gradually put the sector out of business as that cash goes into green industries. Fossil fuel will fund the competition to finish it off. For now, though, getting product to tidewater is essential for both Notley and the federal Liberals.

CHAPTER 10

"BEST INTERESTS AT HEART"

Albertans were in a grim mood in mid-2016, largely because of the punishing regional economy. Much of the rest of Canada was more optimistic. It may be, however, that everybody has cause to hope for a stronger, more collaborative national future. That could come down to two key leaders — Rachel Notley and Justin Trudeau.

They both have lived family histories deeply intertwined with emotional national events and tendencies. Both appear to have learned a great deal from the experience. They have no interest whatever in provoking the regional hostilities that enmeshed their fathers.

Trudeau's father, Pierre, was the last of a long line of Liberal prime ministers who viewed the West as a resource bucket for Central Canada. His 1980 National Energy Program was an epic example of Central Canadian paternalism masquerading as national interest. The NEP provoked a political and constitutional firestorm that lasted for years.

The policy wasn't devoid of merit, however, and one person who perceived this was Notley's father, Grant, then the Alberta NDP leader. He chastised both Ottawa and the province for enflaming the issue into a national crisis. Grant Notley approved of more Canadian ownership in the oil and gas industry, one of Trudeau's goals with the NEP. For that stance he paid personally, with questions about his loyalty to Alberta, and at the polls.

From these different perspectives, Rachel Notley and Justin Trudeau are familiar with the dangers of regionalism. Each refuses to play that tired old card today.

They do the opposite, trying hard to bank the fires.

Trudeau actively appeals for Canadians to rally around Alberta. During a Calgary stop on February 3, 2016, the prime minister said: "Alberta and Albertans have contributed tremendously to Canada's growth, particularly over the past 10 years. Our economy right across the country has benefited. Now, Alberta and Albertans are facing challenging times and, quite frankly, Canadians help other Canadians when they're facing tough times."[1]

When he was questioned about why Alberta should get extended employment insurance benefits when other parts of the country actually have a higher jobless rate, Trudeau added: "I think, looking at the rapid change and the significant shock Alberta has suffered since the falling oil prices, the terrible impact it has had on far too many Albertan families ... there is a need for Canada to step up and support Canadians who are in trouble."

There's no I told you so, no lecture about Alberta as wastrel and environmental laggard. Instead, he uses the plight of his father's old nemesis as a national unity moment. He refuses to put a pejorative regional face on Alberta's economic malaise, although he certainly could. It wouldn't cost him anything, because he has so many MPs from eastern Canada, Ontario, and Quebec, as well as allies in Liberal provincial governments from Ontario to the tip of Newfoundland.

The reality is that with pipelines at issue, it's extremely dangerous to play on regional tensions. Notley won't bite when B.C. premier Christy Clark needles her, or even when Saskatchewan premier Brad Wall presents himself as an alternative Alberta premier. (Unfortunately, the old strategic alliance among western provinces died long before the passing of its main authors, former premiers Lougheed of Alberta and his NDP friend Allan Blakeney from Saskatchewan.)

Like Trudeau, Notley carefully adopts a conciliatory approach. She can snap when necessary; she chided Wall for sounding off about her friendly talks with Quebec. Albertans don't want a pushover premier. But she is careful never to be personal and she leaves doors open to negotiation.

There's a reason for this besides the tension over pipelines and environment. Younger Canadians are far less moved by regional appeals than they were decades ago. They move more freely across provincial borders for work and relationships. Social media, non-existent during the old East-West range wars, foster cross-Canada friendships and understanding. Alberta has also been flooded with migrants from down east who often see themselves almost as dual citizens. Many of these people were happy to get good jobs in Alberta when their own economies were weak. During the Fort McMurray fire they showed their gratitude with comments and donations that moved Albertans deeply.

Trudeau and Notley also seem to recognize that conflict over pipelines isn't really regional or interprovincial. It's environmental and local. Pipeline approval must now be won almost kilometre by kilometre from local populations and stakeholders, as well as from environmental lobbies with the fixed goal of shutting down the oil sands. No major pipeline is likely to succeed against both these hostilities. Indeed, the rejection of Northern Gateway by Canada's federal court happened precisely because the Harper government didn't fully consider indigenous communities on the route.

Trudeau's answer, which Notley endorses, is to give local groups much more input and consultation, to the point of appointing a special envoy from the federal energy minister's office if necessary. If the local objections and fears can be mediated to the point of approval, provincial governments in Ontario, Quebec, and British Columbia will be far more likely to agree.

Notley's contribution to this dynamic is the provincial climate-change plan, with its hard cap on oil sands emissions, phase-out of coal, and province-wide carbon tax. Gary Doer, the former NDP premier of Manitoba, and then Harper-appointed ambassador to the United States, thinks Notley has handled it extremely well. "She's moved up the profile with her climate-change plan," he says. "The premier is bringing environmental, energy, and First Nations together, and that was pretty impressive. That's what people want. They don't want winner-take-all." As the now-retired ambassador who for years promoted pipelines to Americans, he feels Notley "is doing everything correctly by having Alberta partner with the federal government and partner with energy and environmental leaders in her own province. That partnership is crucial … the plan that gets consensus is better than the one coming from on high."

David Taras, political analyst at Mount Royal University, says the stakes are enormous because Notley is taking "a grand gamble — if she does get a pipeline, it will be an extraordinary achievement and it could well save her in the next election. But, with no pipeline, it's basically a failure and the strategy will have fallen apart, losing in investment, markets and tax revenue."

And yet, Notley's calculation is by no means entirely political. It also stems from her conviction that Alberta was in desperate need of change. Her whole NDP crew ardently believes the measures are essential for the environment as well as the economy. Notley says she moved fast on climate policy so it will be entrenched whether the NDP survives an election or not. "We're well underway with the climate-change leadership plan so that win or lose, nobody is going to reverse that thing."

The NDP is also intent on irreversibly changing Alberta's social landscape through direct measures to help the poor; a tax policy tilted toward the middle and lower middle class; increases to the minimum wage; programs to reduce domestic abuse; raising the status of women and First Nations in the workplace and society at large; as well as doing much more besides. But there is still resistance in many pockets of Alberta. Polls in mid-2016 showed Wildrose well ahead of the NDP in popular approval, and the Conservatives not far behind.

Rachel Notley knows that she hasn't yet fully won over her province. It's a remarkable admission to hear from a politician — and also an honest statement — when she voices her hope for the end of her term in 2019: "Albertans will have concluded that we actually are people who are capable; who care about them, who listen to them, and who have their best interests at heart. That's what I want to see."

AFTERWORD

By late 2016, Rachel Notley was facing criticism even from lifelong New Democrats who felt the government had done too much too quickly, without properly preparing the public for one huge change after another. The economy was still shrinking even as the taxpayers faced a comprehensive carbon tax set to take effect January 1, 2017. The conservative right was fomenting a sense of almost hysterical crisis as it edged toward a merger of like-minded parties in time for the next provincial election in 2019.

Notley's own government had been consistently shocked by the length and depth of the economic collapse. The 2016–17 deficit, first projected at $10.4 billon, was expected to total nearly $11 billion. The Fort McMurray wildfire had sucked further billions out of the economy. And yet, the NDP had seemed stuck on every detail of its election platform and program.

But signs began to emerge that the NDP would adapt. Notley hinted that her big-borrowing, big-spending program would be adjusted if the economy didn't turn. Her government was hoping to announce major investments. Approval of a critical pipeline still seemed possible. And there was always hope that oil would recover, once again making Alberta the province that accounted for 20 percent of Canada's GDP.

One thing Rachel Notley would not do was stop being a New Democrat of fiercer temperament than most Albertans anticipated. "It's time for the public interest to govern what the government of Alberta does, and not private interests," she told a cheering union audience in Ottawa on

August 24, 2016. "We got rid of a backward-looking, climate-change denying, deficit-offloading, austerity-loving, failed Alberta Conservative government."

At this point it's impossible to say if Notley can win again. But she has already put her stamp on the country, changed the image of a province that was supposed to be stuck in time, and fundamentally altered Alberta's way of dealing with the federation. It's also likely that by 2019 she will have created an Alberta so fundamentally altered, with the traditional power structure so scattered to the wind, that conservatives will never be able to put the old egg back together again.

NOTES

Unless indicated by a specific note, all quotations in the text are from interviews conducted by the authors. We would like to thank the following for their kind consent to speak with us:

Anonymous interviewees, Frank Dabbs, Randy Dawson, Gary Doer, Laurent Jeff Dubois, Roger Gibbins, Kent Hehr, Chris Henderson, Don Iveson, Brian Jean, Thomas Lukaszuk, David King, Colleen Klein, Ralph Klein, Naheed Nenshi, Jeanette Nicholls, Ron Nicholls, Rachel Notley, Roy Piepenburg, Darryl Raymaker, Michelle Rempel, Jim Stanton, David Taras, Brian Topp, Lori Williams.

CHAPTER 1: "A LITTLE BIT OF HISTORY"

1. Steven Chase, "Policy debates to the fore," *Globe and Mail*, May 25, 2016, A8.
2. Peter Lougheed, in *Alberta: A State of Mind*, ed. Sharpe et al., 261.
3. The White House, President Barack Obama, "Remarks by President Obama in Address to the Parliament of Canada," June 30, 2016, www.whitehouse.gov/the-press-office/2016/06/30/remarks-president-obama-address-parliament-canada.
4. Rachel Notley, quoted by Alexander Panetta, The Canadian Press, April 28, 2016, www.calgaryherald.com/business/premier+

rachel+notley+works+alberta+climate+change+image+washington-Ma/11885825/story.html.

5. Matthew Fisher, *National Post*, "PM Wins Hostage Stance Support," *Calgary Herald*, May 27, 2016, NP3.

6. *Globe and Mail* video, April 28, 2016, www.theglobeandmail.com/news/news-video/video-justin-trudeau-fires-back-at-critics-over-pipelines/article29775213.

7. Kathleen Wynne, transcript from Premier Wynne's Remarks & Availability with Alberta Premier Rachel Notley, May 26, 2016.

8. Rex Murphy, *National Post*, May 7, 2016, news.nationalpost.com/full-comment/rex-murphy-for-fort-mcmurray-better-days-will-come.

9. Annalise Klingbeil, "We Understand What They're Feeling," *Calgary Herald*, May 5, 2016, calgaryherald.com/news/local-news/we-understand-what-theyre-feeling-syrian-refugees-in-calgary-step-up-to-help-fort-mcmurray-fire-evacuees.

CHAPTER 2: THE HOPE-MONGERS

1. David McLaughlin, *Globe and Mail*, October 9, 2015, www.theglobeandmail.com/opinion/ground-game-strategy-get-out-the-vote/article26730749.

2. Danielle Smith, letter, December 18, 2014, assets.documentcloud.org/documents/1382826/smith-resignation-letter.txt.

3. Jim Prentice to Donna McElligot, CBC Radio, March 4, 2015.

4. Rachel Notley to reporters Karen Bartko and Emily Mertz, *Global News*, March 5, 2015, globalnews.ca/news/1865331/premiers-comments-spark-witty-prenticeblamesalbertans-jabs.

5. Gary Mason, *Globe and Mail*, April 22, 2015, theglobeandmail.com/news/alberta/alberta-wildrose-leader-brian-jean-enters-critical-stretch-of-campaign/article24070378.

6. Michael Platt [*Calgary Sun* columnist], *Fort McMurray Today*, March 29, 2015, www.fortmcmurraytoday.com/2015/03/29/new-alberta-wildrose-leader-brian-jean-turfs-candidate-bill-jarvis-over-comments-made-during-leadership-announcement. See also: www.youtube.com/watch?v=AUQzMbBPvGI.

7. Darcy Henton, "Wildrose Drops Candidate in Calgary-Varsity Over Offensive Blog Post," *Calgary Herald*, April 15, 2015, calgaryherald. com/news/local-news/wildrose-drops-candidate-in-calgary-varsity-over-offensive-blog-post.

8. Michael Wood, "Bake of Fire," *Calgary Sun*, April 16, 2015, www. calgarysun.com/2015/04/16/bake-of-fire-wildrose-candidate-apologizes-for-bring-your-wifes-pie-notice.

9. Darcy Henton, "Sleep-Walk Campaign Has Turned into a Fight to Save a Dynasty," *Calgary Herald*, May 2, 2015, calgaryherald.com/news/local-news/sleep-walk-campaign-has-turned-into-a-fight-to-save-a-dynasty.

10. Ibid.

11. CBC, April 8, 2015, www.cbc.ca/news/elections/alberta-votes/nenshi-criticizes-tories-for-early-election-call-1.3025424.

12. *Calgary Herald*, April 24, 2015, calgaryherald.com/news/politics/how-math-is-difficult-or-mathishard-blew-up-on-social-media.

13. Paul Wells, "My name is Rachel Notley," *Maclean's*, May 6, 2015, www.macleans.ca/news/canada/my-name-is-rachel-notley.

14. Karen Kleiss, *Edmonton Journal*, May 5, 2015, www.edmontonjour-nal.com/Analysis+Alberta+Progressive+Conservative+dynasty+fell/11033955/story.html.

15. Gary Mason, "Can Rachel Notley Lead an NDP Breakthrough in Alberta?" *Globe and Mail*, May 4, 2015, www.theglobeandmail.com/news/national/can-rachel-notley-lead-an-ndp-breakthrough-in-alberta/article24233863.

16. Bill Graveland, The Canadian Press, April 28, 2015, www.cbc.ca/news/elections/alberta-votes/rachel-notley-accuses-jim-prentice-of-fearmongering-on-royalties-pipelines-1.3052858.

17. Geoffrey Morgan, *Financial Post*, April 29, 2015, business. financialpost.com/news/energy/cenovus-energy-inc-warns-of-negative-fallout-if-ndp-changes-royalty-structure.

18. Dean Bennett, The Canadian Press, April 30, 2015, globalnews. ca/news/1972826/prentice-says-alberta-ndp-pipeline-policy-will-mirror-mulcairs.

19. Dean Bennett, The Canadian Press, May 1, 2015, globalnews.ca/news/1974648/prentice-says-mulcair-scripts-alberta-ndp-plan-notley-laughs-at-attack.

20. See Elections Alberta, Financial Disclosure, efpublic.elections.ab.ca/efParty.cfm?MID=FP_7&PID=7.

21. Slav Kornik and Caley Ramsay, *Global News*, May 1, 2015, globalnews.ca/news/1973934/edmonton-business-leaders-support-pc-government-ndp-dismiss-them-as-pc-donors.

22. Karen Kleiss, "Tory Backers Rip 'Amateur' NDP Policies," *Edmonton Journal*, May 2, 2015, A4.

23. Dean Bennett, The Canadian Press, May 10, 2015, www.cbc.ca/news/canada/edmonton/rachel-notley-says-it-hit-her-a-week-before-election-that-she-d-be-premier-1.3068407.

24. Angie Klein, April 30, 2015, www.youtube.com/watch?v=lBvHLKiOevM.

25. Jason Van Rassel, *Calgary Herald*, May 4, 2015, A1.

26. Charles Rusnell, Jennie Russell, Meghan Grant, and John Archer, CBC, April 28, 2015, www.cbc.ca/news/elections/alberta-votes/jamie-lall-chestermere-candidate-subject-of-restraining-order-in-2007-1.3052406. See also: Don Braid, *Calgary Herald*, April 28, 2015, calgaryherald.com/opinion/columnists/braid-a-week-from-the-election-pcs-fight-over-snotty-text-messages.

27. Rusnell et al., CBC, April 28, 2015.

28. See Dean Bennett, The Canadian Press, "Jim Prentice Defends PC Candidate in Sex Case," *Global News*, April 29, 2015, globalnews.ca/news/1968720/jim-prentice-defends-pc-election-candidate-convicted-of-soliciting-prostitute.

29. "Disgraced Former Tory MLA Mike Allen Isn't Resigning Yet," *Edmonton Sun*, July 22, 2013, www.edmontonsun.com/2013/07/22/disgraced-former-tory-mla-mike-allen-isnt-resigning-yet.

30. Bryan Passifiume, "Former Wildrose Leader Danielle Smith Speaks Politics During Calgary Political Panel Discussion," *Calgary Sun*, April 26, 2015, www.calgarysun.com/2015/04/27/former-wildrose-leader-danielle-smith-speaks-politics-during-calgary-political-panel-discussion.

31. In Trevor Howell, "Tories, Wildrose Urge Albertans to Avoid Voting NDP, While Notley Calls for Change," *Calgary Herald*, May 4, 2015, calgaryherald.com/news/politics/tories-wildrose-urge-albertans-to-avoid-voting-ndp-while-notley-calls-for-change.

CHAPTER 3: THE MIRROR CRACKS

1. Graham Thomson, "Not the 'Generational Change' Jim Prentice had in Mind," *Edmonton Journal*, www.edmontonjournal.com/graham+thomson+generational+change+prentice+mind/11033314/story.html.
2. James Wood, "Defeated Prentice Faces Tories at Annual Fundraising Dinner," *Calgary Herald*, calgaryherald.com/news/local-news/defeated-prentice-faces-tories-at-annual-fundraising-dinner.
3. Don Braid, *Calgary Herald*, calgaryherald.com/opinion/columnists/braid-a-once-great-dynasty-shreds-itself.
4. Matt McClure, "Watchdog Warns Tory Caretaker Government Against Trashing Files," *Calgary Herald*, calgaryherald.com/news/politics/watchdog-warns-tory-caretaker-government-againt-trashing-files.
5. Ibid.
6. Jim Prentice to PC delegates, quoted in Caitlin Hanson, Michelle Bellefontaine, and Kim Trynacity, "Alberta PC Leadership Vote," CBC News, September 6, 2015, www.cbc.ca/news/canada/edmonton/alberta-pc-leadership-vote-jim-prentice-wins-on-1st-ballot-1.2758180.
7. CBC News, www.cbc.ca/news/politics/enbridge-taps-jim-prentice-to-rescue-northern-gateway-first-nations-talks-1.2560859.
8. calgaryherald.com/news/tories-sweep-all-four-byelections-video.
9. Brian Mason, *Hansard*, December 3, 2014, www.assembly.ab.ca/ISYS/LADDAR_files/docs/hansards/han/legislature_28/session_3/20141203_1330_01_han.pdf.
10. Doug Griffiths, *Hansard*, December 3, 2014.
11. Thomas Lukaszuk, December 2, 2014, twitter.com/LukaszukAB.
12. See: Dave Cournoyer, daveberta.ca/2014/12/alberta-gay-straight-alliance-timeline.
13. Reid Southwick, "Jon Cornish Calls for Compassion in Gay-Straight Alliances Debate," *Calgary Herald*, December 4, 2014, calgaryherald.com/news/politics/jon-cornish-calls-for-compassion-in-gay-straight-alliances-debate.
14. James Wood, "Ron Ghitter Knows all about Human Rights and He Doesn't Like Bill 10," *Calgary Herald*, December 4, 2014,

calgaryherald.com/storyline/ron-ghitter-knows-all-about-human-rights-and-he-doesnt-like-bill-10.

15. Dean Bennett, The Canadian Press, www.macleans.ca/politics/who-is-jim-prentice.

16. *Hansard*, May 10, 2016, www.assembly.ab.ca/ISYS/LADDAR_files/docs/hansards/han/legislature_28/session_3/20150310_1330_01_han.pdf.

17. Ibid.

18. Ibid.

19. Kristopher Wells interview, CBC News, May 10, 2016, www.cbc.ca/news/canada/edmonton/bill-10-to-allow-gay-straight-alliances-for-any-student-in-alberta-schools-1.2989399.

20. Trevor Howell, "Alberta Party Scoops Website," *Calgary Herald*, April 8, 2015, calgaryherald.com/news/politics/alberta-party-scoops-website-for-pc-campaign-slogan-details-are-important-says-leader.

21. Jim Prentice TV address, March 24, 2015, www.alberta.ca/release.cfm?xID=379413AE11E88-B809-F164-A17A06135FC8806B.

22. Dave Cournoyer, March 24, 2015, twitter.com/davecournoyer/status/580563098479783937.

23. Jim Prentice, alberta.ca/release.cfm?xID=379413AE11E88-B809-F164-A17A06135FC8806B.

24. Merwan Saher, Auditor General of Alberta, "Auditor General Releases August 2014 Special Duty Report on the Expenses of the Office of Premier Redford and Alberta's Air Transportation Services Program," August 7, 2014, www.oag.ab.ca/node/437.

25. Matt Dykstra, "Postmortem on the Alberta PC Catastrophe," *Edmonton Sun*, June 13, 2015, www.edmontonsun.com/2015/06/12/postmortem-on-the-alberta-pc-catastrophe.

CHAPTER 4: BRIMSTONE AND FIRE

1. See: policyschool.ucalgary.ca/sites/default/files/research/siren-song-economic-diversification-morton-mcdonald.pdf.

2. Sharpe taped interviews with Ralph Klein, September to December 2010.

3. That's often the first thing people who were interviewed for the book said about former premier Ed Stelmach, before making any observations on his government.

4. Karen Kleiss, "Analysis: How the Alberta Progressive Conservative dynasty fell," *Edmonton Journal*, May 5, 2015, www.edmontonjournal.com/Analysis+Alberta+Progressive+Conservative+dynasty+fell/11033955/story.html.

5. Kevin Libin, "What are the possible outcomes of Saturday's Alberta PC leadership vote?" *National Post*, September 30, 2011, news.nationalpost.com/full-comment/what-are-the-possible-outcomes-of-saturdays-alberta-pc-leadership-vote.

6. Alison Redford, letter to Alberta Teachers' Association President Carol Henderson, September 22, 2011, www.stephentaylor.ca/2011/10/how-did-alison-redford-win.

7. ATA newsletter, October 11, 2011, www.teachers.ab.ca/Publications/ATA%20News/Volume%2046%202011-12/Number%204/Pages/New-premier-pledges.aspx.

8. Sydney Sharpe, *The Gilded Ghetto* (Toronto: Harper Collins, 1994), 72.

9. *Globe and Mail*, October 3, 2011.

10. David Schindler, quoted in the *Calgary Herald*, April 17, 2012, calgaryherald.com/opinion/scientists-respond-to-dani-the-denier.

11. Ron Leech, interview with a multicultural radio station, April 15, 2015, www.cbc.ca/news/canada/manitoba/wildrose-candidate-apologizes-for-white-advantage-comment-1.1127464.

12. Naheed Nenshi, April 18, 2015, www.metronews.ca/news/calgary/2012/04/23/the-sounds-of-the-alberta-election-campaign.html.

13. Allan Hunsperger blog, quoted in James Wood, "Wildrose Candidate Tells Gays in Lady Gaga-Inspired Blog Post: 'You Will Suffer the Rest of Eternity in the Lake of Fire, Hell,'" *National Post*, April 15, 2012, news.nationalpost.com/news/canada/allan-hunsperger-wildrose-blog.

14. James Wood, "Q&A with Premier Redford about $1B Recovery Commitment," *Calgary Herald*, June 20, 2014, calgaryherald.com/news/local-news/qa-with-premier-redford-about-1b-recovery-committment-with-video.

15. Alison Redford letter, "It's Time to Start the Next Chapter of My Life," *Calgary Herald* and *Edmonton Journal*, August 6, 2014.

16. Merwan Saher, Auditor General of Alberta, "Auditor General Releases August 2014 Special Duty Report on the Expenses of the Office of Premier Redford and Alberta's Air Transportation Services Program, August 7, 2014, www.oag.ab.ca/node/437.

17. Ibid.

CHAPTER 5: BORN TO RUN

1. Howard Leeson, quoted in Don Braid, "Political Integrity Endures," *Calgary Herald: Best of Alberta*, August 27, 2008, 25.

2. Alan Kellogg, "Knocking at the Door of the Dome," *Edmonton Journal*, April 14, 2007, www.canada.com/edmontonjournal/news/insight/story.html?id=b13ff6fa-715c-4810-ad19-0195211989d3.

3. Dean Bennett, The Canadian Press, October 18, 2014, edmonton. ctvnews.ca/alberta-ndp-leader-rachel-notley-started-activism-in-childhood-protest-marches-1.2060445.

4. Ibid.

5. Kellogg, "Knocking at the Door of the Dome."

6. Graham Thomson, "Rachel Notley," in *The Canadian Encyclopedia*, www.thecanadianencyclopedia.ca/en/article/rachel-notley.

7. Ibid.

8. Kellogg, "Knocking at the Door of the Dome."

9. Ibid.

10. Ibid.

11. Ray Martin, quoted in Don Braid, "Political Integrity Endures," *Calgary Herald: Best of Alberta*, August 27, 2008, 25.

12. Ibid.

13. Kellogg, "Knocking at the Door of the Dome."

14. Ujjal Dosanjh, quoted in Gary Mason, "Notley's Way: How the Alberta Premier Became Determined," *Globe and Mail*, May 8, 2015, www.theglobeandmail.com/news/alberta/the-alberta-ndps-rachel-notley-she-is-a-child-of-the-party/article24338069.

15. See: web.archive.org/web/20110706164108/www.ndpopposition.ab.ca/rachelnotley/node/4.

16. www.anglicanjournal.com/articles/reginald-rule-187.

17. Kellogg, "Knocking at the Door of the Dome."

18. Ibid.

19. Brian Mason interview, CBC News, October 18, 2014, www.cbc.ca/news/canada/edmonton/rachel-notley-is-the-new-leader-of-the-alberta-ndp-1.2804396. Mason also told the story at the 2016 provincial NDP convention.

20. Rick McConnell, CBC News, May 5, 2015, www.cbc.ca/news/elections/alberta-votes/rachel-notley-a-premier-50-years-in-the-making-1.3062239.

21. Brian Mason interview, CBC News, October 18, 2014.

22. Rachel Notley interview, Kim Trynacity, CBC News, April 17, 2015, www.cbc.ca/news/elections/alberta-votes/rachel-notley-new-democratic-party-leader-1.3013351.

23. CBC News, www.cbc.ca/news/elections/alberta-votes/rachel-notley-a-premier-50-years-in-the-making-1.3062239.

24. Stephen Notley, quoted in Colby Cosh, "How Rachel Notley Became Canada's Most Surprising Political Star," *Maclean's*, May 21, 2015, www.macleans.ca/politics/how-rachel-notley-became-canadas-most-surprising-political-star.

25. Gary Mason, "Notley's Way: How the Alberta Premier Became Determined," *Globe and Mail*, May 8, 2015, www.theglobeandmail.com/news/alberta/the-alberta-ndps-rachel-notley-she-is-a-child-of-the-party/article24338069.

CHAPTER 6: THE PURPLE PRELUDE

1. Shaheen Nenshi Nathoo, quoted in Marcello Di Cintio, *Readers Digest Canada*, May 2012, www.readersdigest.ca/features/heart/politics-20-naheed-nenshi-and-power-social-engagement.

2. Naheed Nenshi, quoted in Kate Torgovnick, "How the Mayor of Calgary Decided to Run for Office," *TedBlog*, May 29, 2014, blog.ted.com/mayor-of-calgary-naheed-nenshi-ran-for-office-after-giving-tedx-talk.

3. Chima Nkemdirim, quoted in Marcello Di Cintio, *Readers Digest Canada*, May 2012, www.readersdigest.ca/features/heart/politics-20-naheed-nenshi-and-power-social-engagement/2.

4. @KyleMLA, October 18, 2010, 9:21 p.m.

5. www.worldmayor.com/contest_2014/world-mayor-2014-winners.html.

6. globalnews.ca/news/1374259/nenshi-on-the-2013-flood-five-memorable-quotes.

7. Don Iveson, quoted in Slav Kornik, *Global News*, October 22, 2013, globalnews.ca/news/917542/social-medias-impact-on-iveson-victory.

8. Chris Henderson, quoted in Paula Simons, "How the Race was Won: Iveson Campaign Courted Young Edmonton Families," *Edmonton Journal*, October 21, 2013, www.edmontonjournal.com/technology/Simons+race+Iveson+campaign+courted+young+Edmonton+families/9068802/story.html.

9. Ibid.

10. Lauren Strapagiel, Postmedia, May 29, 2013, o.canada.com/news/rob-ford-vs-naheed-nenshi-understanding-torontos-jealousy.

11. Mayor Nenshi blog, April 23, 2016, calgarymayor.ca/stories/on-mayor-nenshis-comments-about-uber.

12. Jason Markusoff, Postmedia News, February 3, 2015, news.nationalpost.com/news/canada/canadian-politics/calgarys-naheed-nenshi-named-best-mayor-in-the-world-by-u-k-research-group-he-is-an-urban-visionary.

CHAPTER 7: BIG DREAMS IN BAD TIMES

1. www.albertandp.ca/platform.

2. David King, "Don't Be Too Quick to Dismiss New NDP Cabinet's Ability," *Calgary Herald*, May 23, 2015, calgaryherald.com/opinion/columnists/king-dont-be-too-quick-to-dismiss-new-ndp-cabinets-ability. Reprinted with permission of the *Calgary Herald*, and David King.

3. James Wood, "New NDP MLA in Album Cover Controversy," *Calgary Herald*, May 15, 2015, calgaryherald.com/news/politics/new-ndp-mla-in-album-cover-controversy.

4. Deborah Drever, quoted in Don Braid, *Calgary Herald*, January 4, 2016, calgaryherald.com/news/politics/braid-after-the-siege-and-long-months-of-insults-deborah-drever-speaks-out.

5. Don Braid, "The Strange Path of Shannon Phillips," *Calgary Herald*, June 25, calgaryherald.com/news/politics/braid-the-strange-path-of-shannon-phillips-how-to-back-greenpeace-and-save-capitalism.

6. Peter Lougheed, interviewed by Anna Maria Tremonti, *The Current*, CBC Radio, September 13, 2011, www.cbc.ca/news/canada/edmonton/peter-lougheed-opposes-keystone-pipeline-1.1078801.

7. Peter Lougheed interview, "Sounding an Alarm for Alberta," *Policy Options* (September 2006): 6.

8. Peter Lougheed, interviewed by Anna Maria Tremonti, *The Current*, CBC Radio, January 21, 2008.

9. Ian Austen [*New York Times*], "Oilsands Boom Dries Up in Alberta, Taking Thousands of Jobs With It," *Financial Post*, October 13, 2015, business.financialpost.com/news/energy/oilsands-boom-dries-up-in-alberta-taking-thousands-of-jobs-with-it.

10. Kevin Taft, quoted in Darcy Henton, *Calgary Herald*, January 18, 2012.

11. Canada West Foundation, *Alberta's Energy Legacy*, 2007.

12. Pearl Calahasen, *Hansard*, April 7, 2014, www.assembly.ab.ca/ISYS/LADDAR_files/docs/hansards/han/legislature_28/session_2/20140407_1330_01_han.pdf.

13. *Hansard*, June 22, 2015. See also: aptn.ca/news/2015/06/23/text-alberta-premier-rachel-notleys-apology-residential-school-survivors.

14. *Alberta Government*, June, 22, 2015, www.alberta.ca/release.cfm?xID=382201F08E932-0934-F591-9820A6FA93C90156. See also: aptn.ca/news/2015/06/23/text-alberta-premier-rachel-notleys-apology-residential-school-survivors.

15. Daryl Slade, "Siksika Chief Knows First Hand About Abuse at Residential Schools," *Calgary Herald*, June 26, 2015, calgaryherald.com/news/local-news/siksika-chief-knows-first-hand-about-abuse-at-residential-schools.

16. Kathleen Ganley, quoted in Carrie Tait, "How Alberta Intends to Follow Up on its Apology to First Nations," *Globe and Mail*,

June 26, 2015, www.theglobeandmail.com/news/alberta/how-alberta-intends-to-follow-up-on-its-apology-to-first-nations/article25160763.

17. *Alberta Government*, July 7, 2015, www.alberta.ca/release.cfm?xID=38301C30F2496-A31B-EBFF-5C27272061798EA5.

18. Brian Jean, @BrianJeanWRP, January 21, 2016, twitter.com/brianjeanwrp/status/690209077025071104.

19. Brad Wall, quoted in Don Braid, "Unlike Notley, Wall Tells Provinces to Butt Out of Pipeline Approval," *Calgary Herald*, July 15, 2016, calgaryherald.com/news/politics/braid-unlike-notley-wall-tells-provinces-to-butt-out-of-pipeline-approval.

20. Rachel Notley, quoted in Don Braid, *Calgary Herald*, July 16, 2016, calgaryherald.com/news/politics/braid-notley-counters-brad-wall-without-a-tantrum.

21. Ibid.

22. Wall, quoted in Don Braid, "Unlike Notley, Wall Tells Provinces to Butt Out of Pipeline Approval."

23. July 2015. See: www.canadaspremiers.ca/phocadownload/publications/canadian_energy_strategy_eng_fnl.pdf.

24. See: Lauren Krugel [The Canadian Press], "Poll Suggests Two-Thirds Support for Energy East, but Big Regional Divides," *Calgary Herald*, March 2, 2016, www.calgaryherald.com/business/poll+suggests+twothirds+support+energy+east+regional+divides/11759438/story.html.

25. David A. Dodge, "Report to the Government of Alberta," Bennett Jones LLP, October, 2015, www.bennettjones.com/uploadedFiles/Publications/Articles/ReporttotheGovernmentofAlberta.pdf.

26. Deborah Yedlin, "Dodge's Infrastructure Report Offers Important Economics Lesson," *Calgary Herald*, October 27, 2015, calgaryherald.com/business/energy/dodges-infrastructure-report-offers-important-economics-lesson.

27. Dean Bennett [The Canadian Press], "Red Thursday," *Edmonton Journal*, April 13, 2016, www.edmontonjournal.com/Alberta+braces+Finance+Minister+Ceci+unveils+budget/11851572/story.html.

28. See: "Climate Leadership Plan," November 22, 2015, www.alberta.ca/climate-leadership-plan.cfm.

29. Climate Leadership Plan speech, *Alberta Government*, November 22, 2015, www.alberta.ca/release.cfm?xID=38886E9269850-A787-1C1E-A5C90ACF52A4DAE4.

30. Murray Edwards, quoted in "Alberta's Climate Change Strategy Targets Carbon, Coal, Emissions," CBC News, November 22, 2015, www.cbc.ca/news/canada/edmonton/alberta-climate-change-newser-1.3330153.

31. Steve Williams, quoted in "Alberta's Climate Change Strategy Targets Carbon, Coal, Emissions."

32. Grand Chief Tony Alexis, quoted in "Alberta's Climate Change Strategy Targets Carbon, Coal, Emissions."

33. Mike Hudema, quoted in "Alberta's Climate Change Strategy Targets Carbon, Coal, Emissions."

34. Shell Global, "Climate Change and Energy Transitions," www.shell.com/sustainability/environment/climate-change.html.

35. Brian Jean, *Hansard*, November 23, 2015, www.assembly.ab.ca/ISYS/LADDAR_files/docs/hansards/han/legislature_29/session_1/20151123_1330_01_han.pdf.

36. Jim Dinning, quoted in James Wood, "Former Tory Finance Minister Jim Dinning Backs Carbon Tax Idea," *Calgary Herald*, June 1, 2016, calgaryherald.com/news/politics/former-tory-finance-minister-jim-dinning-backs-carbon-tax-idea.

37. @JustinTrudeau, November 22, 2015, twitter.com/justintrudeau/status/668583555002429440.

38. Al Gore, November 22, 2015, www.algore.com/news/statement-by-former-vice-president-al-gore-on-alberta-s-economy-wide-price-on-carbon-announcement.

39. Rachel Notley, quoted in James Wood, "The NDP Will Maintain the Current Royalty Structure for the Oil Sands," *Calgary Herald*, January 30, 2016, calgaryherald.com/storyline/test-notley-to-unveil-royalty-review-this-morning-announcement-starts-at-11-a-m.

40. Greg Clark, quoted in Don Braid, *National Post*, January 30, 2016, news.nationalpost.com/full-comment/don-braid-how-rachel-notley-learned-to-love-or-at-least-accept-albertas-royalties-system.

41. Robert Skinner, quoted in Don Braid, ibid.

42. Lougheed interview, "Sounding an Alarm for Alberta."

43. Rachel Notley, quoted in Darcy Henton and James Wood, "Notley Opts to Leave Her Gun in the Holster Over Pipeline Dispute," *Calgary Herald*, March 1, 2016, calgaryherald.com/news/politics/ notley-opts-to-leave-her-gun-in-the-holster-over-pipeline-dispute.

44. James Fitz-Morris, CBC News, November 30, 2015, www.cbc.ca/ news/politics/trudeau-address-climate-change-paris-1.3343394.

45. Line Beauchamp, quoted in by Kelly Cryderman, "Ontario, Quebec Say They Won't Shoulder Oil Sands Burden," *Calgary Herald*, December 12, 2009, www.calgaryherald.com/business/ Ontario+Quebec+they+shoulder+sands+burden/2336575/story.html.

46. Marg McCuaig-Boyd, quoted in Don Braid, *Calgary Herald*, December 10, 2015, calgaryherald.com/news/politics/braid-bill-6-brought-bullying.

47. Debbie Jabbour, quoted in Don Braid, ibid.

48. Richard Starke, quoted in Don Braid, ibid.

49. Ibid.

50. Rachel Notley, quoted in Darcy Henton, "Premier Accepts Blame for Bill 6," *Calgary Herald*, December 15, 2015, calgaryherald.com/news/politics/ premier-accepts-blame-for-bill-6-wont-point-finger-at-opposition.

51. Jake Edmiston, *National Post*, "Alberta NDP's Ban on Rebel Reporters to Stay for at Least Two Weeks," February 17, 2016, news. nationalpost.com/news/canada/canadian-politics/alberta-ndps-ban-on-rebel-reporters-to-stay-for-at-least-two-weeks-while-it-reviews-policy-government-says.

52. *Constitution Act, 1982, Canadian Charter of Rights and Freedoms*, Government of Canada, laws-lois.justice.gc.ca/eng/const/page-15. html.

53. Jen Gerson, *National Post*, February, 18, 2016, news.nationalpost. com/full-comment/jen-gerson-notleys-about-face-a-rare-reversal-on-a-stupid-decision.

54. Ian Greene, *The Charter of Rights* (Toronto: Lorimer, 1989), 19.

55. Lyman Duff, quoted in Greene, *The Charter of Rights*, 20. See also: www.lawnow.org/the-edmonton-journal-freedom-of-the-press-canada.

56. Darby Allen, quoted in Graham Thomson, *Edmonton Journal*, May 9, 2015, edmontonjournal.com/opinion/columnists/graham-thomson-fort-mcmurray-is-still-alive-fire-chief-declares.

57. Rachel Notley, quoted in Otiena Ellwand, "Despite 'Ocean of Fire' That Raged Around Fort McMurray, About 90 Per Cent of Structures Saved," *Edmonton Journal*, May 9, 2016, edmontonjournal.com/news/local-news/despite-ocean-of-fire-that-raged-around-fort-mcmurray-about-85-per-cent-of-structures-saved.

58. Ibid.

59. Yadullah Hussain, "Expert Warns Oil Talks May Be 'a Yawn,'" *Calgary Herald*, May 31, 2016, B4.

60. Michael Bloomberg, *Calgary Herald*, June 4, 2016, calgaryherald.com/opinion/columnists/bloomberg-action-on-climate-is-being-noticed.

CHAPTER 8: MATH IS DIFFICULT

1. Rachel Notley to supporters and reporters on election night, May 6, 2015, authors' notes via various live feeds.

2. Rachel Notley, quoted in Don Braid, *Calgary Herald*, July 16, 2015, calgaryherald.com/news/politics/braid-notley-counters-brad-wall-without-a-tantrum.

3. Government of British Columbia, "2016 Speech from the Throne," February 9, 2016, engage.gov.bc.ca/thronespeech/transcript.

4. www.ipu.org/pdf/publications/wmnmap15_en.pdf.

5. Charlotte Whitton, quoted in Sharpe, *The Gilded Ghetto*, 49.

6. Rachel Notley, quoted in Mariam Ibrahim, "Rachel Notley Says Persistence Key to Bringing Women into Politics," *Edmonton Journal*, April 25, 2015, edmontonjournal.com/news/politics/rachel-notley-says-persistence-key-to-bringing-women-into-politics.

7. Sharpe, *The Gilded Ghetto*, 176–77.

8. Donna Dasko, quoted in Jane Taber, "Rachel Notley Says Persistence Key to Bringing Women into Politics," *Globe and Mail*, May 13, 2016, A3.

9. Notley, quoted in Mariam Ibrahim, "Rachel Notley Says Persistence Key to Bringing Women into Politics."

10. Stephanie McLean, quoted in James Wood, "Stephanie McLean Moves into Alberta Cabinet Days Before Due Date," *Calgary Herald*, February 2, 2016, calgaryherald.com/news/politics/profile-of-new-calgary-cabinet-minister-stephanie-mclean.

11. Rachel Notley, quoted in Michelle Bellefontaine, CBC News, November 5, 2015, www.cbc.ca/news/canada/edmonton/premier-rachel-notley-vows-mla-will-not-lose-pay-due-to-pregnancy-1.3304765.

12. February 13, 2016. See: twitter.com/ndpstephanie/status/698618501825626114.

13. Ric McIver, quoted in James Wood, "Alberta Legislature Approves Morning Sitting Hours," *Calgary Herald*, November 5, 2015, calgaryherald.com/news/politics/alberta-legislature-approves-morning-sitting-hours.

14. Catherine McKenna, speaking on CBC Radio, soundcloud.com/cbcottawa1/catherine-mckenna-on-ottawa-morning-answers-questions. See also: Jane Taber, *Globe and Mail*, February 11, 2016, www.theglobeandmail.com/news/politics/for-catherine-mckenna-balancing-politics-and-family-means-setting-boundaries/article28737484.

15. Stephanie McLean, quoted in Graham Thomson, "New Cabinet a True Reflection of Alberta," *Edmonton Journal*, February 3, 2016, edmontonjournal.com/news/politics/graham-thomson-new-cabinet-a-true-reflection-of-alberta.

16. Mike Morrison @mikesbloggity tweeted Derek Fildebrandt @ Dfildebrandt, 6March 1, 2016, www.pressprogress.ca/wildrose_mla_derek_fildebrandt_under_fire_after_dismissing_social_issues_as_boring.

17. Brian Jean, interviewed by Michelle Bellefontaine, CBC News, December 27, 2015, www.cbc.ca/news/canada/edmonton/brian-jean-has-his-dancing-shoes-on-waiting-for-a-partner-1.3370921.

18. See: Sharpe, *The Gilded Ghetto*, 217–19.

19. Maria Fitzpatrick. *Hansard*, November 16, 2015, www.assembly.ab.ca/Documents/isysquery/24434e83-c9b8-4c18-b7ad-d0bacf37dcfe/1/doc.

20. Shannon Phillips, quoted in Crystal Laderas, "Government Votes in Support of Calgary-Bow MLA's Bill to Support Domestic Violence Victims," 660 News, December 7, 2015, www.660news.com/2015/12/07/government-votes-in-support-of-calgary-bow-mlas-bill-to-support-domestic-violence.

21. Rachel Notley, March 7, 2016, www.alberta.ca/release.
    cfm?xID=4034736BBB060-9843-168F-59498D9E3AFF267C.

22. Shannon Phillips, quoted in Amanda Taylor, Ali Hardstaff-Gajda,
    and Mahroh Mohammad, "Alberta Ministry of Human Services
    Report Card Gets Failing Grade," *Calgary Journal*, December 12,
    2013, www.calgaryjournal.ca/index.php/news/2007-alberta-
    ministry-of-human-services-report-card-gets-failing-grade.

23. Kathleen Lahey, "For Women, It's the Alberta Disadvantage,"
    Parkland Institute, March 11, 2015, www.parklandinstitute.ca/
    media_for_women_its_the_alberta_disadvantage.

24. Justice Robin Camp, quoted in Daryl Slade, "Ex-Calgary Judge Faces
    Discipline for Comments to Sex Assault Victim," *Calgary Herald*,
    November 24, 2015, calgaryherald.com/news/crime/ex-calgary-
    judge-faces-discipline-for-comments-to-sex-assault-victim.

25. Alison Crawford, "Judge Robin Camp's Rape Remarks Led to
    Appeal Before Peter Mackay Promoted Him," CBC News, March
    19, 2015, www.cbc.ca/news/politics/judge-robin-camp-knees-
    together-1.3322867.

26. See: www.cbc.ca/news/politics/federal-court-judge-robin-camp-
    inquiry-1.3393539.

27. Justice Brian O'Ferrall, quoted in Daryl Slade, "Former Calgary
    Judge Investigated for Comments Made to Alleged Sex Assault
    Victim," *Calgary Herald*, November 9, 2015, calgaryherald.com/
    news/crime/former-calgary-judge-investigated-for-comments-
    made-to-alleged-sex-assault-victim.

28. Cristin Schmitz, "Federal Justice Camp is Facing Public Inquiry,"
    The Lawyers Weekly, January 22, 2016, www.lawyersweekly.ca/
    articles/2594.

29. Justice Robin Camp, quoted in The Canadian Press, "Robin Camp
    Decision in 'Keep Your Knees Together' Case Referred to Review
    Panel," CBC News, December 21, 2015, www.cbc.ca/news/canada/
    federal-court-judge-robin-camp-rape-trial-1.3375509.

30. Ganley, quoted in Alison Crawford, "Judge Robin Camp's Rape
    Remarks Led to Appeal."
    See also: Tabatha Southey, "Justice Robin Camp: Canada's Toughest
    Sensitivity Training Student," *Globe and Mail*, November 13, 2015,

25, www.theglobeandmail.com/opinion/justice-robin-camp-the-toughest-sensitivity-training-student-possible/article27250702.

31. Ganley, quoted in Cristin Schmitz, "Federal Justice Camp is Facing Public Inquiry."

32. Canadian Judicial Council, "In the Matter of an Inquiry Pursuant to Section 63(1) of the *Judges Act* Regarding the Honourable Justice Robin Camp. Notice of Response to the Allegations, July 4, 2016." www.cjc-ccm.gc.ca/cmslib/general/Camp_Docs/2016-07-04%20 Notice%20of%20Response.pdf.

33. Schmitz, "Federal Justice Camp is Facing Public Inquiry."

34. Ibid.

35. Marg McCuaig-Boyd. *Hansard*, December 10, 2015, www.assembly. ab.ca/ISYS/LADDAR_files%5Cdocs%5Chansards%5Chan%5Clegis-lature_29%5Csession_1%5C20151210_0900_01_han.pdf.

36. David Swann, quoted in Darcy Henton, "Farm Safety Bill Passes with Tears, Jeers and Cheers in Passionate Debate," *Calgary Herald*, December 10, 2015, calgaryherald.com/news/politics/farm-safety-bill-passes-with-tears-jeers-and-cheers-in-passionate-debate.

37. Brian Jean, quoted in Darcy Henton, "Farm Safety Bill Passes with Tears, Jeers and Cheers in Passionate Debate."

38. Brian Jean, December 11, 2015, www.facebook.com/brianjeanwrp/ posts/10153325064803716. See also: Phil Heidenreich, "Farm Safety Bill Spurs Death Threats Against Alberta Premier," *Global News*, December 11, 2015, globalnews.ca/news/2395805/farm-safety-bill-spurs-death-threats-against-alberta-premier.

39. Neil LeMay, quoted in CBC News, December 12, 2014, www.cbc.ca/ news/canada/edmonton/police-likely-to-investigate-death-threats-against-rachel-notley-security-expert-says-1.3362620.

40. Rachel Notley, quoted in Erika Tucker, "Online Threats, Not 'Out of the Ordinary,' Says Alberta Premier," *Global News*, October 20, 2015, globalnews.ca/news/2287965/online-threats-of-violence-made-against-premier-rachel-notley.

41. Melanee Thomas, quoted in Kate Adach, "Notley Online Threats Far Exceed Those Aimed at Male Politicians, Professor Says," CBC News, December 14, 2015, www.cbc.ca/news/canada/calgary/rachel-notley-death-threats-1.3363938.

42. Deborah Drever, *Alberta Hansard*, Members' Statements, June 1, 2016, www.assembly.ab.ca/Documents/isysquery/bc53ec79-9ca9-46af-89a6-669d86bb14b7/1/doc.

43. Michelle Rempel, quoted in Ashley Csanady, "The Twitter Trial You Never Heard About: Toronto Man Found Guilty of Harassing Michelle Rempel," *National Post*, January 29, 2016, news.nationalpost.com/news/canada/canadian-politics/the-twitter-trial-you-never-heard-about-toronto-man-found-guilty-of-harassing-michelle-rempel.

44. Richard Stewart, quoted in Tristin Hopper, "He Washed it Six Times," *National Post*, February 24, 2016, news.nationalpost.com/news/canada/he-washed-it-six-times-coquitlam-mayor-richard-stewart-explains-why-he-wore-the-same-suit-for-15-months.

45. Elizabeth Goodyear-Grant, *Gendered News: Media Coverage and Electoral Politics in Canada* (Vancouver: UBC Press, 2013), 168–69.

46. Sharpe, *The Gilded Ghetto*, 53.

47. Ibid., 75.

48. Ibid.,158.

49. Renaud, Marie, twitter.com/MarieFrRenaud?ref_src=twsrc%5Etfw.

50. Clark, Christy, "When I Was 13 a Man Suddenly Jumped Out and Grabbed Me Off the Sidewalk," *National Post*, June 9, 2016. news.nationalpost.com/news/canada/christy-clark-when-i-was-13-a-man-suddenly-jumped-out-and-grabbed-me-off-the-sidewalk-i-stayed-silent-for-35-years.

51. Gary Mason, "Wildrose Pitbull's Antics are a Disservice to Alberta," *Globe and Mail*, May 28, 2016, A1, www.theglobeandmail.com/news/alberta/wildrose-insults-an-ally-alberta-dearly-needs-for-energy-east/article30196332.

52. Ric McIver, *Alberta Hansard*, Members' Statements, May 30, 2016, www.assembly.ab.ca/ISYS/LADDAR_files/docs/hansards/han/legislature_29/session_2/20160530_1330_01_han.pdf.

53. See: Curtis Gillespie, "The Power 50: Canada's Most Powerful Business People 2016," *Canadian Business*, November 17, 2015, www.canadianbusiness.com/lists-and-rankings/most-powerful-people/power-50-2016-introduction.

CHAPTER 9: UNEASY ALLIES

1. Author notes from event, October 18, 2015.
2. Dave Cournoyer, October 18, 2015, daveberta.ca/2015/10/justin-trudeau-rachel-notley.
3. Steven Chase, "Niqabs 'Rooted in a Culture That Is Anti-Women,' Harper says," *Globe and Mail*, March 10, 2015, www.theglobeandmail.com/news/politics/niqabs-rooted-in-a-culture-that-is-anti-women-harper-says/article23395242.
4. Justin Trudeau to Chris Hall, *The House*, CBC Radio, October 6, 2015, www.cbc.ca/news/politics/stephen-harper-niqab-ban-public-servants-1.3258943.
5. Interview with Jason Kenney, July 7, 2016.
6. The Munk Debate, Roy Thomson Hall, Toronto, September 28, 2015, www.cbc.ca/news/politics/citizenship-revoked-revocation-bill-c-24-1.3248920.
7. Ibid.
8. Ibid.
9. James Wood, "Liberals Defend Stance on Revoking Citizenship for Terrorists," *Calgary Herald*, September 29, 2015, calgaryherald.com/news/politics/liberals-talk-immigration-to-win-ethnic-voters-back-into-the-fold.
10. James Wood, "Tory MP Obhrai Says He Has Always Opposed Bill C-24," *Calgary Herald*, October 21, 2015, calgaryherald.com/news/politics/tory-mp-obhrai-says-he-has-always-opposed-bill-c-24.
11. Althia Raj, "Conservative MP Deepak Obhrai: New Rules Turning Tories Into 'Elitist and White-Only' Club," *Huffington Post*, April 7, 2016, www.huffingtonpost.ca/2016/04/07/deepak-obhrai-conservatives-white-only-club_n_9639432.html.
12. See: beta.thestar.com/opinion/editorials/2015/08/03/early-election-call-is-a-cynical-political-ploy-editorial.html.
13. Chaldeans Mensah, quoted in Dean Bennett, The Canadian Press, October 20, 2015, globalnews.ca/news/2287791/federal-election-2015-alberta-remains-a-conservative-stronghold.
14. Author notes, Justin Trudeau Calgary rally, October 18, 2016.
15. www.statcan.gc.ca/daily-quotidien/160222/cg-a001-eng.htm.

16. Andrew Coyne [*National Post* columnist], "Liberated by Defeat," *Calgary Herald*, May 31, 2016, NP3.

17. Gillespie, "The Power 50: Canada's Most Powerful Business People 2016."

18. Justin Trudeau, March 30, 2016. See: globalnews.ca/video/2608177/prime-minister-justin-trudeau-says-decisions-on-employment-insurance-were-based-on-cold-hard-mathematics.

19. Christina Gray, speaking on *The House*, CBC Radio, April 2, 2016, www.cbc.ca/news/politics/alberta-labour-minister-seeks-clarity-on-enhanced-ei-benefits-from-ottawa-1.3517279.

20. Gillespie, "The Power 50: Canada's Most Powerful Business People 2016."

21. Ian Austen, "Canada's New Leadership Reverses Course On Climate Change," *New York Times*, November 26, 2015, www.nytimes.com/2015/11/27/world/americas/canadas-new-leadership-reverses-course-on-climate-change.html.

22. Ibid.

23. Darcy Henton and Chris Varcoe, "'No Power from BC Without Pipeline to West Coast,' Says Notley," *Calgary Herald*, March 4, 2016, calgaryherald.com/news/politics/no-power-from-b-c-without-pipeline-to-west-coast-says-notley.

24. Marg McCuaig-Boyd to *Financial Post* columnist Claudia Cattaneo, March 4, 2016, business.financialpost.com/news/energy/b-c-premiers-proposal-to-export-power-to-alberta-looks-dead-on-arrival.

25. Ibid.

26. British Columbia speech from the throne, February 9, 2016, engage.gov.bc.ca/thronespeech/transcript.

27. Mary Fagan, "Sheikh Yamani Predicts Price Crash as Age of Oil Ends," *The Telegraph*, June 25, 2000, www.telegraph.co.uk/news/uknews/1344832/Sheikh-Yamani-predicts-price-crash-as-age-of-oil-ends.html.

28. Chris Varcoe, "Miserable Alberta Recession No Match for 80s Upheaval," *Calgary Herald*, April 5, 2016, calgaryherald.com/business/energy/varcoe-miserable-alberta-recession-no-match-for-80s-upheaval.

29. Lauren Krugel, "Notley Says Alberta Left to Pick From a Menu of Bad Options After Crude Collapse," *Calgary Herald*, February 26, 2016, calgaryherald.com/news/politics/notley-says-alberta-left-to-pick-from-a-menu-of-bad-options-after-crude-collapse.

30. Ibid.

31. Alberta Government, "The Way Forward," April 24, 2016, 3.

32. Colby Cosh, *National Post*, April 11, 2016, news.nationalpost.com/full-comment/colby-cosh-the-party-is-over-and-i-dont-just-mean-the-new-democratic-one.

33. Gil McGowan on the NDP Leap Manifesto, CBC News, April 12, 2016, www.cbc.ca/news/canada/calgary/programs/eyeopener/gil-mcgowan-on-the-ndp-leap-manifesto-1.3532151.

34. McGowan, ibid.

35. Wildrose leader Brian Jean statement, April 10, 2016, www.wildrose.ca/jean_statement_on_ndp_passing_resolution_on_leap_manifesto.

36. Jen Gerson, *National Post*, April 11, 2016, news.nationalpost.com/news/canada/canadian-politics/alberta-premier-calls-leap-manifesto-naive-and-ill-informed-but-wont-cut-ties-with-federal-ndp.

37. Rachel Notley speech to national NDP convention, April 9, 2016. See: www.cbc.ca/news/canada/edmonton/rachel-notley-ndp-conference-1.3528549.

38. See: Althia Raj, "Mulcair Hints Things May Have Been Different if NDP Convention Wasn't in Alberta," *Huffington Post*, April 18, 2016, www.huffingtonpost.ca/2016/04/18/thomas-mulcair-alberta-ndp-convention-tout-le-monde_n_9721752.html.

39. Harrie Vredenburg and Tim Marchant, "Alberta's Energy Industry," CBC News, April 28, 2016, www.cbc.ca/news/canada/calgary/alberta-energy-industry-roadmap-for-future-1.3555924.

CHAPTER 10: "BEST INTERESTS AT HEART"

1. Don Braid, *Calgary Herald*, February 3, 2016, calgaryherald.com/opinion/columnists/braid-trudeau-starts-alberta-visit-on-the-right-note.

BIBLIOGRAPHY

SELECTED INTERVIEWS

Duane Bratt, August 2, 2016; Frank Dabbs, February 3, 2016; Gary Doer, May 9, 2016; Laurent Jeff Dubois, January 19, 2016; Jen Gerson, April 25, 2016; Roger Gibbins, March 15, 2016; Kent Hehr, March 1, 2016; Chris Henderson, March 14, 2016; Don Iveson, March 14, 2016; Brian Jean, May 17, 2016; David King, May 17, 2016; Colleen Klein, December 11, 2015; Ralph Klein, September–December, 2010; Thomas Lukaszuk, December 14, 2015; Naheed Nenshi, February 24, 2016; Jeanette Nicholls, May 9 and 10, 2016; Ron Nicholls, May 10, 2016; Rachel Notley, March 18, 2016; Roy Piepenburg, February 4, 2016; Darryl Raymaker, March 13, 2016; Michelle Rempel, April 5, 2016; Jim Stanton, May 15, 2016; David Taras, April 27, 2016; Brian Topp, March 9, 2016; Lori Williams, February 22, 2016.

NEWSPAPERS AND MAGAZINES

The Anglican Journal; The Calgary Herald; The Calgary Sun; Canadian Business; The Edmonton Journal; The Edmonton Sun; Fort McMurray Today; The Globe and Mail; The Lawyers Weekly; Maclean's; Metro News; The Montreal Gazette; The National Post; The Ottawa Citizen; Policy Options; The New York Times; Readers Digest Canada; The Telegraph; The Toronto Star; The Vancouver Sun

RADIO AND TELEVISION

APTN News; CBC News; CBC Radio's *The Current*; CTV News; Global News.

GOVERNMENT DOCUMENTS

Primary documents are readily available on the various government websites. These were enormously helpful and used unsparingly. Alberta and British Columbia *Hansard,* as the official record of government debates, were immensely helpful.

In addition, various reports, such as that of the Auditor General of Alberta, are easily accessible.

WEBSITES AND FEEDS

All the political parties have accessible websites with pertinent material such as party electoral platforms, as well as party positions on social and economic issues and news releases.

Social media contain sites of vision or vitriol — and often a combination of both. Politicians and journalists are on Twitter; also look for the witty tweets of those such as Kathleen Smith @kikkiplanet and Dave Cournoyer @davecournoyer.

PROFILES BY JOURNALISTS

Excellent profiles of Rachel Notley by the following journalists are cited in the text and endnotes: Dean Bennett; Colby Cosh; Mariam Ibrahim; Alan Kellogg; Gary Mason; Graham Thomson; Paul Wells.

REPORTS BY JOURNALISTS

The sweeping political changes in Alberta and in Ottawa were followed by some of the best journalists in the country. Their accounts expanded the scope of the book and are duly cited. In addition to the above, they include:

Kate Adach; John Archer; Ian Austen; Rick Bell; Michelle Bellefontaine; Claudia Cattaneo; Steven Chase; Andrew Coyne; Alison Crawford; Kelly Cryderman; Ashley Csanady; Frank Dabbs; Marcello Di Cintio; Matt Dykstra; Jen Gerson; Curtis Gillespie; Meghan Grant; Bill Graveland; Chris Hall; Phil Heidenreich; Darcy Henton; Tristin Hopper; Trevor Howell; Yadullah Hussain; Jeffery Jones; Karen Kleiss; Annalise Klingbeil; Slav Kornik; Lauren Krugel; Kevin Libin; Jason Markusoff; Matt McClure; Rick McConnell; Geoffrey Morgan; Rex Murphy; Alexander Panetta; Michael Platt; Althia Raj; Charles Rusnell; Jennie Russell; Daryl Slade; Paula Simons; Jeffrey Simpson; Reid Southwick; Jane Taber; Carrie Tait; Anna Maria Tremonti; Kim Trynacity; Erica Tucker; Chris Varcoe; Jason Van Rassel; Margaret Wente; James Wood; Michael Wood; Deborah Yedlin.

SELECTED BOOKS

Braid, Don, and Sydney Sharpe. *Breakup: Why the West Feels Left Out of Canada.* Toronto: Key Porter Books, 1990.

Dabbs, Frank. *Ralph Klein: A Maverick Life.* Vancouver: Greystone Books, 1995.

Ford, Catherine. *Against the Grain.* Toronto: McClelland & Stewart, 2009.

Goodyear-Grant, Elizabeth. *Gendered News: Media Coverage and Electoral Politics in Canada.* Vancouver: UBC Press, 2013.

Greene, Ian. *The Charter of Rights.* Toronto: Lorimer, 1989.

Janigan, Mary. *Let the Eastern Bastards Freeze in the Dark: The West Versus the Rest in Confederation.* Toronto: Knopf Canada, 2012.

Leeson, Howard. *Grant Notley: The Social Conscience of Alberta.* Edmonton: University of Alberta Press, 1992.

Macpherson, C.B. *Democracy in Alberta: Social Credit and the Party System.* Toronto: University of Toronto Press, 1953.

Mulcair, Tom. *Strength of Conviction.* Toronto: Dundurn, 2015.

Roach, Robert, ed. *Alberta's Energy Legacy: Ideas for the Future.* Calgary: Canada West Foundation, 2007.

Sharpe, Sydney. *The Gilded Ghetto: Women and Political Power in Canada.* Toronto: Harper Collins, 1994.

Sharpe, Sydney, and Don Braid. *Storming Babylon: Preston Manning and the Rise of the Reform Party.* Toronto: Key Porter Books, 1992.

Sharpe, Sydney, Roger Gibbins, James H. Marsh, and Heather Bala Edwards, eds. *Alberta: A State of Mind*. Toronto: Key Porter Books, 2015.

Taft, Kevin, with Mel McMillan and Junaid Jahangir. *Follow the Money: Where Is Alberta's Wealth Going?* Edmonton: Brush Education, 2012.

Trudeau, Justin. *Common Ground*. Toronto: Harper Collins, 2014.

Tupper, Allan, and Roger Gibbins, eds. *Government and Politics in Alberta*. Edmonton: University of Alberta Press, 1992.

Van Herk, Aritha. *Mavericks: An Incorrigible History of Alberta*. Toronto: Penguin Canada, 2001.

ACKNOWLEDGEMENTS

Any book that depends to some extent on events happening in real time demands patience and flexibility not just from the authors, but also from frazzled editors and baffled friends and relatives. Thanks to the many helpful people at Dundurn, including Beth Bruder, Carrie Gleason, Cheryl Hawley, Michelle Melski, Laura Boyle, who created a wonderful design for the book, and especially the indomitable Dominic Farrell, a keen-eyed editor of patience, wit, and understanding. Thanks also to Cy Strom for his careful copy edit. They caught a thousand glitches and mistakes. Any that remain are all ours.

We are grateful to the political team and editors at the *Calgary Herald*, including Darcy Henton, James Wood, and Chris Varcoe. We thank the *Calgary Herald*, Postmedia Network, and David King for permission to print a portion of his seminal opinion piece.

This book is the result of a great deal of research as well as many interviews, discussions, news conferences, conventions, confessions, coffees, lunches, and frugal dinners. Thanks to all, both named and anonymous, who shared their knowledge, stories, and experience.

On the personal level, this book is only possible with the help, love, and support of Rielle Braid and Jamie Edwards, Gabriel Cardenas Sharpe, James and Rasa Barlott Cardenas, Norma Sharpe, Kholby Wardell, Sam Switzer, Phoebe and Richard Heyman, Margo Helper and Greg Forrest, Jeanette and Ron Nicholls, Jeanine Arseneault and Rob Edwards, Pat and Kerry-Jane Clayton, Carol Ryder, Shosh Cohen, Barb Zack and Tom Oystrick, Jim Stanton and Paula Walsh, John Ashleigh, Christopher Leeson, Carl Sawyer; and, finally and forever, our dear friend, the late Patricia Leeson.

INDEX

BY THE SAME AUTHOR

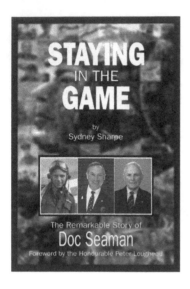

STAYING IN THE GAME
Sydney Sharpe

Peter C. Newman called him "the Totem of the Titans." From a small Prairie town, Daryl K. "Doc" Seaman became an icon of Canadian business and hockey. He is one of the last of a breed of postwar entrepreneurs and sportsmen who forged modern Canada, striking deals on a handshake and always keeping their word.

After flying eighty-two combat missions during the Second World War, Doc Seaman worked in the oil industry with his brothers, turning a small Alberta drilling business into a global giant, Bow Valley Industries. Later, he led a group that brought the Atlanta Flames to Calgary. Still a Flames co-owner, he helped reshape Hockey Canada and restore Canada's glory in international hockey.

Doc Seaman's life is a remarkable saga of courage, resolve, generosity, and success. It ultimately leaves us not only with a deep appreciation of one iconic Canadian but also with a wider understanding of our country.

OF RELATED INTEREST

THE CANADIAN FEDERAL ELECTION OF 2015
Jon H. Pammett and Christopher Dornan

The Canadian Federal Election of 2015 is the tenth volume in a series that has chronicled every national election campaign since 1984.

A comprehensive analysis of the campaigns and the election outcome, this collection of essays examines the strategies, successes, and failures of the major political parties: the Conservatives, the Liberals, the New Democrats, the Bloc Québécois, and the Green Party.

Also featured are chapters on the changes in electoral rules, the experience of local campaigning, the play of the polls, the campaign in the new media, the role of the debates, and the experience of women in the campaign. The book concludes with a detailed analysis of voting behaviour in 2015 and an assessment of the Stephen Harper dynasty. Appendices contain all of the election results.

dundurn.com   dundurnpress

@dundurnpress   dundurnpress

dundurnpress   info@dundurn.com

DUNDURN